A PLUME BOOK

WE DON'T NEED ROADS

NJ Advance/Landov

CASEEN GAINES is the author of *Inside Pee-wee's Playhouse: The Untold, Unauthorized, and Unpredictable Story of a Pop Phenomenon,* which received the 2012 Independent Publisher Book Award Silver Medal in the Popular Culture/Leisure category, as well as *A Christmas Story: Behind the Scenes of a Holiday Classic.* Caseen also directs theater and teaches high school English in New Jersey, where he lives. He aspires to be a Renaissance man and fears being a jack-of-all-trades. He can be found online at www.caseengaines.com.

Praise for *We Don't Need Roads*

"*We Don't Need Roads* is the truly fascinating story of how one of America's greatest movie franchises came to be. Caseen Gaines's in-depth research and unprecedented look at Robert Zemeckis's series proves that the journey to make a perfect movie is anything but perfect. It's a must read for any true *Back to the Future* lover and anyone who wants to peek behind the curtain to see how films get made."

—Adam F. Goldberg, creator of ABC's *The Goldbergs*

"What fun! Deeply researched and engagingly written, Caseen Gaines's *We Don't Need Roads* is the book *Back to the Future* fans have been craving for decades. Geekily enthusiastic and chock-full of never-before-heard tales of what went on both on and off the screen, *We Don't Need Roads* is a book worthy of the beloved trilogy itself."

—Brian Jay Jones, *New York Times* bestselling author of
Jim Henson: The Biography

"Read this book, then watch the movie for the umpteenth time. You'll appreciate *Back to the Future* all the more thanks to Caseen Gaines's muscular reporting and conversational writing style."

—Michael Davis, *New York Times* bestselling author of
Street Gang: The Complete History of Sesame Street

"Even the most knowledgeable *Future* fans will find much to learn from this intricately detailed and exhaustively researched book. But it's not just the depth of Gaines's knowledge and the scope of his interviews that impresses; he clearly adores these films and understands their importance to popular cinema, and that love and understanding shines through the text."

—Jason Bailey, author of *Pulp Fiction: The Complete Story of
Quentin Tarantino's Masterpiece*

"The thirtieth anniversary of the *Back to the Future* trilogy is the perfect time for a book celebrating and examining the greatest comedy, science fiction, time-travel trilogy ever made. With over five hundred hours of interviews with key cast and crew members, Caseen Gaines's book is a delightful way to travel back to the future and relive those wonderful times with Marty McFly, his family, friends, and enemies—not to mention the inimitable Doc Brown. Strap into your DeLorean and get ready for the ride of your life!"

—Marc Scott Zicree, author of *The Twilight Zone Companion*

"*We Don't Need Roads* is essential for any *Back to the Future* fan. Not only does Caseen Gaines offer up a meticulously crafted and entertaining account of one of the most beloved time-traveling franchises in movie history, but he uses his access to take an incisive look behind the scenes of Hollywood filmmaking. A must read for all pop culture aficionados."

—Larry Landsman, author of *Planet of the Apes Revisited*

WE
DON'T
NEED ROADS

THE MAKING OF THE

BACK TO THE FUTURE

TRILOGY

CASEEN GAINES

A PLUME BOOK

PLUME
An imprint of Penguin Random House LLC
375 Hudson Street
New York, New York 10014
penguin.com

LIBRARY OF CONGRESS CATALOGING-IN-PUBLICATION DATA
Gaines, Caseen, 1986–
We don't need roads : the making of the Back to the future trilogy / Caseen Gaines.
pages cm
Includes bibliographical references and index.
ISBN 978-0-14-218153-9 (paperback)
1. Back to the future films—History and criticism.   I. Title.
PN1995.9.B26G35 2015
791.43'75—dc2   2015007982

Printed in the United States of America
10 9 8 7 6 5 4 3 2 1

Set in Fairfield Light

While the author has made every effort to provide accurate telephone numbers, Internet addresses, and other contact information at the time of publication, neither the
publisher nor the author assumes any responsibility for errors or for changes that occur
after publication. Further, the publisher does not have any control over and does not
assume any responsibility for author or third-party Web sites or their content.

for my family
who raised me on a healthy dose of science fiction
inadvertently showing me that all things are possible

The only thing more uncertain than the future is the past.

—Soviet proverb

Contents

INTRODUCTION

Thursday, January 23, 2014

Murphy's Law—noun: *The theory that, moments before an interview with Robert Zemeckis, one's audio recorder will malfunction.*

At nine months into the research phase for this book, I knew I had put off calling Robert Zemeckis as long as I could. I was nervous about speaking with the creative brain behind some of my favorite films like *Forrest Gump, Who Framed Roger Rabbit*, and, of course, that epic time-travel trilogy. There were a million things I wanted to query him about, most of them having to do with the project I was working on. It wasn't so much that I was starstruck by the prospect of speaking with him, but when you have a chance to chat with a visionary whose work you respect and admire, it has a way of putting you on edge.

Or, at least, that's what I attribute my feelings to in hindsight. More likely it was because I had tangible evidence of the benefit of having Robert Zemeckis—or Bob Z, as he's known to friends, colleagues, and *Back to the Future* aficionados—on board for this book. A few weeks earlier, when I reached out to Christopher Lloyd's manager, he asked me if Zemeckis was on board. A line was drawn in the sand: The day I spoke to the director would be the day an interview would be scheduled with the Doc.

Challenge accepted. I hung up the phone with Lloyd's rep and retrieved the index card with Zemeckis's agent's phone number written on it, a three-by-five piece of card stock that had been haunting me ever since I'd scribbled on it four months earlier. Without jumping through too many hoops, I got a hold of Zemeckis's assistant, who promptly scheduled a half-hour interview for us, with only one request: "We respectfully ask that you contain the time to the thirty minutes which we have allotted." No big deal, I thought, until a week later when it was six minutes before our scheduled interview and the software I use to record Skype calls on my computer stopped working.

It was 12:24 P.M. Pacific Standard Time. I was based on the East Coast, but had grown accustomed to working my day around what I reductively referred to as "Los Angeles Time." Each second became more and more important. There was no way I was going to call Bob Z late. Bob G—Bob Gale, cowriter and coproducer of *Back to the Future* and its subsequent sequels—had told me that Zemeckis rarely does interviews on his past work. His rep's words raced through my head, an LED sign outside the New York Stock Exchange. Slowly at first, and then faster and faster, with the print getting larger and larger— THIRTY MINUTES WHICH WE HAVE ALLOTTED. THIRTY MINUTES WHICH WE HAVE ALLOTTED. THIRTY MINUTES. THIRTY MINUTES. MINUTES. MINUTES.

By 12:29, I was stuck with no choice but to use my plan B. I took out my cell phone, deleted a few apps to ensure I had a surplus of memory, and called Zemeckis from my computer, silently praying the microphone on my handheld device was catching everything. I had consolidated all of my questions into six or seven bullet points of topics, deciding it might be easier to let the colloquy unfold naturally, while making sure I got what I needed within the confines of his schedule. And everything did work. Not only was the director a pleasure to speak with, but he was also refreshingly direct about his thoughts on the films and his contributions to cinema in general. Of the many takeaways from our conversation, the most substantial was his continuing pride and astonishment with the enduring legacy of a story that he and Gale had created more than three decades earlier, which wouldn't have seen the light of day were it not for their tenacity and unwavering commitment to their project.

Set up a Google alert for the words "Back to the Future" and a day won't go by without a headline from someplace in the world using the title, often without having any connection to the film. Like *Jaws* a decade earlier, *Future* set a new precedent for how to create a winning summer blockbuster. As Bob Gale likes to remind aspiring screenwriters, the three things that matter most in a story are characters, characters, and characters. For all of its special and visual effects, the true success of the film lies with Zemeckis and Gale's airtight script, and the distinctive characters that were brought to life by their talented cast. For the thirty years that followed the first film's release, the trilogy has continued to capture the imagination of a generation who, in turn, passed these movies on to their children like beloved family heirlooms.

I'm just young enough to have missed the film's theatrical run, but thanks to one of my aunts—who had what seemed like hundreds of VHS tapes when I was growing up—I had the fortunate and, for many *Future* fans, rare experience of being introduced to Hill Valley's inhabitants for the first time in a triple feature. It was a school day, but I had a slight fever and was sent home by the school nurse. With both of my parents at work, my Aunt Stacey, who worked nights, picked me up. "I think you'll enjoy these," she said as I sat on her couch under a blanket with some chicken soup beside me. I doubt she had any idea just how much I would. She put the first film in the VCR as I studied the cardboard sleeve of the box. The design, with that guy I recognized from TV with one foot in this strange vehicle and fire running between his legs, seemed magical. I couldn't stop studying it, looking for clues about what was going to unfold over the next few hours. I knew I was in store for a movie unlike anything I had seen before. As the end credits for the first and second installments started, I raced to switch the cassettes, trying my best to continue the story as quickly as possible. When the words "THE END" appeared on the screen in the last moments of *Part III*, I decided to let the credits roll in their entirety. By the time my mother came to pick me up, my fever was all but forgotten. I couldn't wait to go to school the next day and tell my friends about Marty McFly, his friend Doc Brown, and the wild adventures I had spent close to six hours watching them get into.

I have always been an avid reader of behind-the-scenes books about my favorite films and television shows, as they went into greater detail than the standard promotional "making of" shows that would occasionally pop up on television in the late 1980s and early 1990s. As the thirtieth anniversary of *Back to the Future* approached, I couldn't believe that a comprehensive book on the making of one of the most culturally significant movies of the past three decades had yet to be written. My goal was to change that, not only by chronicling the filmmaking process, but also by showing how these three films left an indelible stamp on the United States and many other countries around the world.

When I set out to write this book, it was important for me to speak with as many people who were associated with *Back to the Future* as possible. The trilogy has been well documented for the past thirty years, in magazines, fan clubs, featurettes on VHS, DVD, and Blu-ray, and countless websites like BacktotheFuture .com, the digital hub for all things about the franchise. As one person put it to me, "What else can you say about a movie that has been written about continuously for the past thirty years?" But even with that abundance of information available, the mythology always felt somewhat incomplete to me. Too few people had retold the same stories too many times. A lot of the behind-the-scenes tales have become so commonplace, whether or not you know them has become a pseudo litmus test among the die-hards to determine how big a fan of the film a new member of their tribe is. And I had a feeling that these stories may have been missing some of their original verve.

Throughout the researching process, I found that my suspicions were true. Many of the anecdotes that have been repeated over the years had been scrubbed clean, condensed to omit significant details, and/or told with minimal context. While interviewing my subjects, I encouraged them to push beyond their stock stories and really remember the past. Or, perhaps more appropriately, the *Future*. And they did. I could feel people discovering things they had long since forgotten, often with startling accuracy. It's difficult for someone to remember everything they did last week, let alone three decades ago, but the more people I spoke to, the more stories were corroborated, and a comprehensive picture of what it was like to be a part of the team that made cinematic history became clearer.

As I learned working on my previous two books, there is rarely a person who works on a film who hasn't accumulated an interesting anecdote or two. To that end, I was fortunate that so many people found it worth their time to spare a few minutes for me. In addition to Robert Zemeckis, Bob Gale, and Christopher

Lloyd, whose manager came through on his promise, more than fifty additional people from all facets of production, including actors, producers, members of the camera crew, editors, graphic artists, costumers, and those involved with special and visual effects, signed on to make this project the largest *Back to the Future* reunion ever assembled. I also spoke with some people who didn't work on the movies, but who are experts on the trilogy's impact, including movie critics, documentarians, and fans who have gone beyond the call of duty to keep the embers glowing for their favorite franchise.

In writing this book, I relied heavily on more than five hundred hours of interviews I conducted over a twenty-one-month period. All of the quotes that appear in the pages that follow come from those conversations. Some of the quotes have been corrected for clarity, which was done extremely judiciously and with significant care for each interview subject. In scenes where conversations are reconstructed, the dialogue comes either from the account of one person or the synthesis of more than one person's recollection of events. All of the information included has either been corroborated against other sources or reflects what had likely happened based on my appraisal of the validity of each speaker and the veracity of their memory. The result is a reconstructed time capsule of the making of the *Back to the Future* trilogy, by those who were there to have experienced it.

As my interview process progressed, I began to realize that this project isn't simply about the making of one film trilogy, but is also about how some of the titans in the movie industry came into being. Even readers who are only casual fans of the films will find interesting pieces of information about the movie business, from the perspective of some of Hollywood's best. At your leisure, look at the list of credits that *Future* alumni amassed

prior to and since working on the films. While you may not recognize every person's name, virtually everyone I spoke with
worked on other movies that have received a substantial bit of
attention over the years, such as *Avatar, Blade Runner, Fight
Club, One Flew Over the Cuckoo's Nest, Star Wars: The Force
Awakens*, the original *Superman* franchise, and *Titanic*, to name
just a few. They are incredibly talented visionaries, some of
whom were already veterans when filming began in 1984, and
others who were just getting started in the business. Regardless
of their previous experience, they worked together to make a
truly timeless film about time travel.

What follows is an amalgamation of their truth—a profile
not only of a film series but, as I was reminded when I spent a
half hour on memory lane with Zemeckis, of the beautifully normal and ordinary people whose creativity and passion produced
an extraordinary trilogy. Some of the decisions they made were
unconventional, yet they paid off, despite the odds. The trilogy
has forever changed the landscape of cinema by redefining what
a summer blockbuster could be, who could star in one, and under
what improbable circumstances a trio of films could have a major
impact around the world. You may not believe *Back to the Future*
is the most important film trilogy of all time now, but after reading
this book I bet you will.

So buckle up, because if my calculations are correct, when
this baby hits eighty-eight miles per hour, you're going to see
some serious shit.

WE DON'T NEED ROADS

1. THINK, McFLY, THINK

Sunday, December 30, 1984

Filming had only been under way for less than a month, but already something wasn't quite right. On what should have been his day off, Robert Zemeckis made his way into the double-wide trailer that would remain parked behind the Amblin Entertainment compound for the next several months. Since all the editing rooms inside the studio offices were delegated to other projects, Steven Spielberg had arranged for coeditors Arthur Schmidt and Harry Keramidas to make the temporary structure their permanent workspace as they pieced together *Back to the Future*, Universal Pictures' film scheduled for release Memorial Day weekend.

The director made his way through the bullpen, which normally would have been buzzing with assistants and apprentices filing film trims and outtakes into the large cardboard boxes that lined the wall. But because it was a weekend, it was a virtual ghost town, with the exception of the two other living souls in the building, Schmidt and Keramidas. The editors were tucked away in the former's makeshift office, seated in front of a modestly sized monitor. Next to them sat a chair—the most comfortable chair in the office—that remained empty except during these visits from Zemeckis. Increasingly, these meetings had become fairly commonplace by this point in the shooting schedule, weeks after their November 26 start date. The production team expected principal photography to wrap after about twenty-two weeks of filming, meaning there would be fewer than three months between the last shot being captured and *Future*'s late May release date. As if the timeline weren't tight enough to begin with, there were several optical effects that would have to be added in postproduction by George Lucas's Industrial Light & Magic (ILM), further constricting the schedule.

To expedite the process, Zemeckis would come into the cutting room at the end of his shooting days and on weekends to look at scenes in the process of being put together. Zemeckis grew to trust his editors, especially Artie, who had been nominated for an Academy Award a few years prior for his work on *Coal Miner's Daughter*, another Universal release. His meticulous editing skills led him to be hired after a serendipitous meeting a few months earlier. "I was working on a film at Paramount called *Firstborn*, and we had two young teenage boys in the movie," he says, likely referring to Christopher Collet and Robert Downey, Jr. "Bob was looking everywhere for somebody to play Marty. He called up the director, Michael Apted, and asked if he could see some film of the two boys. Michael didn't want to let the film out of the cutting room because he was still shooting, and I was close-cutting it as we went along, so he asked Bob to come look at the film on the editing machine with just me."

Zemeckis went over with his producers Bob Gale and Neil Canton to watch the three or four scenes Artie had prepared in advance. The editor ran the film, which, afterward, was met by silence. It seemingly grew louder by the second, until the visitors heard it broken by their host.

"What do you think?"

"I don't think either one of those boys is right for Marty McFly," Zemeckis said. "But I really like the way those scenes were edited." Schmidt's face filled with color, embarrassed that he may have been perceived as fishing for a compliment when he was merely trying to speed up the session and get back to work. He thanked the director for the kind words and the group went on their way. The seemingly inconsequential meeting took on new importance when, about three weeks later, Bob Z called for the editor to come over to his office at Universal for an interview. Schmidt went and was hired.

A second sit-down between Zemeckis and Schmidt soon followed. When there was a lull in the conversation, the editor asked who was cast in the role of Marty, since neither of the young actors they had scouted that fateful day was a match. "So far we haven't decided," Bob Z said. "The guy that I really want is . . ." He walked over to the coffee table in his office and picked up a teen magazine, which he opened to a page with a large photograph of a young heartthrob on it. "That's the guy that I really want to have to play Marty," he said, pointing at the picture. "But he's not available because he's doing his TV show."

Artie didn't know it at the time, but the search for the perfect Marty McFly was an arduous endeavor. When Universal Pictures green-lighted the film, the Bobs immediately set out to fill the pivotal role of *Future*'s protagonist. Although he wasn't in their minds as they wrote the screenplay, once it was finished, they both felt strongly that Michael J. Fox would make the perfect leading man. Today it seems that Fox was born to play Marty, but that was not the case when casting was under way in mid-1984. Yes, the Canadian actor was the linchpin of the popular television sit-com *Family Ties*, but to date he had only appeared in two major motion pictures—Disney's 1980 flop *Midnight Madness* and the moderately successful 1982 film *Class of 1984*, a film with a subtitle that foreshadowed the actor's eventual career-defining role: "We are the future . . . and nothing can stop us!"

In the late summer of 1984, even before the request was made to Michael Apted that resulted in Schmidt's hiring, Steven Spielberg called his friend, *Family Ties* producer Gary David Goldberg, to ask that Fox read the script and consider screen-testing for the role. Spielberg and Goldberg had met in 1979, after Kathleen Kennedy, who was the former's assistant and the latter's old friend from college, introduced the two. While Spielberg was in London filming *Raiders of the Lost Ark*, Goldberg was flown overseas to join him, as the two were collaborating on a screenplay that was ultimately unmade called *Reel to Reel*, a semiautobiographical musical about a first-time director making a science fiction film. By the time *Future* was in preproduction, the two were not only friends, but also neighbors—they both owned beach houses within close proximity of each other in Malibu—and professional allies. Spielberg was one of the first people to see a rough cut of the *Family Ties* pilot back in 1982, and without any puffery, he told his friend that the show was guaranteed to be a hit and that his precocious actor playing the teenage son Alex was going to be a major star. When Zemeckis made it clear that Fox topped his short list of actors for Marty, Spielberg volunteered to give Goldberg a call directly, bypassing the traditional route of phoning an agent to broker a deal.

After a cursory perusal of the screenplay, the television titan decided that Fox wasn't going to be given the pages. Goldberg loved what he read and saw the potential for the film to be a success—but that threatened to derail all he had established with his sitcom. The show was experiencing a meteoric rise in the Nielsen ratings, from forty-ninth place in its first season into the top five within a three-year span, thanks in large part to *The Cosby Show* providing a strong lead-in. When Meredith Baxter, who played matriarch Elyse Keaton on the show, was pregnant with twins, the show's scripts were modified to rely more heavily on Fox's character. The twenty-three-year-old actor, who still had a boyish face and youthful demeanor, became a star, true to Spielberg's prediction, which led to increased attention for the show and teen magazine spreads like the one Zemeckis had on display in his office. Goldberg was confident that Fox would be interested in working on the film, thus distracting him and threatening the show's popularity. He wanted to help his friend, but Michael J. Fox, he said, was off-limits. The search for Marty McFly would have to continue.

So it did. As disappointed as the Bobs were with Fox's lack of availability, they were determined to press on and find the best second choice possible. Nothing about getting *Back to the Future* off the ground had been easy to that point, and as far as they were concerned, this was just the latest setback that they needed to overcome in the same way they always took on their problems—together.

The two had met on the first day of their Cinema 290 class in the fall semester of 1971 at the University of Southern California's School of Cinematic Arts. A fast friendship soon followed. "We were among a handful of undergraduates in a mostly graduate class," Gale says. "We quickly discovered we had similar tastes in film. Bob was the only person I'd ever met who, like me, owned the soundtrack to *The Great Escape*."

They soon realized that, while the majority of their classmates were absorbed with the idea of creating highbrow cinema, they were more interested in making movies that average joes would want to see. More often than not, their free time was spent catching a showing of *Dirty Harry* or the latest *James Bond* flick, not discussing the leitmotifs throughout Akira Kurosawa's career. Movies, they believed, should be entertaining to the general public first and foremost; the added benefit would come when a person reflected on what they had just watched, and realized that there was more than they initially thought had met their eye. Zemeckis had aspirations of being a film director, while Gale dreamed of being a writer, and they decided to develop their common love for moviemaking as a team. Before graduation, they collaborated on each other's student films, including 1972's *The Lift* and 1973's *A Field of Honor*, as well as a screenplay for a horror movie Gale conceived about vampiric prostitutes, *Bordello of Blood*, which, little did they know at the time, would be turned into a movie more than two decades later with a completely rewritten screenplay by A. L. Katz and Gilbert Adler.

Their goal was for *Bordello* to become the first feature they would make together. The two continued to refine the script over their first postgraduate summer, but in order to get a foot in the door, they thought they might try their hand at television. Bob Z took to hanging around Universal Studios, having heard the legend that Steven Spielberg had done the same when he was a young wannabe filmmaker with a dream similar to Zemeckis's. Spielberg, the story goes, hung around the studios so much that he was eventually assumed to have been on contract and was offered a directing gig—a tall tale that makes for great Hollywood lore. While following in his idol's fabricated footsteps, Zemeckis overheard that the television show *Kolchak: The Night Stalker* was nearing cancellation, and established veteran writers were stepping away from the show. Perhaps, he thought, that could provide an opening for two hungry twentysomethings to try their hand at getting one of their stories on the air. The duo banged out a nine-page story treatment for an episode over a few weeks, which Universal purchased. It was the first moment of affirmation that their shared dream of being filmmakers just might come true, and that they might prove their skeptical parents wrong when it happened.

Success knocked swiftly twice more. The Bobs wrote an episode for *McCloud* that was optioned—industry jargon for a producer officially reserving the right, for an agreed-upon time, to purchase a script at a later date—and another script for *Get Christie Love!*, a short-lived series perhaps best remembered now as being name-checked in the opening sequence of Quentin Tarantino's *Reservoir Dogs*. Universal saw potential in the Bobs to be great television writers and offered them a seven-year contract to pen for some of the company's NBC shows, netting each half of the team $50,000 a year through the length of the agreement. Gale's father, who, like Zemeckis's parents, already thought his son was nuts for enrolling at USC with the hopes of becoming a professional filmmaker, was convinced he had raised an idiot when he was told that the Bobs, under the advice of their recently acquired agents and lawyers, were declining the deal.

Instead of relying on that steady paycheck, the two abandoned television and decided instead to concentrate on their big-screen aspirations. They finished another screenplay they wrote on spec named *Tank* and brought it to fellow USC alum John Milius, an uncredited cowriter of the first two *Dirty Harry* films and *Jaws*, who was just a few years away from receiving an Academy Award nomination for his *Apocalypse Now* screenplay. The writer was under contract at Metro-Goldwyn-Mayer (MGM) with a deal to direct two films and produce two others. He was taken with the Bobs' screenplay, but thought they might have a better idea. They pitched another story they had been kicking around, a period comedy set in Los Angeles immediately after the start of World War II. By the end of the meeting, Milius agreed to produce the film, based primarily on the strength of their well-developed concept and enthusiasm. After the Bobs expanded their idea into a formal script, Milius pitched the film to Spielberg, who was already well acquainted with Zemeckis. The director bit, and *1941* began its trek to production.

Bob Z's relationship and friendship with Spielberg began when the former was a student at USC and the latter visited the campus to screen his first film, *The Sugarland Express*. Zemeckis attended the screening, approached Spielberg afterward, and asked if the director would like to see his 1973 student film, *A Field of Honor*, for which Zemeckis had won a Student Academy Award. Within a few days, the two were watching the fourteen-minute short at Spielberg's office. While Spielberg was still years away from becoming a household name at the time of his visit to USC, the director was already establishing a reputation as someone to watch. Sid Sheinberg, who was vice president of production for Universal's television division at the time, saw Spielberg's 1968 student film *Amblin'*, which later inspired the name of the director's production company, and offered him a long-term directing deal. Although *1941* followed the success of *Jaws* and *Close Encounters of the Third Kind*, it failed to replicate those films' profitability at the box office. The movie became Spielberg's first to not recoup its budget in domestic box office gross, though it did return a profit on the studio's investment with overseas markets factored in.

While *1941* was in production, Spielberg signed on to executive-produce *I Wanna Hold Your Hand*, a screenplay the Bobs wrote and which Universal picked up. This time Zemeckis would direct. The movie was released in 1978, and two years later Columbia Pictures released their second film, *Used Cars*. The Bobs put their hearts and souls into both, but while critics loved them, as with *1941*, the movies failed to connect with the general public. "It wasn't that *Hand* and *Used Cars* weren't well received—we had dynamite sneak previews for both," Gale says. "We simply never had audiences show up on opening day."

"Zemeckis's early films he made with his writing partner Bob Gale just have such an incredible kinetic energy," film critic Leonard Maltin says. "They seem to be supercharged with adrenaline. That's what I think about first and foremost. I love *Used Cars*, and I'll never understand really why that didn't become more. Even over the years it never really built the following that it deserves, but I don't know why. Is it too snarky? Too cynical? I don't know. Maybe just the name *Used Cars* connotes something that people don't find appealing."

Although Columbia Pictures only made a minuscule profit on *Used Cars*, with the movie earning $11.7 million against an $8 million budget, Frank Price, the head of the studio, wasn't ready to give up on the two young filmmakers. The movie had received the highest ratings in test screenings in the studio's history, and what did it matter that few people saw it, really? Those who did thought it was hilarious—the studio head included. Shortly after the film was released, Price asked the Bobs to bring their next idea to him as soon as they had one—which, as it turned out, was sooner than expected, as an idea had been marinating between the two filmmakers.

Just a few weeks before Price approached them, Bob G was in his hometown of St. Louis to do some publicity for *Used Cars* and attend the local premiere of his film. While visiting his parents' house, he discovered his father's 1940 University City High School yearbook. Before he was the patriarch of the Gale family, Bob's father was the senior class president, a fact the filmmaker hadn't known until he stumbled across his dad's black-and-white photo. As Bob stared at the face on the printed page, he realized his own time as a student must have been very different from his father's. The younger Gale, who graduated from the same school in '69, would never have run for student government. Although he achieved straight-A's, he wasn't one of the eggheads. He loved music—not rock and roll, like some of the other students, but movie scores. His spare time was spent reading comic books or science fiction novels, making movies, or working in the art studio. Girls were interesting but expensive, so he didn't date until his senior year. As a student, he had a wide range of interests, but making speeches in front of his peers and hanging up GO WITH GALE or BET ON BOB posters in the hallways was not among them. The young filmmaker's mind went into overdrive while he stared at his father's yearbook photo. He couldn't help but wonder: If he and his father had attended school at the same time, would they have been friends?

The Bobs had been trying to come up with a time-travel story since they'd begun collaborating on scripts, having both been influenced heavily by H. G. Wells's *The Time Machine*, as well as Rod Serling's *The Twilight Zone* television series, but couldn't come up with an original idea worthy of being told. However, as Gale packed the yearbook away, he thought he had come up with the germ of a great idea. When he returned to Los Angeles, he shared his thought with his collaborator. Zemeckis saw the potential in the concept and started adding his own extemporaneous suggestions into the mix: *What if your mom, who always said she had never kissed a boy while a teenager, was actually the school slut?* They quickly fleshed out some additional details of their story and brought the idea to Frank Price.

It took the studio head less than three minutes to realize that their project was a winner. During the pitch, Gale sensed that Price was interested, but it took Zemeckis a bit longer to read the tea leaves. The director's enthusiasm led him to prattle on with minor plot details and gags that the duo had come up with. After a few minutes of monologue, his partner gave him a nudge, stopping Bob Z just long enough for the two to be offered a development deal at Columbia to expand their idea into a screenplay.

Within a few days, the two got to work. "Bob and I always sat in the same room, usually our office, and talked through everything," Gale says. "We would first outline the movie on index cards and put them up on a corkboard on the wall. Once we had a structure and plan for the film, we'd start with the first scene and talk it through. We'd work out the dialogue in each scene together, and I'd make detailed notes."

"It was a true collaboration," Zemeckis adds. "We were very much in sync, and when a good idea got sparked, it was pretty much just back-and-forth, talking everything through. We said everything that came to our minds; we were never worried that we might be saying something that wasn't a good idea or a valid idea. Anything that we thought of, we would run it up the flagpole for the other guy because you just never know. You never know what might spark another idea."

"Because I could type and Bob couldn't, each night I'd type up the day's work into script form," Gale continues. "When we started writing the first draft, I was using a manual typewriter which I'd had since I was a college freshman and I still have to this day. I don't recall if I made carbon copies as I typed, or if we xeroxed the pages the next day. Either way, the result was that Bob Z had a copy of what I typed up. We moved into the next scene, and when I was typing that day's work, Bob would review the typed pages I'd given him that morning, making notes, revisions, whatever. I never read what I typed until there was a complete script. That way, I could read it from beginning to end and get a sense of the pace, which Bob could not do, since he dealt with it scene by scene."

This process continued until, on February 21, 1981, the two completed the first draft of *Back to the Future*. While the main crux of the story that materialized on-screen is present—boy has crackpot inventor friend, crackpot inventor has time machine, boy is accidentally sent back in time and disrupts his parents' first meeting—there are several significant differences between that screenplay and what made it to the screen. In this script, Marty McFly was a video pirate, running a secret black market operation with his friend Professor—not Doc—Brown, who had a pet chimpanzee named Shemp. His girlfriend's name is Suzy, his mother's is Eileen, Marty travels back to 1952, and his parents have their first kiss while the band Lester & the Moonlighters plays Eddie Fisher's 1951 single "Turn Back the Hands of Time" at the Springtime in Paris dance.

Frank Price still thought the general conceit of the movie was good, but believed the screenplay was too rough around the edges. The Bobs, ever hopeful, went back to their office with index cards in tow. "Inevitably, our opinion regarding our own first rough draft was that it was terrible," Gale says. "This was true with every script we'd ever written. We proceeded to revise, deconstruct, and overhaul the work."

A second draft was completed on April 7. Price thought their second go-around was better, but he passed on giving *Future* the green light. *Used Cars* was a raunchy comedy, Zemeckis's only R-rated film until 2012's *Flight*, and Price was hoping the Bobs would bring him another picture that fit that mold. A quaint movie about a kid trying to fix up his parents might make a good film, but as far as Price was concerned, he didn't know anyone besides himself who would be interested in seeing it. The script was given back to the filmmakers in what is known in the industry as a turnaround deal, an arrangement whereby a studio—for example, Universal—can purchase the rights to a script developed at another studio—like Columbia—so the original studio can recoup their initial investment.

Which was precisely what happened. The Bobs were free to take their script to other movie studios, which initially proved to be less than fruitful. From Paramount to Universal, 20th Century Fox to Warner Bros., every executive they met with asked them a variation of the same question: *What about Steven?* Spielberg was interested in executive-producing *Future*—he saw the potential in Zemeckis and Gale's script and the ingenuity of their idea—but the Hollywood heavyweight was asked to stand down during the pitch process. The Bobs liked working with him, but their first two films had underperformed. They were afraid that if that precedent continued, they would never be given an opportunity to make another for a major studio. Even worse, they would be perceived among those in the industry as two people who scored undeserved opportunities to waste studio money because of their friendship with one of the most profitable directors of the past decade. Thus, Zemeckis asked his friend for some space in an attempt to prove he could stand on his own two feet.

As the Bobs continued to shop the film around to every studio in Hollywood and back again, they frequently heard that *Future*'s script was too saccharine to attract the rebellious youth of the 1980s. Although history would ultimately prove them wrong, one can't fault the uniform thought process of notoriously risk-averse film executives. In the four years that it took for the duo to convince a studio to finance and release their picture, R-rated teen comedies like *Fast Times at Ridgemont High*, *Porky's*, and *Risky Business* were all huge hits at the box office. Not only that, but three time-travel films also hit cinemas—*The Final Countdown*, *Somewhere in Time*, and *Time Bandits*—and only the latter was a modest success. The record was set and well corroborated: raunchy comedies made money; time-travel movies did not. All of the studios passed on it primarily for those reasons, except for Tom Wilhite, the vice president in charge of development for feature films and television at the Walt Disney Company, who had his own complaints. The suit was appalled by the scene with Marty and his teenage mother sharing a brief, awkward kiss in Doc's yellow Packard convertible. The movie was officially a nonstarter—too provocative for Disney and not provocative enough for any other studio.

Although the Bobs both hoped to see *Back to the Future* made, reality soon set in. It was nice to continue to pursue a dream, but it was better to have money so they could eat. The Bobs got an opportunity to set up *Gangland*, a gangster movie for a short-lived feature film division of the ABC television network, but about five weeks into preproduction the company killed the picture. The project wasn't one that either Bob was particularly jazzed about, but it was the final straw for Zemeckis. He was tired of running on the hamster wheel—developing an idea, writing a script, pitching to studios, and then repeating the process, only to watch a green light go red, or fail to turn green at all. He informed his partner that he would direct the next decent script that came by. Gale understood. No hard feelings.

As if he spoke it into being, a screenplay that appealed to Zemeckis's interests soon landed in his lap. He was offered to direct Michael Douglas, Kathleen Turner, and Danny DeVito in

1984's *Romancing the Stone*, a romantic comedy-action film about a woman from the big city embarking on an adventure that takes her through the jungles of Colombia. The film, which marked the director's first collaboration with Dean Cundey, was shot primarily on location in Mexico. Although the director and cinematographer got on well, the shoot was occasionally problematic, with Turner frequently becoming frustrated with Zemeckis's style of directing. She thought he was a bright-eyed kid fresh out of film school, more preoccupied with the cameras and special effects than he was attentive to his actors. The director not only failed to impress his leading lady, but he, more detrimentally, failed to win any accolades from the studio executives at 20th Century Fox.

"He wasn't the Bob Zemeckis that we all know now, with all the fabulous films. He had made those other two movies, which, financially, had not done well at all," Clyde E. Bryan, who served as first assistant cameraman on *Romancing the Stone*, says. "Instead, the studio executives were counting on a picture called *Rhinestone* to be a huge hit. It was with Dolly Parton and Sylvester Stallone. It was an awful combination, a terrible movie. They put tons and tons and tons of money into that movie. They spent almost no money on *Romancing the Stone*, and at one point they had sent the bonds people down there to pull the plug on it. It was, at that time, not a very expensive movie, nine or ten million dollars. They just had no idea about how it would perform."

"It was kind of a different film for the period," Cundey says. "When they saw the first rough cut of *Romancing the Stone*, one of the guys at the studio said that he thought the film was unreleasable." While the director continued to work with his editors on the final cut and reshoots, the bottom was falling out beneath him. He was pegged to direct another film for Fox, the science fiction/

fantasy film *Cocoon*, but after the producers of that project received a tip that *Romancing the Stone* was anticipated to perform poorly in theaters, Zemeckis was fired. It was clear: Zemeckis's chances were running out. He needed a hit or he would be denied any further opportunities to direct another motion picture for a major studio.

Then, despite the forecast, the sky opened up. *Romancing the Stone* was released in theaters on March 30, 1984, earning a respectable $5.1 million in its opening weekend. The following week it performed even better. Contrary to industry expectations, the movie was not only a financial success, but it was Fox's only hit of the year. By the time the film ended its theatrical run, it had grossed over $76.5 million domestically, nearly four times what *Rhinestone* brought in. Almost instantaneously, Zemeckis became a director in demand, with *Back to the Future* becoming a hot property by extension. The Bobs were back and it was no longer a question of whether or not their time-travel movie would see the light of day. The only question was which studio would be financing it.

Zemeckis didn't want to give any of his fair-weather Holly-wood friends who had rejected *Future* over the preceding years the courtesy of producing his picture. The answer, then, was to go back to the only person who had believed in the project from the start—Steven Spielberg. He had recently entered the record books with *E.T. the Extra-Terrestrial*, which had banked $359 million to surpass *Star Wars* as the highest-grossing film of all time. Although his stature in the industry had risen dramatically since he'd first read the Bobs' *Future* script, the producer still wanted in. *Back to the Future* became the first project set up at Amblin Entertainment that Steven Spielberg would not direct himself—a testament to the trust the mentor had in his mentee.

After joining the *Back to the Future* team, the executive producer pitched the project to Universal, where the Amblin offices were located. Serendipitously, Frank Price was now president after having left Columbia in 1983. Spielberg held a grudge against the executive for passing on *E.T.* when he was still at his previous movie company, and stated that if Universal wanted to be a part of *Back to the Future*, Price would have to be involved as minimally as possible. "Frank Price never had an intimate relationship with Steven," Sid Sheinberg says. "He was very much under the influence of a fellow by the name of Marvin Antonowsky who came from the world of research. The problem with the world of research is that sometimes you come to the wrong conclusions." In a highly unusual move, Sheinberg appointed himself to chief executive in charge of looking out for the studio's investment in the film. After four years of rejections, the Bobs finally got the green light they had been hoping for.

With the ball finally rolling, a production team had to be rounded out. With Spielberg came Frank Marshall and his former assistant Kathleen Kennedy, two producers who, in 1981, cofounded Amblin after they achieved success with *Raiders of the Lost Ark*. Although the Bobs had a relationship with Spielberg, it was clear that this was a project that would have interested the Amblin Trio even if it had arrived at their offices unsolicited. "I thought the screenplay was terrific," Frank Marshall says. "I couldn't understand why no one wanted to make it. It's one of the best scripts I'd ever read."

Frank Marshall suggested Neil Canton join the team, whom he had previously worked with on 1972's *What's Up, Doc?* "He had this script and asked me if I would read it," Canton says. "I read it, loved it, called him the next day, and told him. It made me laugh. I was moved by it. The idea of a time-travel story was something that I totally was in love with." Later that day, Canton, Zemeckis, and Gale met for lunch in Burbank. The three hit it off and the production team was complete.

After four years of tinkering with the script, which was still in its second draft, Zemeckis and company officially started preproduction. The director invited some of the *Romancing the Stone* crew to join him, including Dean Cundey, Clyde E. Bryan, and composer Alan Silvestri. However exciting it was that things were under way, there were still some matters to deal with regarding the script. Sid Sheinberg wanted the name of Marty's mother to be changed from Eileen to the first name of his wife, actress Lorraine Gary, who appeared in both Spielberg's *1941* and *Jaws*. He was also adamant that Professor Brown be nicknamed "Doc" instead, as it was shorter and more accessible. Of utmost importance was that Shemp, the scientist's pet primate, had to go. "Sid *hated* that," Gale says. "He told us he'd looked it up and that movies with chimps never made money. I challenged him, pointing out Clint Eastwood and *Every Which Way But Loose*, but Sid retorted that the simian was an orangutan, not a chimp. So we gave Doc a dog instead. Probably a good idea—everybody likes dogs." Rewrites resumed, with Sheinberg's changes, along with many others, materializing in a third draft, which was completed that July.

But just as it seemed like everything had finally fallen into place, things started to get complicated. With Michael J. Fox unavailable to play Marty, casting directors Jane Feinberg, Mike Fenton, and Judy Taylor met with what felt like an unremitting list of newly established actors and potential stars-to-be, including Johnny Depp, fresh off of a substantial role in 1984's *A Nightmare on Elm Street*, and Brat Pack member John Cusack. George Newbern, who is perhaps best known for his role in *Father of the Bride* (1991) and its sequel released four years later, flew in from

Chicago to audition. Charlie Sheen, who had made a stellar debut in 1984's *Red Dawn*, also read for the role. Canadian pop star Corey Hart was given the opportunity to screen-test, but declined. Perhaps as a public sign of regret over his decision and an attempt to associate himself with the franchise, the singer's official website still trumpets that the casting triumvirate wanted to meet with him, even though he was completely uninterested in the role at the time. None of these actors were ever seriously considered; they were just a few of the many to circle through the revolving door of the casting office, only to be quickly sent out the other end.

C. Thomas Howell and Eric Stoltz ascended to the top of the casting directors' list of Marty choices. By the time of his audition, Howell had accumulated a string of successful roles in hit films helmed by Hollywood royalty like Steven Spielberg (*E.T. the Extra-Terrestrial*) and Francis Ford Coppola (*The Outsiders*). The Bobs preferred him, believing he gave the strongest screen test of everyone who auditioned, an opinion generally shared with the casting directors and members of the film crew. "I remember C. Thomas Howell's audition really well because, if I had been in charge, I would have picked him," Clyde E. Bryan, first assistant cameraman, says. "He was the only one that made that character seem real to me. There were three or four different tests for Marty, but the only two I remember were Eric Stoltz, mostly because of his piercing blue eyes, and the fact that the hair and makeup department dyed his hair, and C. Thomas Howell, who I thought was hilarious in the part. Based on C. Thomas Howell's screen test, he was the right choice."

Eric Stoltz had become a protégé of writer Cameron Crowe after appearing in 1982's *Fast Times at Ridgemont High* and accumulated several other films on his résumé, including the writer's 1984 follow-up *The Wild Life*. Ironically, none of his high school comedies were responsible for him being on the McFly short list. What attracted the attention of the suits at Universal was Stoltz's star turn as Rocky Dennis, a teenager living with a skull deformity, in Peter Bogdonavich's *Mask*, another Universal picture. Although the film had yet to be released at the time *Future* was casting, studio head Sid Sheinberg had seen the picture and anticipated its success by a mile. While his foresight was not always correct, in this instance he accurately predicted what was to come. When *Mask* was released in March 1985, it opened to commercial and critical acclaim. Stoltz's performance was applauded in the press as being emotionally visceral despite the actor being concealed in heavy facial appliances. The actor would go on to be nominated for a Golden Globe for his performance, but for now he was a soon-to-be-discovered secret, a star whom Sheinberg hoped would remain in Universal's solar system for a long time to come.

Because of his history with Spielberg, Sid Sheinberg had taken a special interest in *Back to the Future* and the Marty McFly casting deliberations. He communicated the choice between the two finalists as deciding between "chicken salad," Stoltz, and "chicken shit," Howell. Sheinberg registered his official vote for the former, which, in the end, proved to be the only vote that mattered. Zemeckis had final say on casting, sure, but with that Memorial Day mandate from the studio hanging over his head, each calendar page tossed in the garbage while casting deliberations continued came at a high cost. Not only that, but disagreeing with the studio head was probably not the best foot to get off on. Sheinberg was so positive that Eric Stoltz would be right for the role that he told the Bobs that if it didn't work out, he would allow them to replace their leading man. The matter was settled. Stoltz was offered and quickly accepted the role.

Filming began and continued for four weeks. As Christmas approached, production didn't stop completely. Gale and Canton took advantage of the holiday hiatus, and cameras rolled inside Whittier High School, the location used as the fictional Hill Valley High, while the students were on break. But the winter did put a small freeze on the schedule, which the director used to his advantage. He tasked the editors with putting together a very rough cut of all the footage shot to date, which the three of them would screen prior to the year's end. It wasn't until that Sunday in late December, when Bob Z and his two editors were staring pensively at a monitor, that the problem that had been bubbling under the surface reached a full boil. Before that moment, the director knew there would be reshoots. Days earlier, he had provided Artie Schmidt and Harry Keramidas, who was brought on board shortly after filming began when it became apparent that editing would be more time-consuming than originally thought, with notebook pages of shots he suspected would have to be revisited. Zemeckis would be paying special attention to those sequences while watching this comprehensive, yet rough, edit of about an hour's worth of footage—a month's worth of fruits from their collective labor. Although Bob Z had been upholding his end of the bargain, coming into the trailer during lunch breaks and after shooting to check on the scenes that were being cut on a daily basis, he sensed that the film might not be gelling as a whole the way he had hoped.

"Bob does not like to see his movie in any kind of long form until he's worked on every scene and has each scene where he wants it," Keramidas says. "He once said that he gets so depressed on watching the first cut of his movies because he feels like there's so much more that he needs to get out of it."

"Movies are like little pieces at a time—little moments that have been put together, and sometimes you can't get a sense of how the performance is going until you see some of those moments put together," Neil Canton says. "Maybe there was a reason Bob went to the editing room when he did. Maybe deep down inside he was worried. Maybe down inside he said, *I want to go see this, because I'm not sure if this is working the way I want it to,* or there was a little voice in his head saying, *Go to the editing room, Bob. Go to the editing room.* Either way, I'm just very, very thankful that he did."

So, the day before the coruscating sparkling ball was set to drop in Manhattan, Zemeckis was seeking to confirm if the voice in his head was correct. The three watched in silence, with the director analyzing each frame through his large eyeglasses. There were minor aspects of many shots that bothered him. The unrelenting side effect of Zemeckis being a disciple of David Lean, director of picturesque cinematic films including 1957's *The Bridge on the River Kwai,* 1962's *Lawrence of Arabia,* and 1965's *Doctor Zhivago,* was that he believed every frame of a film had to be worthy of being hung on a wall and heralded as a piece of fine art. But attention to detail was the least of his worries in this case. The problem wasn't the forest, but one specific tree— the largest redwood in sight. Bob Z watched as Eric Stoltz first walked across the 1950s Hill Valley town square in a T-shirt, high-collared black jacket, and dark jeans. He ran across the street, the sky above him overcast. Zemeckis not only was failing the Lean test, but his score was falling faster with each passing second. Everything in the frame was the antithesis of perfection. It was dark, dreary, and devoid of any humor, a mirror reflecting the director's mood. The confirmation was complete.

"It was very agonizing," Zemeckis says. "You don't want to have to admit this horrible truth. There was no moment where it was, 'Oh, I know what the problem is.' It was always a gnawing suspicion that just got worse and worse in my mind, and then I finally had to admit to myself that it wasn't working in the way that it needed to."

The rough-edit screening continued, with Zemeckis barely making a sound. The three sat in silence once the monitor stopped broadcasting the film, with Bob Z deep in thought. After a few minutes passed, Artie spoke up.

"What do you think?"

The director knew what he thought, but was uncertain as to whether he should say it.

"Well, I don't think Eric . . ." Zemeckis paused for a minute, and then reconsidered and rephrased his answer. "There's a hole in the middle of our screen. The lead actor doesn't work."

In that moment, it was hard to pinpoint exactly what the implications of Bob Z's statement were. Was this simply a case of a nitpicking director venting, or did this mean that the picture was destined to be dead on arrival before it had even come to term? Having watched the totality of the shot footage, even more than what Zemeckis had screened, the editors weren't immediately sure what the problem was. "I had accepted the fact that Eric Stoltz was Marty McFly," Schmidt says. "What I thought of his performance didn't seem to make much difference to me at that particular point because I knew that Bob had looked high and low for somebody to play Marty and finally settled on Eric. Who better to know what Marty McFly's character was supposed to be other than both Bob Zemeckis and Bob Gale?"

While Artie was trying to figure out the why, Harry took to figuring out the where, as in, where he was going to find his next gig when this one went belly-up. Keramidas got the job on *Future* after being recommended by Schmidt, whom he worked with on 1978's *Jaws II*. The working relationship between the two wasn't only good, it was great, but it now appeared their professional reunion was to be short-lived. "I was afraid I was going to lose my job," Keramidas says. "I was having my first big break on a big Hollywood movie with the best script I had ever read, and probably the best script I ever did read in my whole career in terms of how well it was realized and how much it resonated page to page, scene to scene, and all I could foresee in that moment was a shutdown."

However oblivious the editors were to Zemeckis's discontent with Stoltz, there were others who saw red flags. "I kind of sensed for about three weeks prior to the fact that they weren't happy and were looking for a solution," cinematographer Dean Cundey says. "While I heard a couple of rumors, there was nothing concrete for any of us in the circle to go by just watching on the set. Bob would want something that would make you say, 'Yeah, that's pretty funny,' and Eric would say, 'Well, no, I don't think I can do that.'"

Back to the Future is hard to pin down in terms of genre, with significant comedic, science fiction, fantasy, and even musical elements. While there are moments of romance and pathos, the film would certainly not be considered by many to be a hard-hitting emotional drama. But that fact might have been lost on its original lead actor. From the first day of shooting, the director had to put in extra effort to try and coax out of Stoltz the comedic performance that he and Gale had imagined would be there during the writing process.

"Eric didn't get it," Clyde E. Bryan says. "Eric did not understand the physical, pratfall type of humor that Bob was looking for, that Steven called 'Daffy Duck humor.' Eric didn't like that. It wasn't part of his style, for sure, so it was this constant tug-of-war—'This is what I want,' 'I don't get it,' 'Why should I fall down when I'm putting my pants on?' Eric is a fine actor. I've worked with him before and since then, but he's a very method actor, which doesn't really work for Bob's style of shooting."

Almost half a decade earlier, in 1981, Eric Stoltz moved to New York after dropping out of the University of Southern California. He studied with Stella Adler, Peggy Feury, and William Taylor, respected and revered acting teachers, before returning to Los Angeles the following year. Consistent with Adler's preferred approach to the craft, he devoted himself to the "method," a process by which a performer uses a number of techniques to embody the thoughts and feelings of the character he or she is portraying, in order to achieve a more realistic performance. Stoltz learned to parse a script and look for subtext, skills that may have been put to limited use in his earlier film roles, but lessons that paid dividends and led to his excellence in *Mask*. That movie may have caused him to get the role of Marty, but it was obvious from day one, at least to Lea Thompson, who played Marty's mother, Lorraine Baines McFly, that Stoltz's approach may have been all wrong for the lighter fare that the Bobs were going for.

"The story is really kind of intense if you think about it," she says. "If you break down the script as a fine actor, you get confused by that stuff. They needed an actor to keep those balls up in the air so people would just stay with the story and not think about the darker aspects of it. I remember after the read-through, everyone was like, 'That was so great,' and he brought up the point that it's really kind of strange and sad that all the people Marty loves remember a past he didn't live. He remembers a completely different past. I don't remember how he said it, but I was like, 'Don't do that! Don't say that, Eric!' He just wasn't the right fit for the part."

The ill fit of his acting chops might have been something the actor was actually aware of. Several in the crew believed he was frustrated working on the project, as there was little similarity between Marty McFly and the actor portraying him. At one point, Stoltz purportedly said in the makeup chair before shooting that he didn't understand why he was in the film, because he wasn't a comedian and didn't think he was funny. He fancied himself as more of a trained and serious actor. The response from the makeup artist was simple: "You're an actor? Well, then act, dammit."

But that's not to say that he wasn't trying. Stoltz did all he could to get into character and excel in the role. After shooting, he frequently met with Paul Hanson, a guitar instructor at Hollywood's Musicians Institute hired by Bones Howe, the film's music supervisor, to learn how to finger-sync on the guitar for the "Johnny B. Goode" number at the Enchantment Under the Sea dance. "He was staying at the Universal Sheraton, and I would go up to his room," Hanson says. "Then he would come over to my house in North Hollywood. He was a really cool guy. He was a fellow *Star Trek* Trekkie like me. I taught him for maybe a month or so—maybe not that long, but it seemed like that—a couple of times a week." The actor wasn't a musician and had difficulty working his way around the electric instrument, but after a few weeks he became passably proficient. The actor also spent many hours working with Bob Schmelzer, his skateboarding coach. He was much better on a skateboard, so much so that Schmelzer, who was also hired to be one of Stoltz's doubles on the film, thought the actor added a touch of punk edginess to the movie whenever he rode through a scene on four wheels. Stoltz was comfortable and confident on a skateboard, having known how to ride before taking the *Future* gig, which made those moments among the best he experienced during his time working on the movie.

While he clearly sensed that the actor wasn't gelling despite his efforts, Zemeckis tried to make the best of it. Directing, he feels, is a series of compromises. If you're shooting on location, you hope you have well-spaced cumulus clouds against a clear backdrop of cornflower blue, but if you don't, you make your peace with the sky you get. You try your best to remain on schedule, but if not, you move as quickly as you can and try and catch up at a later date. If an actor isn't meeting your standards, try harder to get him to, and then, if all else fails, hope the next shot is better, add some more notes to your legal pad, and press on. But as the director watched the rough cut on the day before New Year's Eve, 1984, he knew keeping Eric Stoltz in *Back to the Future* was a compromise he could not make.

"What do you think we should do, Artie?"

"If you really think this is a big problem, then you should get these scenes in front of our producers as soon as possible, tomorrow, on Monday, and if they agree with you, then you should show the scenes to Steven. If Steven agrees, get the scenes in front of the executives at Universal." Artie looked at his number two, who was peering over the list of shots Zemeckis wanted the editors to trim or use alternate takes of. Zemeckis was not only unhappy with Stoltz's performance, but also the cut-together footage, which he thought was not ready to be shared with anyone else.

"We don't have any time to make any of your changes, so I'll take complete responsibility for the way those scenes are edited," Schmidt continued. "You can tell the producers and Steven and the studio heads that it's not your edit, but we just wanted to get these things in front of everybody because of Eric's performance."

Bob Z sat for a moment, and then got up and left the room, passing all of the cardboard boxes that housed what would soon be mostly unusable footage. He thought about it the whole way home. At this moment, Robert Zemeckis and Marty McFly had two significant things in common—they both were chiefly responsible for fixing the future, and they both needed some assistance and support in doing so. He picked up the phone and called his producers, telling both Bob Gale and Neil Canton the same thing: "Good news, bad news. The good news is that everybody else in the movie is really, really wonderful, the bad news being that Eric is kind of lost in the movie. He doesn't have the everyman quality that we had all been hoping for."

The following day, the two producers joined Zemeckis in watching the footage. They too saw the hole in the screen. The next step was to bring the cut to Steven Spielberg and ask for his support in raising their concerns and request to recast to Sid Sheinberg. The director took the footage to the screening room at Amblin and watched it with his executive producer. When it was over, Zemeckis asked if he was crazy for seeing what he saw. The answer was an emphatic no. Spielberg could write a long list of positive attributes about what he had just watched, but Eric Stoltz's performance would not have been on it.

Zemeckis may not have been eager initially to have Spielberg on his *Future* team during the pitching phase, but with this problem on his hands, Bob Z was glad to have his old adviser still standing beside him. Spielberg screened the footage for his partners Kathleen Kennedy and Frank Marshall, who quickly joined the bandwagon of Zemeckis supporters. "I thought it was a brave conversation for Bob to have at a point when there was still something that we could do," Marshall says. "We were really young. It'd be terrifying now, but it presented itself as a challenge. What do we do? How do we fix this? That's what producers do. Our job is to help directors get their vision up on the screen, whether they have a different vision than they originally had or not. Our challenge was, how do we do this? Can we actually pull this off?"

With all of the producers in tow, Spielberg counseled Zemeckis and his producers to line up a replacement as soon as possible. No matter what they did, they had to keep moving forward on the filming schedule so the studio wouldn't smell blood in the water and pull the plug altogether. While the problem was clear, the solution was more opaque. The search for Marty McFly had been arduous from the beginning, and there was no indication that trying to line up a replacement actor—especially while operating secretly—would yield any greater success. With their backs against the wall, Steven Spielberg offered to make a Hail Mary pass. He shut his office door behind him, sat behind his desk, and made another call on the film's behalf to his friend Gary David Goldberg over at *Family Ties*.

2. ERASED FROM EXISTENCE

Thursday, January 3, 1985

It took Michael J. Fox less than an hour to hang up the phone, get dressed, leave his house, fly down the highway, and get to NBC Studios in Burbank. He had made the drive to Gary David Goldberg's office dozens of times before, but there was something about the urgency and vagueness of the producer's call that made Fox sure this was not going to be a usual visit. He arrived feeling as if he had been called down to the principal's office, and worried he had inadvertently done something worthy of reprimand. Goldberg was already behind his desk. He skipped the pleasantries, further putting Fox on edge. The television producer had a lot of respect for his star and shot straight with him. Goldberg told Fox about *Back to the Future*, how the film's production team had wanted him from the start, and how Goldberg had kept the script from him. While much of this was new information for Fox, the producer was surprised to know the actor was already familiar with the movie and had wanted to be involved since the film's preproduction stages.

Back in mid-August, when Meredith Baxter was put on bed rest as her due date neared, *Family Ties* went on a brief hiatus so her character wouldn't be absent for half of the season. During this time off, Fox was offered, and accepted, the lead role in *Teen Wolf*, a campy teen horror-comedy produced by an independent film studio that promised the actor the three things he was most in want of—a decent paycheck, a starring role, and a four-week shooting schedule. While filming in Pasadena, Fox saw a crew scouting the location where the *Teen Wolf* team had temporarily set up shop. The actor struck up a conversation with the visitors, who said they were working on a new movie, *Back to the Future*, which Steven Spielberg was involved with. The actor was immediately self-conscious of his situation, burdened by afflictive prosthetic makeup, running around the street like an animal in this low-budget piece-of-trash movie that was almost destined to be a flop, while Crispin Glover, whom Fox had recently worked with on an episode of *Family Ties*, was going to be appearing in a $14 million Spielberg picture. Fox thought he was at least as good an actor as Glover was. Why wasn't he offered a chance to audition for the film?

But now it all made sense. The television producer took the script out of an oversize manila envelope safely guarded in his desk drawer. When Spielberg approached Goldberg about Fox for the second time, things were different on both ends. "We assured him we would adjust our shooting schedule around that of *Family Ties*," Bob Gale says. The actor in demand now had a little more flexibility in his series' shooting schedule, since Meredith Baxter had given birth to her twins and returned to *Family Ties* full-time. Additionally, the sitcom would soon be ending its production for the season, not beginning it, as was the case when the filmmakers were initially looking to cast. Spielberg quickly forwarded a revised copy of the script to the television studio and asked that the actor read it that night.

Fox took the script and considered its title quizzically. Given the erratic situation surrounding *Family Ties* in the summer of 1984, the actor couldn't blame the show's creator for seeking to protect his property. Goldberg asked Fox to read it overnight and report back the next day if he was interested. If so, it would mean working eighteen-hour days between both projects, sometimes even longer. Weekends would be dedicated almost entirely to shooting the film, at least until the TV show wrapped for the season close to four months later. And by the way, he would have to start next week.

The actor grabbed the thick stack of pages and made a makeshift scale out of the palm of his hand, bending his forearm at the elbow to assess the weight. It was much heftier than any of his sitcom scripts. He got ready to leave his boss's office, but stopped to let the producer know a decision had already been made, without the script even being read. Michael J. Fox was in. The *Future* production team had cleared their most important hurdle to date. Now they were going in for the kill.

Thanks to a 4:30 P.M. call time on Wednesday, January 2, the producers had time to see the Great and Powerful Wizard of Universal, Sid Sheinberg. Not only would letting Eric Stoltz go be an expensive venture, as they would have to pay him his already-agreed-upon salary and there would be overages due to essentially starting over, but it would also further derail the film's release date. Initially Sheinberg hoped to have the movie in theaters by Memorial Day, but he had already acquiesced and scheduled the film for a mid-July release. A casting change of this magnitude would derail the release of the movie by at least another month. While Sheinberg had given his blessing that they could replace Stoltz if it didn't work out, everyone involved knew it was a bold request, even for someone with as much capital in Hollywood to spend as Steven Spielberg. Replacing an actor midstream wasn't completely without precedence—Harvey Keitel was replaced with Martin Sheen after Francis Ford Coppola was unhappy with the first week of photography on *Apocalypse Now*—but never with so much footage, money, and time that would go to waste. "We went to Sid Sheinberg and put our cards on the table," Bob Gale says. "After he saw the footage, he reluctantly agreed."

But Sheinberg disagrees with the producer's claim. "It was an easy decision," he says. "What would you do if you had a project that had two people making it, Bob and Steven, that you had a very high regard for? They never really said, 'We think it's bad.' They were saying, 'It's not funny. It's not working the way we see it.' It didn't take me one minute. They wanted me to go down and look at film, and I said, 'You guys must be crazy. You think I'm going to take the two of you on? Life is too short. If you guys feel the way you do, make the change.' I think if I would have said, 'Continue making the movie that you don't think is working,' then I would have been an idiot for sure."

While Zemeckis is quick to acknowledge that casting Stoltz was his error, Sid Sheinberg feels culpable for the casting decision. "I was responsible for Eric being hired, but I don't consider that to be a character flaw," Sheinberg says. "It's just that my perception of the role originally was to use actors as prototypes. I saw the role as Jimmy Stewart, which is one kind of a comedy. They saw the role, 'they' being Bob and Steven, as Bob Hope. With the wisdom of hindsight, they were right. Of course, we don't know what would have happened if Eric Stoltz had ended up completing the picture. It may have also been successful."

Secretly, steps were taken to make the transition as smooth as possible. Fox met with the production team and was caught up to speed on his character. Marty McFly, a guitar-playing teenager, seemed like a part right up the actor's alley. He already knew his way around the instrument, and although he wasn't the best rider in the world, he owned a skateboard and was willing and eager to spend more time on one. Initially he found the story a bit confusing to follow, but he thought the writing was exceptional. Whatever happened with *Teen Wolf*, which had yet to be released, and his two previous films, was irrelevant in his mind from this point on; his film career was going to start on his first day of shooting *Future*.

Meanwhile, production kept moving along with the original McFly. Years later, when Eric Stoltz was asked to reflect on his time working on *Back to the Future*, the actor recounted that it felt like a long winter. Perhaps he was remembering the evening of January 7, when art imitated life and Stoltz and Marty's experiences finally became one. The cast and crew shot at Griffith Park, a location production manager Dennis Jones hyperbolically noted that, at night, is the coldest spot in the known universe. Just hours earlier, Zemeckis got the approval to move forward with transitioning away from one lead to the other. Few people knew it at the time, but the actor was soon to be given severance and sent on his way. That evening, Stoltz shot a scene in the sequence before lightning strikes the clock tower. Marty is at the white starting line getting ready to take off in his vehicular time machine. He slams on the gas, but nothing happens. He feels the simultaneous frustration and disappointment that his perceived destiny, his future, isn't within reach as he originally thought. He tries again, but nope. He keeps turning the key, trying to coax the vehicle into motion. Ultimately he slams his head into the center of the steering wheel in exasperation, the car starts, and he prepares to drive. He looks ahead, eyes focused, throws the car into gear, and—

"Cut. Thank you, Marty. We'll take it from here." The actor

got out of the car and his stunt double took his spot, presumably to complete the journey while Stoltz was pushed to the sidelines as another McFly took his place.

The next day, production moved to the Puente Hills Mall, the large shopping center in City of Industry, located in the San Gabriel Valley region of Los Angeles County, which served as the location for the fictional Twin Pines Mall. The cast and crew were scheduled to shoot the scene with the time machine's first temporal displacement, where Doc sends his dog Einstein one minute into the future. The pageant continued, with the crew continuing to accumulate largely irrelevant footage of Stoltz, unknowingly practicing for Fox's turn at the take, as unit photographer Ralph Nelson snapped photographs that would remain under lock and key for decades to follow. Doomsday came just forty-eight hours later. The majority of those called to the mall that night had no reason to suspect that this shoot would be any different from the ones that preceded it. The lead actor arrived on set at 5:30 P.M. and headed directly to hair and makeup. He then stepped in front of the cameras for his final time, presumably to feed lines to Christopher Lloyd, who played his costar Dr. Emmett "Doc" Brown. Production manager Dennis Jones filled out a report on each shooting day with codes listed to represent how each actor's time was spent on that particular day and whether or not he or she was needed back at a subsequent time. On January 10, in the column for Stoltz, Jones wrote the letter *F* in black ballpoint. In this case, it stood for *finished*, but a number of other words could certainly have stood in its place, *fired* among the most gentle.

It was decided beforehand that members of the production team would let the principal cast know about the change slightly in advance of the big announcement to the rest of the crew. Bob Gale spoke with Crispin Glover, who was cast as George McFly, and Thomas F. Wilson, who played bully Biff Tannen, while Neil Canton was responsible for talking to Christopher Lloyd and Lea Thompson. Frank Marshall and Kathleen Kennedy called Eric Stoltz's agents. Robert Zemeckis broke the news to Stoltz himself as Spielberg waited in the wings.

Exactly what transpired between the director and his outgoing leading man during their conversation has been kept between the two of them, but Zemeckis acknowledges that the actor took the news hard, as was to be expected. For Canton, the night that he had assumed would be filled with unhappiness got off to a surprisingly lighthearted start when he received a much-needed laugh from his old friend Christopher Lloyd. "I knew Chris because we had worked together on *Buckaroo Bonzai*," he says. "He was funny. When I told Chris that we were going to be replacing Eric in the film, he looked at me and said, 'Well, who's Eric?' I said, 'Marty,' and he said, 'Oh, I really thought his name *was* Marty.' To this day, I don't know if Chris was just pulling my leg." Canton's amusement came from the fact that, on set, Stoltz adhered to his method acting instruction and refused to answer to his real name, to the frustration and eye-rolls of many in the crew. Those on the production team didn't find the actor's request as grating as the rest on set did. "We almost always called him Marty," Bob Gale says. "We thought it was silly, but we figured if it helped him do his job, it was harmless. There were a few people on the crew who'd worked on *Mask,* and they called him Rocky, the name of his character in that film."

While Lloyd may or may not have realized that this was simply Stoltz's way of staying in character, Tom Wilson was clear that Eric Stoltz was his name and being a pain in the ass was his game. The origin of the frequently awkward and hostile working relationship between Stoltz and Wilson can be traced back to when the former was required to push the latter while filming the scene in the school cafeteria. According to Wilson, the lead used all his force take after take, unwilling to play pretend. Despite repeated requests from Wilson to take it easy, Stoltz didn't, forcing the heels of his hands into the supporting actor's collarbone with increasing strength.

Action! Push. Cut. Again. Action! Push. Cut. Again. Action! Push. Cut. Again. Action! The result was a perfect shot and a number of bruises on Wilson's collarbone. A score had been created and the bully of Hill Valley High was seeking to settle it in a few weeks. Wilson, who was appearing in his first major motion picture—he'd had a small role in an indie film called *L.A. Street-fighters* that he was eager to forget—felt he was in no position to complain to the director, but made a mental note to retaliate when they got around to filming the scene when Biff punches Marty outside the Enchantment Under the Sea dance. Wilson would never have his chance to deliver Stoltz's comeuppance.

For Lea Thompson, the news of Stoltz's dismissal was bittersweet. "It was hard for me because I was really good friends with Eric," she says. "Eric is such a different actor, and he could be very difficult. It was a time when we were emerging from the seventies. All the young actors wanted to be like De Niro and Pacino, which was good in a lot of ways. Now a lot of young actors are just like businessmen. It was a different time. But it was not the right movie to behave like that. Eric had such an intensity. He saw drama in things. He wasn't really a comedian, and they needed a comedian. He's super-funny in real life, but he didn't approach his work like that, and they really needed somebody who had those light chops."

However, as disappointed as she was to hear that he was being removed from the project, the news did come as a small relief, especially considering her own minor indiscretions at the time of filming. "My boyfriend at the time was Dennis Quaid, and he was overseas making a movie," she says. "We hadn't seen each other in a while and I really wanted to see him. I was not supposed to go away, but I had a week or two off, so I slipped away against the rules after I was explicitly told not to leave town. I was in Munich. That was a long time ago, so I called my answering machine just to check in, and it was like, 'Beep! This is Steven Spielberg. Beep! This is Frank Marshall. Beep! This is Bob Zemeckis. Beep!' and I was like, 'Oh, my god, I'm getting fired! Oh, my god! Oh, my god! Oh, my god, they found out that I ran out of town and I'm in trouble!' I was trying to get a plane ticket until I finally talked to Neil and he told me what happened."

"I was just super-relieved it wasn't me," she continues, still laughing about it after almost three decades. "I disobeyed the rules. They wouldn't remember that because I never told them I was out of town."

Some of the actors who worked most closely with Stoltz had a feeling that something was off-kilter within a week of the announcement. Tom Wilson remembers there being an odd atmosphere and uncomfortable buzz around the set in the first few days of 1985. Christopher Lloyd also had a sense that things were not clicking the way they should have been. "I felt for Eric. He was a really good actor," he says. "Although he was doing the part well, he was not bringing that element of comedy to the screen."

As surprising as the announcement was, some on the crew had sensed that a big change was forthcoming once shooting resumed after the Christmas holiday. "There were signs, especially the last week or so," Cundey says. "When we would set up a shot and we would shoot Chris Lloyd's angle, but we wouldn't do the reverse on Marty. I'd say, 'Don't we need the angle?" and

Bob would say, 'No, no, no, let's not worry about that.' It didn't take long for me to see that we were saving our energy for what would come next."

"I got a phone call from one of the producers—I don't remember if it was Bob Gale or Neil—basically saying, 'Larry, don't change the set from 1955,'" production designer Larry Paull says. "They said they weren't done with it, there may be some changes, and they couldn't go into it any further, but I was to stop what I was doing."

The formal announcement came during the late-night "lunch break," around 10:30 P.M. After Zemeckis dismissed Stoltz from the set, the cast and crew were assembled. The full production team of the director, Bob Gale, Neil Canton, Kathleen Kennedy, Frank Marshall, and Steven Spielberg were present, an unusual show of force that tipped everyone off that something serious was imminent.

"We have an announcement," Zemeckis said into his bullhorn. "It's probably going to be shocking—kind of good news, bad news." The crowd was starting to grow uneasy, he could tell. "I'll give you the bad news. We're going to have to reshoot most of the movie because we've changed the cast and there's going to be a new Marty: Michael J. Fox."

The director saw the reactions. They weren't gleeful, per se, but they didn't seem to be as angry or worried as he had feared. Someone from the crowd shouted, "That's certainly not the bad news!"

"Okay, well, then that's the good news. I guess the other good news is that we're going to continue on." He paused. "So it's only good news and good news."

With only a half hour designated for break, things quickly returned to as close to business as usual as they could be after

Zemeckis's megaphone address. However, while Zemeckis and company had planned a surprise for their crew, an unexpected surprise was still in store for one member of the inner circle. After the announcement, Neil Canton's pager went off. He went to the nearest pay phone and dialed. "Hurry home." It was his wife. He did as instructed, excusing himself, racing out of the mall parking lot, and heading westbound on California Route 60. The next time he would return to work, he would not only have a new leading man, but also a baby daughter.

Eric Stoltz's name remained on the production report for the following day, but with no call time or code letters written in to indicate that he was requested to report on set. When the next week began, two strokes of Wite-Out were applied to the call sheet, eliminating *Marty* and *Eric Stoltz* from the top of the cast list. Michael J. Fox would be reporting for duty that Tuesday to the mall, exactly where Eric Stoltz had left off. There could be no greater sign that things were going to continue as seamlessly as possible than that.

But much to the production team's disappointment, there was some collateral damage that came with the Stoltz decision. It's hard to imagine anyone unhappier to hear about Stoltz's ousting than Melora Hardin, who was cast as Jennifer Parker, Marty's girlfriend. Hardin, now best known for playing Jan Levinson on NBC's American version of *The Office*, had yet to shoot a frame of footage for *Future* before she found herself on the losing side of a lesson in causality. The Bobs realized that her height— five foot five—might appear awkward to the audience next to Fox, who is an inch shorter. Initially, they thought they might have been overthinking the matter. What's an inch? Plenty of guys had girlfriends who were taller than them. But just to be sure, they decided to poll the crew. As it turned out, women felt strongly that Jennifer shouldn't tower over her boyfriend in physical stature, which was enough to convince them to recast.

Months before Bob Z made that announcement in the mall parking lot, Hardin, who had starred in the forgettable 1977–1978 NBC series *Thunder*, and had guest roles in a number of unforgettable shows such as *The Love Boat*, *Diff'rent Strokes*, and *Little House on the Prairie*, was brought in to audition for *Back to the Future*. A callback followed, which included a "chemistry read," a process by which two actors are put together to see how well they interact and look together on-screen. With Stoltz already hired, Hardin and two or three other finalists took turns reading short excerpts from the script—known in the industry as "sides"—doing their best to show that they had what it took to play the part of Marty's love interest.

While hardly new to the acting world, the young actress, who had just celebrated her eighteenth birthday a few weeks earlier, felt that this audition was special. Hardin was ecstatic when she learned she would be sharing the silver screen with Stoltz. In the weeks following her hiring, production began. When Stoltz and Crispin Glover were filming the scene in Hill Valley High cafeteria where Marty first tries to convince George to ask Lorraine to the Enchantment Under the Sea dance, Hardin was called to the set. Photographs were taken of her that were later to be developed into a pocket-size print for Marty to carry around in his wallet. "I remember being at the school where they were filming," she says. "I said hello to everybody. Everyone was like, 'We're so happy to have you on the set! We're so happy you're in the movie!' They were very warm and sweet, and meanwhile it was all falling apart and I didn't even know it."

The state of things became apparent when she received a large bouquet of flowers and a conference call at home with both

Bobs on the line. "They called me together and said that they were so sorry," she says. "It had nothing to do with me, but that they had to recast Eric. I was just too tall for Michael J. Fox, but they had loved me and promised we would work together again in the future." The actress burst into tears, prompting her newly former bosses to console her over the phone. "It was one of the hardest things I ever had to do," Bob Gale says. "I have no problem firing someone for cause, but having to let her go because she was three inches too tall was a very tough conversation."

"Bob Gale and I have had lunch a couple times over the years—just recently, in fact—and talked more about it," Hardin says. "I can only imagine how horrible that was on their end of it. It's hard to do those things. But they would have had to have Michael J. Fox standing on a box every time he shared a scene with me. That would have been a little weird."

The Jennifer Parker vacancy caused by the second casting shake-up led the production team to offer the role to eighteen-year-old Claudia Wells—for the second time. In the summer of 1984, during the initial casting of the role, Wells was offered the part; however, a funny thing happened on the way to Hill Valley. ABC picked up *Off the Rack,* a pilot she appeared in starring Ed Asner and Eileen Brennan, as a midseason replacement with a six-episode order. The network demanded she give her full attention to the series, which precluded her from appearing in the film. Much like with Michael J. Fox, Stoltz's bad luck created her good fortune. By the time the casting debacle occurred, *Off the Rack* was not renewed, and Wells was available again. She gladly accepted the role, playing alongside a new lead actor who, for the record, is her same height.

Just days after the big announcement, on the evening of Tuesday, January 15, Michael J. Fox made his way to the set to shoot his first scene. The actor had already spent the greater portion of the day at the television studio. When he was done, a driver picked him up and took him to City of Industry. He arrived at 6:30 P.M., was put into hair, makeup, and wardrobe, and made his way to the parking lot at 7:15 P.M. He was expected to shoot for three hours, spend fifteen minutes changing back into his street clothes, get picked up to be taken back home, and catch a short nap on a pile of blankets in the back of a station wagon with a teamster behind the wheel. He would make it to bed a little after 1:00 A.M., continue sleeping for five or six hours, and then be picked up to go back to Paramount Studios on Melrose Avenue to begin the process all over again the next day. Although Fox's marathon workdays have since become the material of cinematic lore, at the time, burning the candle at both ends didn't faze the actor in the slightest. As he told the Bobs when he first met them after accepting the role, he relied on his youth and enthusiasm to compensate for his lack of a good night's sleep.

With the bright movie lights illuminating the Puente Hills Mall parking lot on that January evening, Christopher Lloyd and his new costar engaged in some awkwardly pleasant small talk. Meanwhile, special effects supervisor Kevin Pike's team began laying the foundation for the forthcoming bit of cinematic magic that the two would participate in. Dean Cundey prepared for the shot, while Bob Gale and Neil Canton conferred with Robert Zemeckis. From a bird's-eye view, the producers appeared to be nonplussed, but both were excited over Fox's arrival and relieved that their unconventional maneuver to save their film was going according to plan.

With the lot properly lit and the camera and its operators in place, the producers took a step away from their director. The effects team ignited a mixture of gasoline and pyrotechnic fluid, which had been tested beforehand to ensure it wouldn't destroy the parking lot asphalt. On the blacktop, two adjacent straight lines went ablaze near where the talent would be standing. The actors took to their marks, got set, and when they were ready to go, second assistant cameraman Steve Tate stepped in front of the camera lens and snapped the clapper board. Bob Z gave the word—"Action!"—through his megaphone. Gale and Canton watched closely. Less than a minute into Fox's first shot, those on set could almost feel a weight ascending from everyone's shoulders. *We might just pull this thing off after all . . .*

Zemeckis had gotten used to making compromises, both small and large, in the preceding thirty-four days of shooting. Firing Stoltz was simultaneously a humbling and courageous decision, requiring him to navigate through the channels to rally support behind him, from his editors up to the studio head himself. It was an amazing show of leadership for the thirty-three-year-old director, at a time in his career when he was still considering himself lucky just to have work. Even if it was an intimidating decision to make, when he saw Michael J. Fox turn to face the camera and ask Christopher Lloyd the now-famous rhetorical question—*You're telling me you built a time machine . . . out of a DeLorean?*—the director knew that he had been vindicated. The hole in the middle of the screen had been plugged.

It was a decision that was applauded by both cast and crew. "Bob is really good at seeing the way a project should go and trying to get it to go down that road, as opposed to another director who might be afraid of getting fired himself, just going along and letting the bad actor sort of drive everything," Dean Cundey says. "Bob has that confidence in knowing what the movie needs and to be able to request it. I think that's one of his great qualities, especially with the *Back to the Future* circumstance—the fact that he was just convinced that the decision should be made, and then guided it to that decision."

From the first moments on set, it became clear that Michael J. Fox was perfect for the role for a variety of reasons, both tangible and intangible. Perhaps it was that Marty suddenly became eight inches shorter. With him and the six-foot-one Doc no longer virtually seeing eye-to-eye, there was a greater visual reminder to the audience that their hero was, in fact, a teenager attempting to navigate through an imposing world—both in 1985 and, especially, in 1955. It could also have been the quick and quiet costume change, a substantial departure from the character's original pseudo-militant black turtleneck jacket to a goofier and brighter layered ensemble comprised of a patterned, casual buttoned shirt, a denim jacket, and an orange puffy vest that people of the past understandably kept mistaking as a life preserver. *Back to the Future* stopped becoming just another film project, and with a new leading man in the DeLorean's driver's seat, it started to feel more like something special.

"Michael came on and there was just a different sort of chemistry and feeling amongst most of the crew," Dean Cundey says. "He was this very boyish character that Doc Brown could relate to. Eric was somehow older and more restrained."

"Everyone felt a new sense of energy because of Michael," Neil Canton says. "Like, 'Oh, wow, this movie's better. It's funnier. He's such a much more likable character.' I think everybody kind of felt that way."

"There are films where you realize that it's just not working," Cundey adds. "*Back to the Future* was one of those films where, when the change was made to Michael, the film came to life."

Although she was happy production wasn't stopping, Lea Thompson initially found herself less than enthused about Fox's arrival. The twenty-three-year-old actress had been working for several years, accumulating credits in more than a half dozen high-profile films like *Jaws 3-D*, *All the Right Moves*, and *Red Dawn*. While she was relatively new in the business, having only been acting professionally since she reached adulthood, she knew that making films was serious work—and she struggled to see how Michael J. Fox would live up to the challenge. "I was really snotty then," she says. "I was like, 'Oh, my god, a sitcom actor?' I was so snotty about it. After I actually did a sitcom, I realized it was the hardest thing in the world."

But despite her early skepticism, Thompson was soon won over by her new costar. Fox was not only an asset to what materialized on-screen, but he also elevated the mood of the set. "Michael was a real prince, and it was always really fun to work with him," she continues. "He just had a way of getting a laugh when they needed a laugh. I've only worked with a couple actors like that—him and Walter Matthau. I just always enjoyed his kind of old-fashioned, Buster Keaton, fall-off-a-chair, crack-your-voice technique, which was impeccable."

"Michael was very outgoing and very happy to be there," Bob Gale says. "I remember him introducing himself to the crew, and being very friendly and gregarious. As I recall, Eric took his meals in his trailer, but Michael ate with the company."

J. J. Cohen, who played Skinhead, a member of Biff's gang, recalls the second pass at shooting the "I'm your density" scene in Lou's Café highlighting a significant difference in the acting styles of the two men to have played Marty. During the Stoltz shoot, the actor punched Biff at the conclusion of that scene as if he really meant to hurt him, perhaps another moment that Tom Wilson filed away in his brain when plotting his revenge for the actor's unrelenting method technique. However, when Fox played the part, he added a facial reaction and slight shake of his hand to suggest that the punch had hurt before running out the door. It's a small difference, but one that illustrates why the Bobs were lucky to have had an ally in Steven Spielberg and why the decision to replace Stoltz was so important. Marty is a reactive character, and if Fox was better at playing those moments, Sid Sheinberg was right in investing the extra cash to get the best man for the job.

"The main difference I saw between the two actors was that when Michael did a scene with Chris, he was very funny," production designer Larry Paull says. "He was able to hold on to his end. When Eric did a scene with Chris, it became Doc Brown's scene. That was the difference."

"A lot of times, you need to cast people to fix your story problems just by them being who they are," Lea Thompson says. "If the story problem is that the character does all these terrible things, but you need the audience to like them, you have to find someone really likable so people don't notice that. That's what Michael did. He fixed the problems we were having just by being funny. He kept a lightness to the story that was important."

Although Fox's arrival was primarily greeted with enthusiasm, the cast and crew were aware of the sacrifices they too would be making. On the day of the announcement, those outside of the production team believed themselves to be halfway through the shooting schedule. It had become routine for people to ask each other about what gigs they had lined up for when the shoot was over. Little did they know, the film wouldn't be wrapped until late April, months beyond the industry average. Additionally, Fox's *Family Ties* schedule ensured that twilight and weekend shoots would become the norm, an extra burden for all to bear.

Because there was no precedent for taking more than a month's worth of footage and scrapping the lion's share of it, a unique set of opportunities and challenges were put forth for the crew. Steven Spielberg loved the majority of what Zemeckis had accomplished when he watched the rough edit, so when reshoots began, there was a simple mandate that came down from his office—keep on doing what you've been doing. This was easier said than done, especially with a lead actor who operates as in-the-moment during shooting as Christopher Lloyd does. After all, how do you heed Spielberg's advice if you perform differently each time the director calls a scene into action? "I was really taken aback and very concerned after Eric was fired that I wouldn't be able to do it again," Christopher Lloyd says. "I put everything into being Doc Brown for six weeks, and I was very worried I wouldn't be able to live up to my own performance, so to speak."

Of course, his concerns were for naught. Doc Brown was fully realized on the page in Zemeckis and Gale's script, but the character truly came alive in Christopher Lloyd's hands. The actor was instrumental in crafting the mad scientist's look—a hybridization of composer Leopold Stokowski and Albert Einstein—and his commitment to his performance resulted in some of the most memorable moments in the film. "Chris was amazing," Bob Gale says. "He never did a take exactly the same way, so we'd have all of these different variations on the line readings, and they were all wonderful. It was a good problem to have in the editing room."

"I am sort of the kind of actor who is always worried that I didn't do it well enough, each take," Lloyd says. "I am always second-guessing myself. I tend to do that, but watching *Back to the Future*, I am much better than I thought I was when I did it."

For the crew, revisiting the old material provided them with an opportunity to make small improvements and further elevate the storytelling. According to Cundey, filming with Fox became a bit of a puzzle, with him and Zemeckis matching shots with Marty in them with salvageable close-ups of other actors from the Stoltz era. "We would go back and re-create the scene with the advantage of not having to shoot every angle again, because they didn't need it," Cundey says. However, there is much debate as to whether or not his statement is accurate. The Bobs have consistently maintained that the entire film was reshot, perhaps with the exception of some second-unit photography, which would have included establishing shots, footage that included stuntmen, close-ups of the time machine, and other cutaways. According to Arthur Schmidt and Harry Keramidas, absolutely no footage from the Stoltz era was used. However, Tom Wilson concurs that some shots were only done once, primarily because he remembers that Michael J. Fox never punched him in the face when Biff gets decked by Marty in Lou's Café after George tells Lorraine that he's her density. The fist coming toward the camera, Wilson is positive, belongs to Stoltz. In examining the scene, it is obvious that the largely obscured actor who punches Wilson is several inches taller than Fox. Perhaps it's just a stunt double, but it might also be a ghost from *Back to the Future*'s past.

There were also some modifications made while the film was in transition to accommodate the new budgetary limitations and the physical differences between Stoltz and Fox. For instance, the Bobs had written a scene to open the movie in which Marty sets off a fire alarm to get out of serving detention so he can go to audition with his band. The classroom set had yet to be built at the time of the casting change, so as a cost-saving measure, they devised a different concept for the beginning of the movie. Additionally, one of the last sequences Stoltz shot was with Crispin Glover, as George McFly is hanging laundry. Marty takes his duffel bag filled with clothing, hangs it from a clothesline in the backyard, and teaches his father to punch by practicing on the suspended sack. The scene was supposed to end with George hitting the bag in a goofy way, breaking the hanging mechanism and a window in the process, thus foreshadowing the left-handed punch Biff receives later in the film outside the Enchantment Under the Sea dance.

"We never got that far into it, but when Michael came into our world, we had to reinvent some of the things that we had shot," Kevin Pike says. "But the clothesline and everything that we had put together at the location in Pasadena was still there. For all of us, it was a no-brainer. We were just going to do the same thing over."

When it came time to shoot the scene with Fox, the props department resupplied a bag. The special effects team rigged it from the attachment on the clothesline, and the cast and crew got into place. The actors took to their marks and Zemeckis called action. Then Zemeckis ordered the scene stopped. A call was made from a nearby pay phone to Pike.

"There's a problem."

"What could the problem be? All you have to do is hang the bag." Then it hit him. Fox couldn't reach the clothesline, as the height was set for Eric Stoltz. Because the mechanism was already set up to the top, and the bottom was cemented into the ground, the special effects team took a few inches from the middle of each post and welded the ends back together. As far as growing pains go, this was an easy problem to resolve.

With the movie on the right track, those financially invested in the film began taking the necessary steps to make up for the losses incurred during the first several weeks of shooting between

November 1984 and the beginning of January 1985. The decision to release Stoltz from his duties came at a $3.5 million price tag and a release date pushed even further back from July 15 to August 16. Since Zemeckis and company had taken their eggs and put them in the Michael J. Fox basket, all hands were required to help carry the extra weight. The publicity team did their part by operating with a three-pronged defense. The first step was to keep any bloodhounds in the media far away while the transition from Actor A to Actor B took place. An interoffice memo was sent from production manager Dennis Jones on the day that Stoltz was let go, advising all involved with the production to direct any questions about the casting change to either David Forbes, the publicity representative for Amblin, or Kimberley Coy, the unit publicist, to avoid improper dissemination of information and fueling of what he referred to as "the gossip mill." All complied and, subsequently, the chattering class was kept at bay. Mostly.

"Hollywood did think we were a movie in trouble," Bob Gale says. "We're glad we didn't have to deal with the Internet and shows like *E! Entertainment* suggesting that the movie might turn out to be a train wreck."

"It was news at the time," says film critic Leonard Maltin, who worked for *Entertainment Tonight* between 1982 and 2010. "It got a lot of attention, and then once the film came out and it was so good and so successful, it was discussed that much more."

The second challenge was for the studio to simultaneously champion Stoltz's role in *Mask*, which was still two months away from being released, while tactfully explaining his departure from *Future* to all who asked. Luckily for Universal, *Mask* seemed in no way deterred by "the gossip mill," even with director Peter Bogdanovich getting involved in a very public squabble with the studio over edits made to the movie before its release. There were the occasional questions about Zemeckis's film that came up in interviews with Stoltz, but he consistently maintained that his departure was due to creative differences and that he and the filmmakers were on amicable terms, a position he has more or less stuck with for the decades following the film's release.

The final step was to contour *Future*'s promotional strategy for its new release date in the late summer, a time of year when people tend to stop visiting movie theaters in exchange for taking one more vacation before Labor Day. The difficult date, coupled with its newly expanded budget, created an even greater challenge for Universal to make a return on its investment. The Amblin publicity team did their part by opening conversations with Drew Struzan, the highly sought-after artist who designed the iconic illustrated posters for the *Star Wars* trilogy, along with those for dozens of other films. Struzan had a long-standing working relationship with the Amblin Trio—Steven Spielberg, Kathleen Kennedy, and Frank Marshall—and the three felt that a one-sheet featuring his arresting artwork might just generate the interest they would need to get the attention of the public. The artist agreed to lend his unique touch to the film's promotional campaign, to the delight of not only the executive producers, but also longtime Struzan fan Robert Zemeckis.

By the time production wrapped at the end of Michael J. Fox's first evening shoot, the double-duty schedule that would be followed for the next several weeks had been set. By 4:35 A.M., the crew was dismantling their equipment in the mall parking lot. The sun would be coming up soon, and since the shopping center was still fully operational during the day, it wouldn't be long before employees started filing into the mall to prepare for the day's business. Michael J. Fox was already tucked away in bed, hours away from being woken up and driven to the *Family Ties* set. As much as Christopher Lloyd was sorry to see Eric Stoltz go, the veteran actor became even more alive with Fox at his side. The two quickly realized they had a shared bond, not only in their shared love for the Bobs' story and screenplay, but also in their mutual frustration with their other costar—the stainless-steel beast on four wheels that required a small army to keep it functioning for the duration of the film shoot.

3. DO IT WITH SOME STYLE

Thursday, January 24, 1985

The white 1984 GMC Value Van, marked with the words DR. E. BROWN ENTERPRISES—24 HR. SCIENTIFIC SERVICES, sat parked on the smooth black asphalt as a dozen or so men busied themselves in its immediate vicinity. The ground, which had been hosed down by the special effects team moments earlier, reflected the bright lights used to illuminate the parking lot, an old movie trick to give depth and texture to evening shots. White smoke seeped out of the top of the vehicle, foreshadowing what was soon to come. As the rear aluminum ramp began to descend, it revealed that the interior body of the box truck was completely engulfed in a haze of thick white mist. Two red brake lights pierced through the cloud. Then, the details of the DeLorean DMC-12 came into better view: the bumper; the smooth gray body, which was begging to have a hand run across its side; and the California license plate with OUTATIME imprinted between two large exhaust vents. With a subtle fluidity, the camera ascended, showcasing a mess of wires, screws, connectors, and coils, along with a nuclear reactor, cleverly retrofitted from the hubcap of a Dodge Polara from the 1960s. In just a few moments, Christopher Lloyd would hop out of the car and greet Marty, setting into motion the experiment with Einstein and a scene filled with exposition about the rules of time travel and the way his invention worked.

In life it may be impolite to show off, but in the movie business, it is encouraged. This extends not only to film stars, but also to filmmakers and how they choose to shoot a scene. When executed well, essential information to drive the narrative forward can be given by what is included, or omitted, in a single frame. This is not only true for this moment in the film, but throughout the entire movie. For example, the first time the audience sees Michael J. Fox in *Back to the Future* is in a close-up of the actor with guitar in hand and reflective aviator sunglasses, epitomizing teenage male coolness circa 1985. In that same opening sequence, the camera slowly pans across a variety of different clocks, establishing the motif of time. After George McFly rescues her character from Biff Tannen's rape attempt in Doc's car outside of the Enchantment Under the Sea dance, Lea Thompson is filmed from above—so she has to look up at the camera, mirroring the way she now looks up to George for his heroic action—in a shot that showcases her beauty. The DeLorean time machine's first glamour shot sought to communicate to the viewer that while the car may look like the DMC-12 most in the audience were familiar with, it was capable of a lot more than just driving.

Consider the shot's placement in the film. After Marty arrives at the Twin Pines Mall, he pets Einstein, and is interrupted by Doc's white box truck's rear lift unfolding automatically. Before long, the DeLorean time machine is fully exposed, having pierced through a cloud of white smoke. As visually interesting as this moment is, from a practical standpoint this moment in the film's narrative seems to stretch the limits of common sense. Doc Brown presumably entered the car and drove it into the truck, sure, but how did the cabin become filled with smoke? Why did he trap himself with no escape route? How did he even lift the gate in the first place, and how did he know when to let it down? It appears to be the theatrics were all to impress Marty, except Doc is surprised to see his friend standing beside the car once the car's gull-wing door opens up. While there may be a convoluted theory as to why the scientist went through these lengths—chalk it all up to his eccentricities?—the most logical reason for the shot is that it was meant to captivate the audience with a few seconds of automotive eye candy and generate a few moments of wild speculation within a viewer's mind as to what function the time machine's exterior components served. "It's a classic reveal," special effects supervisor Kevin Pike says. "There are a lot of ways that you could have shown that car to the audience, and a lot of ways that Doc Brown could have shown the car to Marty. There's no story point that says that the truck had to be full of smoke because of some plan that Doc had that didn't go right. That was all Bob Zemeckis's dream. He puts power into all of these little pieces that we would jump through hoops, as best we could, to satisfy. That is pure art going on there."

Although it is a decision that has received far less attention over the three decades following the film's release than the one to switch lead actors midstream, the Bobs' most significant last-minute change might have been transforming the time-traveling chamber into a car. In the earliest draft of the *Future* script, the chamber was driven around in the back of a pickup truck. Before settling on the clock tower lightning strike as the energy source to send Marty back to 1985, the original climax of the film saw Doc and Marty driving the chamber to a nuclear test site as an explosion went off. It was an interesting idea, but they sensed they could come up with a more compelling ending to their movie than showing a truck driving across the desert to await an explosion. When they were writing *Back to the Future*, the Bobs had a simple set of governing rules: check your ego at the door, write a film that both of us would want to see, and if someone thinks they can improve upon an idea, it must mean there's a better one out there. During the summer of 1984, their rules led them toward an inspired concept: What if Doc Brown's time-travel device wasn't just on wheels, but was also a little dangerous? They had just the perfect car in mind: the DeLorean DMC-12.

Since its founding in 1975, the DeLorean Motor Company, headed by former General Motors vice president John DeLorean, was marred by controversy and misfortune. DMC struggled financially to produce vehicles up to par by quality control standards, and was unable to move enough units to stay afloat. By early 1982, the American car market was in shambles—the worst the country had seen since the Depression era. Sales of all vehicles slowed dramatically, with luxury cars taking the largest hit. Thousands of DMC-12s, the only model the company produced, languished in the Irish factory where they were constructed, unable to be sold. The company went into bankruptcy that May. While this was a damning blow to its founder, it paled in comparison to the allegations that the millionaire, while jet-setting around the world to try and attract investors for his fledgling empire in its waning days, agreed to participate in a cocaine trafficking ring. Undercover FBI agents had videotaped their interactions with DeLorean, and on October 12, 1982, he was arrested. Two years later, as the Bobs were working on their fourth draft of the *Future* screenplay, he was cleared of all eight counts. The defense successfully argued their client was a victim of entrapment. Regardless of its controversial reputation, the Bobs thought the stainless-steel vehicle would be the perfect vessel for Doc Brown's invention. It didn't look like anything else on the road, and its notorious creator added an air of mystique to the vehicle. Spielberg was fine with the original chamber concept, but since the Bobs were enthusiastic about their new idea, he was supportive of their decision to make the change.

It could easily be argued that the most important character, and the biggest diva on set, was the DeLorean. The vehicle was heralded as a stroke of creative genius when integrated into the screenplay, yet it required a significant amount of attention, some due to the demands of the script, while others were the result of the inherent limitations of the DMC-12 model. "It was tight and uncomfortable," Christopher Lloyd says. "Usually we had to shoot with the windows closed. One time we were in there with Einstein, Doc's dog. He did not smell too good. We got pretty close and it got pretty stagnant in there." Despite the cramped quarters, Lloyd recognized the DeLorean's value. "It looked great. It was streamlined, it was futuristic—it was Doc's car, plain and simple. It was the ideal vehicle for his mission."

When the DeLorean was written into the movie, the aesthetic value of the vehicle was paramount. In the fourth draft of the screenplay, the Bobs wrote that the time machine was modified with "wicked-looking units," making it look and feel "dangerous." It was noted that there were coils along the front and rear of the body, but besides that, the Bobs were otherwise unspecific as to how the car would look. They were perhaps equally nonplussed about how a DMC-12 would handle the rigors of their production schedule. They had heard of the many problems that plagued the DeLorean Motor Company, and the reports of the cars' poor craftsmanship, but neither Bob had personal experience with the car. As cameras started rolling on *Future*, they discovered that the vehicle's performance was as horrible as its design was unique. "It was a cool-looking car, but it really wasn't a good car," Neil Canton says. "There's a reason why it never really became a successful seller."

The final look of the movie car, with its abundance of gadgetry, is the result of the art and special effects departments harvesting the best of the talent they had available. Once the change was made from a chamber to a DeLorean, illustrator Ron Cobb was pegged to spearhead the design concept for the new and improved time machine. The artist came to Spielberg's attention by way of director John Milius, who was a fan of Cobb's paintings and political cartoons. By the time Spielberg was looking to hire a production artist on *Raiders of the Lost Ark*, the social critic had made the transition to working on feature films like the original *Star Wars* and *Alien*, assisting the production designers and special effects teams with concept art. Milius brokered a meeting between Cobb and Spielberg, who hit it off, and Cobb was hired to work on *Raiders*.

By the summer of 1984, Cobb was regularly at the Amblin offices, the quaint compound at Universal that Sid Sheinberg took to calling "Taco Bell" because of its southwestern architecture, which Spielberg himself designed. The Bobs' offices were across from where Cobb was regularly sketching with other animators, putting *Back to the Future* on his radar. He thought the concept for the movie was interesting, a feeling that was confirmed when Spielberg approached him directly as the movie's principal photography start date loomed ahead, just a few months away.

"Could you be a part of this time-travel movie and come up with a design for a time machine that's made out of a DeLorean?"

"A DeLorean?" Cobb hadn't heard many details about the film and was struck by the oddity and ingenuity of the concept.

"That's really good, I like that. But why a DeLorean?" Spielberg wasn't entirely sure. As far as he knew, the Bobs just thought it would look interesting. Either way, Spielberg's answer, or lack thereof, was irrelevant. The illustrator wanted in, regardless of why the DeLorean was picked.

There were very few parameters put on the artist as he prepared to start his first drawing. It was important that the car look not only like it could actually travel through time, but that it look like an inventor had built it in his garage. Cobb had always been interested in science, and his previous cinematic work had included science fiction elements, but now he felt he had a real opportunity to go into overdrive. He took appraisal of the list of requisites: The car had to have a nuclear reactor in the back, appear to be street-legal, and include a flux capacitor, the mechanism by which, in the fantasy of the film's narrative, time travel was possible. In between the other projects he was working on, he came up with "bogus physics" to explain how the vehicle's many supplemental parts, which the Doc could have harvested from junkyards and hardware stores, would actually make the machine travel through time.

"A movie car should tell you instantly how it works, just by looking at it," he says. "When someone invented the paper clip, you could immediately understand how it was used. It didn't have to be explained. I wanted that sense for the DeLorean. Like the grid around the car—I knew right away that everyone would buy it because it *looks* like something you'd need to punch through hyperspace and arrive in the fifties."

Cobb completed three detailed design sketches and submitted them to the art director, Todd Hallowell. Once Larry Paull, the film's production designer, was hired, he was given the sketches so he could figure out how to best realize them on-screen. There were only six or seven weeks in the schedule before the DeLorean would be needed for production, so there was no opportunity for significant changes to the design. "I didn't have time or the energy, quite candidly, to dot every *i* and cross every *t*, to execute it exactly the way he had designed it," Paull says. Andrew Probert, one of the film's production illustrators, was called in to make further revisions to the design concept, as Cobb was assigned to work on other Amblin projects. Probert had previously worked on *Battlestar Galactica* and *Indiana Jones and the Temple of Doom*, but he was perhaps best known in the industry for his significant contributions on *Star Trek: The Motion Picture*. Probert gave a second pass at the design, relying heavily on what Cobb had come up with. DeLorean Design 2.0 was complete within a few days.

Michael Scheffe, another freelance artist, was hired and tasked with synthesizing Cobb and Probert's artwork into the final concept for the time-traveling vehicle, which he worked on just around the time Kevin Pike was hired as special effects supervisor. Scheffe's design blueprints were very close to what materialized on film largely because, before he was hired for the film's art department, he had spent a day inventorying parts that might work for the time machine with visual effects supervisor Mike Fink. Fink was brought on to *Back to the Future* as a liaison between the art department, based out of Amblin, and Kevin Pike's shop, Filmtrix, located a few miles away on Chandler Boulevard in North Hollywood, where the DeLorean would be built and the other effects would be worked out. On one of his many excursions for add-on components, Fink purchased the parts that would be used for the flux capacitor, but he found the process of making the regular excursions to shops and junkyards too arduous to go at alone. He invited Scheffe to join him on one such adventure, and the two spent an afternoon driving to supply houses, with Scheffe dutifully keeping a running list of appropriate parts that could be used to bring the sketches to reality—where they were located, how many of each piece was in stock, and what the prices were. Since three cars would be used for production—the A (or hero) car, with full amenities; the B car, which would be used primarily for stunts and distant shots, which wouldn't require all of the interior elements; and the C car, which would be used for process or effects shots—it was essential that multiples of all of the various knickknacks that would be attached to the car be available. The goal was to present the list to Pike, have his team decide what they thought was useful, and then make purchases, so as not to waste time and money getting pieces that wouldn't be used.

Fink wanted to offer Scheffe an assistant job, but it wasn't meant to be. The budget was tighter than expected and couldn't accommodate hiring a number two. Scheffe had had fun, and he didn't regret spending a day or two doing some window-shopping for a movie car without compensation. After all, the illustrator had designed KITT, the talking car for the *Knight Rider* television series, so the opportunity to be back in the saddle working on a futuristic vehicle, albeit briefly, wasn't a bad way to log some volunteer hours for a major motion picture. But in typical *Back to the Future* fashion, Scheffe didn't stay separated from the project for long. A few days later, he received a phone call.

"Mike, I just got an offer to work on another film." It was Fink. "Would you be interested in taking over my job?"

"Are you kidding? Of course."

"You're going to have to go and talk to the art department and show them your portfolio. They'd have to make sure that you're the right guy, but I think you'd be a shoo-in." Before the week's end, Scheffe was at Amblin meeting with Todd Hallowell and Larry Paull. They were impressed, not only by his experience and designs, but also his surprisingly relevant educational experience. Before becoming an artist, the illustrator went to school to learn how to build airplanes, a background that the art director and production designer felt would make him the perfect person to take Cobb's and Probert's sketches and realize them into working blueprints that Kevin Pike's crew could use for the build.

"They wanted to know I was someone who can take responsibility for finding stuff and someone who would respect the feeling of those original sketches," Scheffe says. "Plus, there were some changes they wanted to make to the drawings. They had the right feel to them, but there were some things that had to be adjusted. Like, could you really get a two-shot, where two actors are in frame at the same time, or was stuff going to get in the way between the driver and the passenger? I took the job and started running around, taking pictures of stuff and sketching what it would look like if we used this or that piece."

The design of the DeLorean time machine might serve as one of the clearest examples of how collaborative the moviemaking process is. The Bobs wrote a DeLorean into the screenplay, the art department and production designer commissioned original sketches by freelance illustrators, then, before the actual build could begin, the designs were further refined, based upon both the budget and availability of the parts, and with consideration toward the overall functionality of the vehicle during the shooting process. All the while, the clock kept ticking and the cash kept flowing. To further complicate matters, the direction of the final vehicle design could have changed at any point depending on an innumerable number of factors. "If you're in commercial art or design, there's a real delicate balance," Scheffe says. "If you don't care about the thing you're working on, it's not going to be good. If you put your heart and soul into it, it'll be better, but if you put every bit of your identity and self-respect, you're making yourself awfully vulnerable. There's a balance where you want to be inspired, you want to be engaged, but you also don't want to take too big a fall if things don't go well, so you protect yourself. That's why you make the rough sketches. That's why you polish things up as things go along. Usually you don't have a big shock of, 'Let's tear this up and start over again,' because people know where you're going and you're part of that process. It's not done like fine art might be done, solely for the love of the expression that you put into that painting. It's done because the client has a need and you're lucky enough to be employed to fill that need and to make whatever changes are necessary. You have to be flexible enough so that if someone changes their mind or changes direction, you're able to say, 'Okay, this is a change and I'm going to do it.'"

Once Scheffe's sketches were done, they became the working version for Pike and his team to use. Three cars were purchased from a local collector, and parts were culled from a variety of vendors. The shopping was divided up, with members of the team showing up to work on a given day with pieces they had found that matched the drawings they had been given. The result, they hoped, would be a vehicle that appeared to be simultaneously haphazardly and meticulously put together. "We had a crew of about ten, fifteen people in my shop that built the cars and made sure they looked good," Pike says. "It had to look homemade, like Doc Brown made it in a garage. Plus, we had to make sure that the car still worked after we took stuff off and put stuff on—that all the gags worked and we didn't destroy the car. It had to move and have functionality for all the effects to help tell the story that they created. The car was unique in that a lot of people were looking at it and coming up with ways it could work. You just can't put a piece of metal on the back and say, 'This is going to be the plutonium chamber.' It has to work. The 'plutonium' has to be able to go into the engine somehow. There's a lot of logistics with each decision that's made, whether in function or in design."

Larry Paull visited the shop once or twice a week to ensure the team would make their deadline and to offer feedback on the aesthetics. As go-between, Scheffe made daily visits. "Kevin had a great crew, and of course, they had to suffer with my sketches," he says. "But they did a great job and everyone had a can-do attitude. I still remember all those people in his shop. I remember the electronics guy, the welders. There was a spirit on that show of, 'We're going to make this work.' People tried so hard, and you can see it. You can really see it in everything."

The Filmtrix team's work with the time machine wasn't limited to the vehicle build. The crew was responsible for managing all aspects of the vehicle's mechanics, from wiping fingerprints from the stainless-steel body, to replacing dented fenders with pristine ones from the other cars. The A car received the most attention, of course, as it was the one that would be seen the most in close-up shots where the actors' faces were visible. Throughout the shoot, the C car was systematically cut into pieces to accommodate filming. Consider the perspective shot when Marty first travels to 1955 and hits the scarecrow on Old Man Peabody's Twin Pines Ranch, where the camera is serving as Marty's eyes looking out the front windshield of the DeLorean. Because a camera is large and requires multiple operators, it would have been impossible to fit the device and requisite personnel into the

DeLorean's tight backseat. The only possible solution, to capture the shot in the way Zemeckis intended, was to remove the rear of the car and film from behind Fox's head.

But for all the visual spectacle of the DeLorean, its greatest achievement may be its vibrant display as it prepares to travel through, and returns back from, time. This was achieved through a perfect synergy of the special and visual effects departments. For an example, one needs to look no further than the scene at the Twin Pines Mall when the DeLorean is first revealed. Getting the time machine up to eighty-eight miles per hour wasn't the effects team's only challenge, although, perhaps contrary to what conventional wisdom might suggest, even that cinematic feat required some finagling. Although *Back to the Future* fans have attempted to figure out the significance of Marty having to travel at that speed to transport himself through time, the Bobs are quick to note that the number was chosen for only one reason: It would be easy for the audience to remember. This somewhat arbitrary decision inadvertently created a problem for the effects team. Thanks to a 1979 law set by President Jimmy Carter's National Highway Traffic Safety Administration, all cars released after September of that year were to have a speedometer that topped out at eighty-five miles per hour, in an effort to encourage drivers to travel at safer speeds. The legislation was overturned less than two years later, but its legacy lasted in all models of the DMC-12, as production had ceased by the time of repeal. With the magic number that time machine had to hit being out of range, Pike not only replaced the manufacturer's speedometer with one that went beyond the regulated amount, but added a digital display for additional good measure.

While working on his round of design sketches, Ron Cobb mentioned that he believed the time machine would go out through the time portal at a burning-hot temperature, but come back cold. To that end, the special effects team lit fire trails whenever the DeLorean was beginning a journey. For shots of its return, the car would have to endure a somewhat complicated process to make it appear encased in a thin layer of ice. "When the car got cold, one of the obvious flaws in design was that the gas condensed in the cylinders of the rods that held the doors up, causing them to sag," Pike says. "When we loaded it up with ice and made it heavy and colder yet, Michael would open the door and stand up. When he'd go to get back in, the door would sag and he had to be very careful he didn't hit his head. We had a crew with hair dryers that constantly reheated those hydrogen-filled pistons to keep that from happening. I remember that when he shifted in the car in excitement, he would bang his elbow against the mechanism on the console. It was tight quarters, but it was a time machine. It wasn't a luxury Cadillac or something."

Because of the height differential between Eric Stoltz and Michael J. Fox, some of the custom parts added to the car were harder to utilize than they otherwise would have been. For one, when Marty attaches the electrical conductor hook to the back of the DeLorean before the scene where lightning strikes the clock tower, Fox was initially unable to reach the female end of the connector due to the protruding exhaust vents on the back of the vehicle. In order to accommodate their new leading man, a wooden step was fashioned to provide Fox with some extra lift.

After filming each time-traveling sequence, the footage was given to Arthur Schmidt and Harry Keramidas, who would continue editing with Zemeckis's regular supervision and approval. When Keramidas was brought on board, the two editors looked through the script and decided that they would each take one of the action sequences in the film—the Twin Pines and clock tower scenes—and work on them individually. Artie chose the mall parking lot scene, while Harry took the other. While Editor A was working on his major sequence, Editor B would tackle the other dialogue-heavy scenes as they came in, and vice versa.

Because both scenes rely heavily on optical effects that had to be added by ILM in post, the sequences required the editors to think beyond what they were seeing at the editing bay in front of them, just as they would have to anticipate how sound effects and an orchestral score would complement the moving pictures. "You have to use a lot of imagination to visualize what those effects are going to be, and how long a cut needs to be in order for those effects to be incorporated into the shot," Arthur Schmidt says. "Because visual effects and animation are very expensive, you're always asked to turn over a shot to its, hopefully, exact length with no extra frames. The reason is so that the visual effects people or the animators don't have to do any extra work that, obviously, is time consuming and also costs money. It sort of requires you to make educated guesses."

After each editor put the scene he was working on together, Zemeckis and visual effects supervisor Ken Ralston of ILM, who had cut his teeth on the first two *Star Wars* films and the first two sequels to the *Star Trek* film series, would review the footage together. The primary goal was for the two of them to determine where the finishing touches would be added in each frame by the effects house. However, in true Zemeckis fashion, sometimes advice would come from a third party. The notoriously collaborative director believes no one has a monopoly on good ideas, allowing everyone on his set to bring suggestions forth to enhance the project. To that end, when Schmidt completed work on the Twin Pines sequence, the editor was given an opportunity to contribute his two cents into the effects process.

Zemeckis asked Schmidt what he thought should happen visually as the DeLorean traveled through time to 1955. The editor hadn't given it any thought whatsoever—after all, visual effects were out of his jurisdiction, and he assumed Ken Ralston and his team had the answer to that question all sorted out. Again Artie thought quickly on his feet. "Sparks?" He was trying to imagine it. "Wouldn't there be sparks?" Zemeckis and Ralston agreed and sent the edited sequence to Wes Takahashi, one of ILM's animators, with the instructions that sparks be integrated into the look of time travel.

Yet when the finished footage arrived at the animator's station, the director was still unclear as to exactly what he wanted time travel to look like. Before Takahashi was given the assignment of designing the time slice—the visual effects that appear as the DeLorean prepares to move from the future to the past and vice versa—visual director Phil Norwood had designed a visual look whereby the DeLorean would start to react like a popcorn kernel in a microwaved bag. Three-dimensional cubes would protrude out of the stainless-steel body until the vehicle exploded through time. But Zemeckis wasn't too fond of the idea. He still didn't know exactly what he wanted, but he did have one piece of advice for Takahashi: "I just want it to feel like there's a Neanderthal sitting on the hood of the DeLorean, chipping away at the fabric of time with an ice pick."

"Well, that's something we've never seen before."

"I need to have something—some huge event that would then be followed by an explosion and implosion!"

With some clearer direction, the animator studied the DeLorean for clues as to where he might start. He looked at all of the vehicle's add-ons and thought the ornamental molding around the car might be better if, during time travel, they glowed a cool blue hue. From there, the animator threw in the kitchen sink. There were comets that shot out and bounced off an invisible plane in front of the car, emitting more neon. He added light explosions and sparks that opened up the time slice until the DeLorean would finally pierce through. Electricity flew and smoke contrails seeped out. Tracks of fire would emerge from the wheels, and then, once eighty-eight miles per hour was hit, Zemeckis's explosion and implosion would occur. Throughout the process, Takahashi walked the line, hoping to not provide so many effects that the sequence would appear cartoonish, while also not holding back so much that it would lack the excitement time travel would need. "With some directors it's a lot more challenging," he says. "You show them fifty or sixty different iterations, and by the time we'd get to sixty-one, they would say, 'Okay, actually I like the second one best. Why don't we go back?' It's all up to the director. Some you're attuned with, and they're a lot easier to please. I lucked out with Zemeckis. On the time-traveling scenes, we were on the same wavelength."

John Ellis served as supervisor at the optical department, the branch of ILM responsible for matching the effects to the camera focus and adding coloration to each shot. Takahashi would do his work on black or white paper, and then hand it over to Ellis's team for the finishing touches. "I would say—and I hope nobody is checking any records of my time cards—it probably took a week to do one shot," Takahashi says. "And we're just talking about the ten different animated elements generating the time slice effect." While he was spending a significant amount of work creating the look of the DeLorean's passage through time, it was equally important for the animator to focus his efforts on creating lightning for the clock tower scene. The Bobs' script called for "the most spectacular bolt of lightning in the history of cinema," a truly monumental task for an animator to pull off. For all of the impact that moment has on-screen in the finished film, Taka-hashi still sees an abundance of unrealized potential in his work.

"I never liked the animation that was finally approved of the gigantic bolt of lightning that hit the clock tower," he says. "That one shot went through numerous iterations. 'The biggest bolt of lightning in cinematic history'? Well, that could be interpreted many ways. If you make electricity too fat, it's just big white space and you lose all dimension, which, to me, never really worked. I started out trying to have this electricity start way off in the background and just creep up quickly towards the foreground and hit the clock tower. I was doing a lot of conceptual painted designs of lightning over color photos of the clock tower, and Bob Zemeckis chose this S-shaped one. That's what I animated, but it wasn't very convincing to me as animation. I wish I could have submitted other designs, or maybe just taken a little longer on that one shot, but given that I was the person who was doing all the electricity in the movie, I was pretty strapped for time."

The attention given to the clock tower sequence is fitting, given that the scene is arguably the most important one in the film. The narrative structure of *Back to the Future* sets up two goals for the main character: One, Marty has to fix his parents up, and two, he needs to return to 1985. As a result, there are two separate resolutions to these problems. When George kisses Lorraine at the Enchantment Under the Sea dance, the emotional climax of the film is realized. Marty's parents will fall in love and, providing our hero achieves his second goal, all will be fine. From a storytelling standpoint, this makes the sequence depicting the greatest thunderstorm in Hill Valley history the scene with the most import in the film. If Marty misses the lightning strike, his existence will still be threatened, and all the time spent connecting his parents will be undone. The sequence was meticulously story-boarded ahead of time, because of the effects that would be added in postproduction. They were then shot on film and cut together, so the editors would have a working guide of how the finished scene was supposed to look. It was a lengthy sequence to put together, but one that Zemeckis and company were unwilling to compromise on. The end result is one of the most iconic shots in cinematic history. As a testament to the significance of the lightning strike to the franchise, it is the only piece of footage that appears in all three installments of the trilogy. "It was good for me," Bob Yerkes, the circus performer who served as Christopher Lloyd's stuntman in this scene, says. "I got paid for the other shows and didn't have to do any extra work."

But as captivating as that sequence is to watch, it was difficult to film. As Marty is shouting up to Doc to warn him about the Libyan terrorists, Michael J. Fox was required to yell take after take as an industrial-strength wind machine blew in his face, making it impossible for him to hear his own voice. Meanwhile, Christopher Lloyd experienced his own difficulties. While Bob Yerkes slid down the wire from the tower to the ground, the remainder of the shots were up to Lloyd to handle. "We hung Chris from a harness off the clock tower for one shot," Bob Gale says. "Today we'd have used a green screen." The close-ups of the actor were obtained on a soundstage at Universal; but for the long shots, the actor had to venture up to the top of the high building that overlooked the Universal backlot.

"I was on break before we got around to shooting the clock tower sequence, and, by myself, climbed the stairs up to the top," Christopher Lloyd says. "That's when I realized that where I was supposed to film was just a ledge." The actor, who is afraid of heights, took one look at the ground, and came to a conclusion:

There was no way he was going to stand up on that ledge to film. He thought of a solution and took it to Bob Z.

"I was thinking . . ." The actor paused. The director looked back at him quizzically. Zemeckis was preoccupied with other business at the moment, and Lloyd knew it, but he had to get his feelings off his chest as soon as possible so the crew could start to work out a solution. "I was thinking that I could do the scene kneeling down."

Zemeckis's response was simple: "No fucking way." He wasn't angry, per se, but he made it clear that Doc Brown was not going to crawl along the clock tower ledge during the film's most important scene. When it came time to get that shot, the stunt team attached one end of a cable to Christopher Lloyd; the other was on a crane. If the actor had lost his footing atop the ledge, he would have fallen no more than a few feet before he was caught. With a secure system in place, the actor felt relatively confident during the shoot. His fear of heights would still remain, but at least he had evidence of one time he had overcome it.

With the scene in the can, Harry Keramidas got to work. He used the storyboards that were shot and edited together as his foundation in cutting the sequence. As footage came into his workspace, he switched out the storyboard footage. At any time, Zemeckis could see how the scene would look in its finished state, since the storyboards were filmed and used as placeholders until the entire sequence was put together. Because of the time required to see this project through to completion, the clock tower sequence wasn't done all in one clip. Instead, Keramidas bounced back and forth between that and the other—meaning shorter and easier—scenes to edit as they made their way to his trailer workspace. Overall, the process took weeks, with Zemeckis continuing to make his regular visits during his lunch "break" and after filming wrapped to give notes.

In terms of the production schedule, it made sense to front-load these scenes. Not only were they a beast to film; they would also require a significant amount of attention before the movie hit the theaters. If practice makes perfect, perhaps it was best that portions of each of these were worked out first during the Stoltz era, then revisited weeks later when all involved had a firmer grasp of the director's vision and expectations. Of course, it was also important for each scene to work in terms of audience buy-in to the story. Introduced within the first few minutes of the film, the clock tower was an important character in its own right, helped in large part because of the scene with Marty, Jennifer, and an overly passionate representative from the Hill Valley Preservation Society played by Elsa Raven.

"When I was called in, I auditioned for Mr. Zemeckis in a tiny little room," she says. "It was longer than a closet, and it was just the two of us. When I started reading, it startled him because I yelled out, 'Save the clock tower!' and Mr. Zemeckis was standing two feet away from me. He kind of recoiled, and I said, 'Well, she's got to reach the people. She's got to be loud!'" The two got to talking and realized they had something in common: They had both worked with Steven Spielberg before—she on *The Twilight Zone: The Movie*. "That made the difference," she says. Although she only received the pages of the script her character appeared in, and only had a minimal idea of what *Back to the Future* was about, she was aware of the gravity of the scene in setting up the importance of the blue flyer her character gives Marty. When Doc of the 1950s mentions to Marty that only a bolt of lightning could generate the 1.21 gigawatts required to send the DeLorean back to the future, it's likely that careful observers in the viewing audience might remember Raven's character and the piece of paper containing the details of the infamous Hill Valley storm.

"Maybe it's subconscious, but I think sometimes the fun and charm of the *Back to the Future* films is the fact that there is dramatic irony, which I think is such a great tool," Dean Cundey says. "The fact that the audience knows something the characters don't. It's like you're always making the audience feel smarter than the characters."

In the run-up to the film's release, Michael J. Fox took to describing the movie as one that audiences should plan on spending $20 to see, four times the average going rate for a multiplex ticket at the time. His reasoning was that it would take several viewings to catch all of the hidden gems the Bobs had incorporated into their script, such as the film titles on the Hill Valley cinema marquee and the ledge of the clock tower either appearing wholly intact or broken, depending on whether the characters were in the timeline where Doc had chipped the ledge or not. "Bob Zemeckis is still my directorial hero," Lea Thompson says. "He was so smart and so awesome to watch work. I just remember him being so detail-oriented and so into the story and the idea of giving the audience their money's worth with every single shot. I have nothing but incredible respect for him."

Sometimes Zemeckis's detail-oriented eye led to more work for the cast and crew. "Special effects are interesting," Harry Keramidas says. "Sometimes they look like visual effects, but they're actually done practically, like when we were doing the skateboard chase in 1955. Bob would go back and reshoot things. While we were editing that scene, he said, 'Wouldn't it be great if we had sparks coming off at the back of the skateboard when Marty tries to stop it?' He went back and did that shot again and that was a physical effect. We had sparklers at the end of the skateboard. Kevin Pike was the guy who was doing a lot of those effects on the first film, and he did a great job."

"Back in those days I was much more of a taskmaster. I would make my actors hit those marks and always be in their light, and now I've kind of—I don't care as much anymore," Zemeckis says. "I wouldn't allow there to be a camera bobble in any of those films. If the camera jiggled one frame, I'd have to do the take again. But nowadays, audiences are so different. I don't think they appreciate the attention to detail. Maybe subconsciously they feel it, but maybe they don't. Having a perfectly composed shot doesn't matter if you are watching it on an iPhone, does it? You wouldn't see it."

With the majority of the heavy lifting done for the clock tower scene, Zemeckis and company moved right along, back to the Hill Valley set, left relatively untouched from the Stoltz era. As Michael J. Fox stepped out into the Hill Valley square, with bright orange vest, the clock tower high above, and period cars driving down the street, someone on the production team called the director's attention upward. Zemeckis looked up to the bright blue sky. The most beautiful clouds he had ever captured on film were suspended above the backlot, as if ordered out of a catalog and hung by the art department. In and of itself, the weather would have been enough to please the director, but there was added satisfaction in this moment. Fox, in his bright costume and with the equally bright landscape behind him, was a marked departure from the footage Zemeckis and his editors had screened months earlier. The Bobs had written what they hoped would be received as a lighthearted story, and at least for the time being, it seemed they were taking steps in the right direction toward realizing that vision on-screen.

4. ROCK 'N' ROLL

Thursday, March 14, 1985

Lea Thompson sat in her dressing room—a small yet comfortable section of a trailer hooked onto the back of a semitruck in the lot of the United Methodist church on Franklin Avenue in Hollywood. For a location shoot, this was quite the convenient spot, less than ten minutes away from home base at Universal. Today had the potential of being arduous and taxing, with several principal actors called, dozens of extras, and an auditorium devoid of air-conditioning. With the seemingly ceaseless shooting schedule just a little over a month away from its conclusion, this week—when the Enchantment Under the Sea dance was being filmed—was one that Thompson was looking forward to.

She sat awaiting the call that she was needed on set, singing loudly to no one in particular. Scattered around her were magazines, which she regularly thumbed through when she wasn't reviewing her lines. Occasionally she stumbled across an ad that caused her eyes to widen, because she found it to be offensive or misogynistic, outmoded or obsolete. But these were trappings from a different era, not magazines from the 1980s.

Every actor has a different process by which they prepare to create magic in front of the camera. Some prefer to be called "Marty" at all times, while Thompson preferred to close herself off from the rest of the world for just a few moments and immerse herself in Lorraine Baines's reality. She found the character to be foreign to her, a marked departure from the role she had just previously played in *Red Dawn*: a tomboy feminist who also happened to be a ballet dancer. Playing the seemingly naive yet sweetly seductive and soft-spoken character didn't come naturally, so excelling required some additional homework. While others might have been catching up on the latest issue of *People* or *Time*, she was reading *Look* and *Life* from the early to mid-1950s, which she had gone to great lengths to find and transport with her each day to the set. She kept a small purse nearby with vintage coins inside, which she would regularly remove from their container, look at, and pass between her fingers, as if studying them for clues as to whom their previous owners had been and how to best channel their spirits. She would take out the lipstick she had purchased especially for the film, a classic shade of pink, and when she was feeling particularly out of character, as she was at this moment, she would play music from the period loudly and sing along: "Please turn on your magic beam / Mr. Sandman, bring me a dream . . ."

"They eventually put the song in the movie, thank God," she says. "It was so goofy, but it would put me in the mood to be Lorraine. For some reason, the old Lorraine was just in my body. I think I was playing one of my girlfriends' mothers or something. That was really easy for me, but it was the young Lorraine that was actually really hard. To really commit to that silliness and not wink at it? To play that innocence was really very hard, so singing 'Mr. Sandman' and reading those magazines really helped."

While the actress focused on her own makeshift time-traveling methods to transport herself to the middle of the century, Robert Zemeckis had a much taller order ahead of him. The sequence at the dance encompassed many elements, such as corralling dozens of extras and filming choreographed songs with complicated camera moves. Over the course of this week, the production team would film several musical sequences, including an elaborate showstopping number by Michael J. Fox. There would be shots using a jib, a mechanism by which a camera is attached to a weighted boom with a seesaw-like device. This enables an operator, who sees what the camera is capturing by watching a monitor, to capture sweeping shots that have to travel a distance. The jib was useful in filming the shot during Marty's "Johnny B. Goode" performance that goes from the back of the gymnasium, through a dancer's legs, to a close-up of Fox's fingers strumming away on his cherry-red Gibson ES-345 guitar, an instrument that wasn't made commercially available until three years after the dance takes place. Despite the difficulty with the camera—Dean Cundey hadn't had much experience using that particular bit of equipment and was initially skeptical that the footage would be usable—the inclusion of those challenging shots in the dance sequence adds just the right amount of fun and excitement to a moment already filled with energy. Zemeckis was still proving himself every day on the set, but his visionary sensibilities as a director, and that USC training that so annoyed Kathleen Turner during the filming of *Romancing the Stone*, were coming together.

"By the time I got to *Back to the Future*, I had pretty much been through any kind of baptism by fire that a director could go through," he says. "From being immersed in an ensemble cast of young actors, to having to do movies on a very, very small budget, to all the rigors of giant stunts and shooting in the jungles of Mexico. I was ready for anything that could be thrown at me. I would say I certainly knew my way around the camera by then. You learn from every movie. Certainly *Back to the Future* wouldn't have been anywhere near as good as it is if it had been my first film."

There were challenges and more compromises to make, sure, but part of what made this scene fun to work on was that it hadn't been tested out during the Stoltz era. "When I was cast, they had shot most of the movie up until the Enchantment Under the Sea dance with Eric Stoltz before they replaced him," Harry Waters, Jr., who plays the musician Marvin Berry, says. "By the time I showed up on the set, it was all new material that everybody was excited about. It was like, 'Okay, now we're getting to something new.'"

Waters first heard about the film back in November of the previous year, while he was taking low-paying theatrical jobs in between the occasional television commercial and guest appearance on television series. While he was appearing in *The Me Nobody Knows*, a 1970 Broadway musical that was being staged in Los Angeles, his agent landed him an audition for the role of the lead singer of the Starlighters, the all-black band that plays during George McFly and Lorraine's first kiss. Although he was somewhat jittery about auditioning for a major motion picture, let alone one with Steven Spielberg's involvement, he felt he could nail it. When he made his first trek to Amblin, the other fifteen or so people waiting to be seen didn't faze him. He went in, sang his sixteen bars a cappella, and left feeling confident.

But after a while, those feelings of confidence started to dissipate. Weeks passed, and Waters and his agent hadn't heard back from the film's producers. The actor scored a callback audition for *He's the Mayor*, an upcoming ABC series, and kept his fingers crossed for that gig to come through as he continued his stage work. In December, a phone call came. Waters was wanted back at Amblin. The actor warmed up his voice and was prepared to sing again. But his follow-up didn't go as planned, as, instead of having an audition proper, the actor was called into an interview with Bob Z. "It was just the two of us chatting," Waters says. "Our conversation became about what I was doing. I said I was doing the musical and working with a friend of mine on a piece of theater about black storytelling. I had no expectation that I was going to land the role. I figured they were going for actors with name recognition, because that's what I had experienced before I even moved to L.A. The industry usually goes with people that have a known track record." Their sit-down lasted for about twenty minutes. The director thanked him for coming in, the actor expressed what an honor and opportunity it was to have had the chance to audition, and the two went in their separate directions. Before heading home, Waters took the opportunity to survey Universal Studios—after all, who knew if he would be back again?

Less than half an hour after getting back home, his phone rang. It was his agent. Waters was one of two finalists being considered for the lead in *He's the Mayor*, and his agent told him that he could no longer sit on the fence. The start dates were around the same time for each project, and the actor would be unable to do both. In the off chance that both came through, which would he pursue? The answer came quickly. He wanted to work with Zemeckis.

On New Year's Eve, the actor received the offer to appear in *Future*. For Waters, who would go on to become an associate professor of theater at Macalester College in Minnesota, the road to his first major motion picture role is one that bears a lesson worth remembering. "I always remind my students that I wasn't sitting around waiting for the next audition before *Back to the Future,*" Waters says. "I was always working on my craft, so when I went into auditions I had something to talk about. It wasn't, 'Oh, my god, I've got to get this job right now because I'm not doing anything else.'"

The role of Marvin Berry is small, but because of Waters's performance, and Robert Zemeckis and Bob Gale's screenplay, it is one of several unforgettable bit-player parts in the film. During the writing process, the Bobs gave particular attention to their characters, believing wholeheartedly that an audience will forgive a fault in your film if they are engaged with the people on-screen. The Bobs were especially aware of the potential of smaller featured roles to be significant catalysts within the story, and they were determined to create each with a unique style and point of view. "Often, we imagine a particular actor in a role," Gale says. "It's not necessarily an actor we think we'll cast—sometimes we'll imagine a movie star from the past in the role, just so that there's a voice in our head. James Cagney talked a certain way, which was different from James Stewart, which was different from Bogart, or John Wayne or Burt Lancaster or Brando or Al Pacino. That's a trick that helps us give a character a certain voice. And when even a small role has enough for an actor to sink their teeth in, it attracts better actors, and gives them more to work with. We always encourage actors to make a part their own, and that's when you can have magic happen. Plus, Bob Z has a natural ability to bring out the best in his casts, and to know the type of things to have actors do that will make audiences remember them. It's something we learned from watching Billy Wilder, Frank Capra, and John Ford movies."

James Tolkan was hand-selected by Bob Z to play Principal Strickland. The character has no lines in the Enchantment Under the Sea scene, but has a great bit of physical comedy immediately after the "Johnny B. Goode" number, where he is seen removing his hands from his ears because of the music that Marty accurately speculates his audience isn't ready for just yet. Due to a continuity error, Tolkan can actually been seen doing this movement twice within a short period of time, no doubt one of the compromises Zemeckis had to make with his editors in the futile effort to make a flawless film. Curiously, the character's first name has been a source of debate among fans of the film since its release. When George Gipe wrote the movie's novelization, he christened Strickland with the name "Gerald," an eponym not cleared with the Bobs. They both hated it, but since their script failed to provide a first name for the character, Gipe's decision prevailed. When the filmmakers set out to write the *Back to the Future* sequels, Zemeckis suggested putting a nameplate on Strickland's door identifying his initials as s.s., to evoke the Nazis. Decades later, when Telltale Games released their video game inspired by the film franchise in 2010, Bob Gale was given an opportunity to finally establish the principal's first name once and for all as "Stanford."

Prior to appearing in *Future*, Tolkan had parts in a number of films, including Sidney Lumet's *Serpico* (1973), Woody Allen's *Love and Death* (1975), and Stuart Rosenberg's *The Amityville Horror* (1979), but had resisted moving to Los Angeles to seriously attempt breaking into the movie industry. In 1984, he was performing in David Mamet's *Glengarry Glen Ross* on Broadway when he received a telephone call from Zemeckis, who had seen the actor in the 1981 movie *Prince of the City*, asking him to join his cast. There was no audition, and according to what he was told during their conversation, no one else was considered for the role of the no-nonsense school administrator with a hatred for slackers and a love for discipline. "I'd always said, 'I'm never going to Hollywood until Hollywood sends for me,' because I was a New York actor for all these years," Tolkan says. "I just said, 'Okay, this is a chance for me to go to L.A. and see what it's like there.'"

The actor spent several days filming at Whittier High School alongside Eric Stoltz in the early days of production, in scenes that were reshot months later. Revisiting old material didn't bother him much. In fact, the actor initially had a very laissez-faire attitude toward the movie in general. It didn't appear to be anything special while filming, and while enjoyable to work on, it certainly did not seem a project predetermined for greatness. The story was wonderful, but the actor found the production to be relatively modest. The trailers were small; the lead actor was a bit disconnected, and then was changed midstream. For all the hubbub among the industry chattering class of this being a Spielberg picture, Tolkan's impression was that the executive producer's involvement was minimal. "Steven Spielberg was more interested in the picture he was working on at the time called *The Goonies* than he was interested in *Back to the Future*," he says.

The two movies were indeed in production during the same time between the fall of 1984 and the spring of 1985, though accounts of Spielberg's involvement on both projects vary. Although Bob Gale recalls Spielberg essentially leaving both Zemeckis and *Goonies* director Richard Donner alone during filming—"Steven knew Bob Z and Donner knew how to make movies, and he had too much professional respect to get involved"—it's been widely reported that Spielberg was incredibly hands-on when it came to *Goonies*, occasionally seeming like less of a producer and more of a codirector. With the dust settled after the Stoltz shake-up on the *Future* set, and *Goonies* based out of Warner Bros. Pictures in Burbank, Spielberg found himself spending less time with the

Bobs and more time with Donner and his young cast. As shooting continued, Frank Marshall, who also served as *Future's* second unit director, became the primary representative from Amblin to check in on how production was going.

While James Tolkan's presence at the Enchantment Under the Sea dance enhances the scene, it's easy to argue that the most important bit players to the sequence at hand were Mark Campbell, Paul Hanson, Brad Jeffries, and Tim May, who didn't appear in this scene physically, yet stole the show with their contributions to the "Johnny B. Goode" musical number. Mark Campbell was a recent transplant to California by way of New Orleans when he was hired to sing "Johnny B. Goode" for the film. His name had been passed around among those in the music scene as being a talented session singer, and within just a few weeks of moving to the area, he received a call from *Future's* music supervisor, Bones Howe, asking him to come audition.

"We've got two or three people we're considering," the producer said when the singer arrived at the recording studio. "But your name kept coming up from a bunch of friends of mine." During the audition, the singers all performed one after the other. Campbell went into the booth and did his thing. He knew he had done the best job of everyone in the room, but Bones wanted the singer to give it a second try. "Okay, check it out," he said. "You're singing it like you've always sung it, probably, and you're from New Orleans. Just remember our guy, Michael, is probably from, I think, Ohio." Neither the actor nor the character is from the midwestern part of the United States, but it didn't matter. The correction was perfect for the singer. He pulled back his accent and sang it with a little less funk. The singer left and received a call later that evening. He was hired and would be recording the track the next day.

After recording the song, the singer received a follow-up call from Bob Gale. The producer told him that, in an effort to keep up the mystique and illusion that Michael J. Fox was actually singing, Campbell wouldn't be receiving a credit on-screen. "I told him I understood. I got it," Campbell says. "I just wanted to do a good job and fool the audience as much as everybody else did. I didn't think anything of it. What's really great for me is that Bones Howe kind of took it personally. He went, 'You're not getting credit? No, no, no, no. That ain't right. I'll tell you what we're going to do. I'm going to figure something out, and I'll get back to you.' About two days later, he called me and told me I would be getting a very, very small but very nice percentage of the soundtrack." Additionally, when the film was released, Mark Campbell's and Tim May's names did appear first on the small list of "special thanks," a move that the singer believes was the result of Bones's advocacy.

Michael J. Fox knew his way around a guitar, having played in bands in high school. Like a lot of teenage musicians, he briefly, but seriously, considered pursuing platinum records as a career, prior to catching the acting bug. However, even with his skills, he wasn't asked to play the high-octane musical number. Instead, noted studio musician Tim May played a custom 1979 Valley Arts Stratocaster guitar with a rosewood body, maple neck, and ebony fingerboard on the track. Like the other three-quarters of the illusion-making team, Paul Hanson was hired during the Stoltz era. Bones Howe had called the Musicians Institute in Hollywood in search of talent, and asked the secretary if she knew anyone who could play guitar with his or her teeth, and might be interested in teaching an actor how to finger-sync along with the prerecorded track.

"Oh, you've got to get Paul." Her response was immediate because, serendipitously, Hanson had stopped by the receptionist's station just a few hours earlier to socialize and show off, imitating Jimi Hendrix while rubbing the top row of his teeth against the guitar strings. She gave Bones his number and he was hired. Rehearsals with Stoltz went well, and the two developed a strong working relationship. Stoltz was a hard worker and a nice guy, but he wasn't as confident or musically competent as Hanson would have liked. There was a marked difference in guitar practice when Fox was brought on board. If things were starting to simmer before, they reached a full boil with the new leading man.

"He would come over, mostly in the evenings," he says. "The thing that I thought was really cool about him is that his memory was so good. I attributed it to the fact that he had to memorize lines all the time being an actor, but he could have actually had a career as a guitar player. The lessons would be about an hour, and we would drink Canadian beer. Moosehead, I think."

For Fox, the opportunity to play rock star for a few hours a week in between shooting *Family Ties* and *Back to the Future* was a relief. Not that he ever needed much of an excuse to put his feet up and let loose, but now he could smoke a few cigarettes, throw back a few beers, and talk about his favorite musical idols, all in the best interest of his job. The two spent time practicing alongside May's recording, and Hanson made a cassette tape of "Johnny B. Goode" at half speed so the actor could practice at home, during his downtime at the television studio, or in his trailer at the film set. Fox's accuracy and the speed at which he picked up the notes impressed his teacher. And moreover, Hanson enjoyed the company. Although he wasn't on the A-list himself, he got a kick out of being a part of the lifestyle, even if it was just for a few hours a week. "At some point, I remember he bought a red Ferrari," he says. "He drove it over to my house in North Hollywood and parked it on the front grass when I had a party. It was pretty cool having that on our lawn."

When it came time to film the dance number, the actor felt prepared when he took to the stage. The shots were planned out, and Fox had a loose idea as to what he was going to do, but Zemeckis gave him the freedom to play and feel inspired. The section at the end of the song, where Marty imitates contemporary artists of the three decades between the film's past and present, materialized differently on-screen than what was originally scripted, where the character was supposed to move his pelvis like Elvis, strut like Mick Jagger, and moonwalk like Michael Jackson—a visual joke that would eventually turn up in *Back to the Future Part III*. While specific artists were named in the screenplay, they were listed simply as a blueprint for the reader of what the Bobs would be aiming for. When the time came to rehearse the number, Fox and choreographer Brad Jeffries worked together to come up with homages to guitarists that might be a more appropriate fit for the scene. Like Hanson, the dance instructor met with Fox for several rehearsals prior to filming and was present on set. In devising the song's climactic finale, he set high expectations within Fox's comfort zone, figuring out what movements he could naturally execute that would also be immediately recognizable to the audience. *Future* was Jeffries's first film as choreographer— he had served as assistant choreographer on the film adaptation of *A Chorus Line*—and he was taken by Zemeckis's ability to hire the best people to do jobs on the film and then step out of the way while they worked. Within the controlled chaos at the United Methodist church, the director seemed both in charge and at a far enough distance away to give everyone breathing room.

Filming the Enchantment scene was a highlight for Fox and many of the others present those days. Harry Waters, Jr., and the

Starlighters, made up of David Harold Brown, Tommy Thomas, Lloyd L. Tolbert, and Granville "Danny" Young, would jam between takes, sometimes playing Whodini's 1984 funk hit "Freaks Come Out at Night" for their mostly white listeners. It was true that music was the great unifier, as everyone danced, despite being incongruously dressed in 1950s party clothes. "It was my first film I ever worked on, and it was just so casual and cool," Hanson says. "I was surprised. The cast was awesome. Bob was a pretty mellow director. Amblin had just hired a brand-new catering company, so these guys, they were really trying to show off how good they were. There was Bundt cake, hot dogs, just food all the time."

Perhaps the only actor to experience any significant amount of discomfort was Lea Thompson, all stemming from her costume, which she had a love-hate relationship with. As great as Lorraine's pink dress looks on-screen, and as beautiful as the actress felt when she saw herself in it, it was uncomfortable to wear and even harder to dance in. Even worse still were the extended periods of downtime where she was unable to change in between takes. "I would take it off and walk around in a corset bra and a crinoline underskirt," she says. "My mother came to visit and she was freaking out because there were, like, two hundred extras sitting there and I'm in my bra. My mom was so scandalized, but the dress was really tight." Although it was an annoyance, the actress has held on to the dress for the past three decades, with it proudly hanging in a garment bag in her closet. "My kids used to want to wear it for Halloween, but they couldn't fit in it," she says, while letting out a genuinely incredulous laugh. "I was tiny!"

For all of the fun involved in shooting the Enchantment Under the Sea dance, there was a bit of stress caused by a clearance that came at the eleventh hour, jeopardizing the gag in the middle of "Johnny B. Goode" where Marvin calls his famous cousin backstage. While the Bobs always intended on having Marty play the song, dating all the way back to the first draft of their script written almost half a decade before filming, they had difficulty getting Chuck Berry on board. Perhaps it was a dispute over money, or maybe the rock 'n' roll pioneer had a problem with the film's revisionist history, a white teenager inventing rock and black musicians just copying his lead. With the set dressed, the crew in place, and the actor waiting for the word, the real Berry wavered before granting his approval for his name to be used in the scene, as the team waited impatiently throughout the day. "His doubts went away when we paid him to use the song," Bob Gale says. "I think it was fifty thousand dollars—a lot for a song back then."

Filming was slightly delayed because of the uncertainty, so once the okay was given, everyone had to move quickly. "I was the only actor on set," Waters says. "We're all in that little corner off-stage in the auditorium of the church. They said, 'All right, action!' I do the line, which has now been documented on at least twenty different sitcoms, cartoons, YouTube videos, everything. *Family Guy* has four versions. I did it in one take and he said, 'Great, cut, print.' We were done and the crew cheered. When it finally showed up in the film, I was amazed. I only gave the line that one time, which is rare for any sort of shooting. I always get to have that as a feather in my cap. I got to do a famous line in this historic movie, and I did it in one take."

However, that wouldn't be the only plume in Waters's headpiece. Alan Silvestri, the film's composer, asked the actor if he would be interested in providing the vocals on the track for "Earth Angel" that would be used during filming. At the time, the request struck the actor as odd. After all, Michael J. Fox had spent months practicing alongside a recording of studio musicians playing "Johnny B. Goode." Why hadn't they hired someone to sing during the moment when George and Lorraine share their first kiss? Despite the curiousness of the situation, the actor agreed. As far as he was concerned, if Zemeckis or any other member of the creative team asked him to jump, he was going to put his legs to work before asking, "How high?"

Waters and his brother, who was visiting from Denver, went to the recording studio in Hollywood. The actor went into the booth, put on the headphones, and listened to the playback. For a musical theater performer, this stirred mixed emotions. It was fun to croon in a studio, but he was out of his element. There were the occasional off-key notes, and after fourteen takes of varying levels of acceptability, recording wrapped. The two were invited to stick around and watch Bones mix the song, scrapping portions of the flawed takes and fusing them with moments of vocal excellence. When Waters heard the track while filming, he thought it sounded decent enough, but still expected the vocals to be replaced by a "real musician" by the time the movie hit the theaters, with his recording only used as a reference for him to lip-synch along with on set.

It wasn't until June 26, three months later, at the cast and crew screening at the Avco Center Cinemas on Wilshire Boulevard, that he realized he hadn't been dubbed over in postproduction. For the first few minutes of watching himself sing, Waters was so engulfed in the story that he hadn't recognized the sound of his own voice, but once Marty's parents kissed, and the violins came in—a decision made to heighten the emotional impact of the scene, even though there are no violinists onstage—the actor realized he had been listening to himself all along.

Mark Campbell attended the screening with his mother, who flew from New Orleans to share the moment with her son. When the "Johnny B. Goode" scene started, the audience was captivated. His mother couldn't have been happier. The woman in the seat directly in front of her turned to her date and said, "I didn't know Michael J. Fox could sing," which resulted in her getting a swift correction from the proud parent. The singer was a little embarrassed, but mostly proud that the trick had been pulled off. *Yup*, he thought. *We fooled 'em, all right.*

A week and a half after that screening, the *Back to the Future* soundtrack was released. Initially, it failed to catch on, barely making an impression on the album charts. By September 7, after several months wading in the kiddie pool, it made a splash into the top 20 on the Billboard 200. By the following month, it moved to its peak position of number twelve, fueled not only by the success of the film, but by Huey Lewis and the News' "The Power of Love," which was inescapable on radio and in television spots during the summer of 1985. The song reached the top spot on the Billboard Hot 100 singles chart and stayed there for two weeks—the first of the band's releases to hit number one—and was certified Gold by the Recording Industry Association of America (RIAA). Like Ray Parker, Jr.'s "Ghostbusters" a year before, it is hard to tell which was the chicken and which was the egg in appraising the tandem success of the song and film. Did people request the song on the radio because they enjoyed the movie, or rush to theaters because of the single?

"In those days it was part of the marketing," Robert Zemeckis says. "It was done by design, to be able to have a really cool song— a good song—played in heavy rotation on the radio. Every time the deejay comes on it's, 'That was "The Power of Love" by Huey Lewis from the movie *Back to the Future*!' That's advertising. That was the whole reason. The only thing that's better than that is to have the song be called 'Back to the Future.' Then you'd get it. Back in the eighties, that's what you did. We only had so many outlets back in the day."

Shortly after the film was green-lighted at Universal, Zemeckis and company called Bob Brown, manager of Huey Lewis and the News, to set up a meeting. The production team wanted music to complement the film, as the Bobs had done for their previous collaborations. For *I Wanna Hold Your Hand*, the Beatles back catalog provided not only the soundtrack, but also inspired the name of the picture. On *Used Cars*, country singer Bobby Bare sang the titular track. But this time, the filmmaking partners wanted to do better. Not only did they want an original song, but one by an artist who might add some additional cachet with the demographic they were hoping to target. Huey Lewis and the News' profile was on the rise, with *Sports*, their third album, reaching the top spot on the Billboard 200 in the summer of 1984. The record spawned four top 10 hits, including "I Want a New Drug" and "The Heart of Rock & Roll." Having Lewis in their camp couldn't hurt, and the Bobs were grateful that the lead singer and his manager agreed to meet with them to discuss collaborating.

Lewis and Brown made their way to the designated location on Universal property, sitting patiently inside a building at Amblin with a sign affixed to its exterior that read MOVIES WHILE U WAIT. AND WAIT. AND WAIT imprinted on it. Before the waiting became too intolerable, they were invited into an office. "We just wrote this movie," Zemeckis said. "The lead character is this guy named Marty McFly, and his favorite band would be Huey Lewis and the News."

"Whoa, cool." Lewis felt humbled. He wasn't familiar with the director's work, but being at Universal Studios, feet away from

Steven Spielberg's office, and hearing someone say they wrote a character who would be a fan of his was music to the singer's ears.

"So we thought—"

"Maybe we could get you guys to write a song or something?" Zemeckis was eager to make the ask.

"Wow, that's great. That's flattering," Lewis said. He looked at his manager, then back at the filmmakers. "But we don't know how to write for movies or whatever." Before the Bobs had a chance to respond, he quickly took appraisal of the offer: Amblin, Universal, Steven Spielberg, *Back to the Future*. It all sounded intriguing enough, and maybe not all that hard to do. But there was one nagging question: What kind of song could they possibly want for a movie with that title? "Even if I wrote a song, it wouldn't be called 'Back to the Future.'"

The Bobs seemed pleased by the answer. Rejections come quickly in the film business, and the singer's response was far from that. Just as Gale had known Frank Price was interested in giving him and Bob Z a development deal to write *Future* at Columbia Pictures, he also knew that Lewis was on the line. This time, his partner sensed it too. The duo went in for the kill. "No, no, no, no, we don't care what it's called," Zemeckis said. "We just want a song."

The singer thought for a moment, then confirmed the Bobs' intuition. "Okay, cool. I'll send you the next couple things we write." Lewis's manager sent a tape over to Zemeckis's office a few weeks later. In the singer's version of the story, that song was "The Power of Love," which the director loved at the first listen and wanted to put in the film. Zemeckis, however, has stated throughout the years that a different song was sent over, and he asked Lewis to send another track, something in a major key. "The Power of Love" was the second submission, not the first.

"But I don't remember that," Lewis says. "'The Power of

Love' is in a minor key in the verse anyway." Either way, it was agreed that the song would be offered to Universal for the film. A few months later, when Columbia Pictures came courting the band to contribute the title song to *Ghostbusters*, which was nearing its release, Lewis and his team declined. They had already pledged their allegiance to Zemeckis and company.

The vocals for the song were recorded at the Record Plant in Sausalito, California, nearly four hundred miles northwest of Los Angeles, near San Francisco; the instrumental track was laid elsewhere beforehand. Journey was next door, working on their *Raised on the Radio* album. Lewis did multiple takes within two hours, and as per usual, he and his band immediately started mixing the record. Zemeckis, his producers, Michael J. Fox, and Christopher Lloyd took a field trip to preview the song's rough draft. "I have to admit, I really didn't know his music at the time," Lloyd says. "I also do not know exactly why the actors were there, because we do not sing."

"We sat them down, played the song," Lewis says. "It was a work in progress; the mix wasn't great. I remember being nervous as shit about the whole thing. But they liked it, I think. We got by somehow."

Lloyd remembers the singer still being largely unfamiliar with the plot of the film, at one point asking the actor, "*Back to the Future?* What the fuck is that?" Before the visitors headed back to Los Angeles, the band's frontman saw an opening, while Zemeckis and his producers were away, to approach the two actors. With genuine curiosity, and perhaps a dash of skepticism, he asked them a question that had been on his mind for some time: "Is this movie going to do anything?"

It would have been impossible to say at the time, but by the end of the summer of 1985, the answer became obvious. Once the film was released, the single helped elevate the band's profile, validating Lewis's decision to take a crack at writing for film. "It's our biggest hit," he says. "The wonderful thing about 'The Power of Love' is that *Sports* was a huge hit in America, but in Europe, not so much. As an American act, we made some noise over there, but 'The Power of Love' was our first international hit. That enabled us to tour Europe and Asia."

"People just connected with it," Neil Canton says. "They were the right choice. The song made people feel good and, I'm sure, brought people into the theater. It's hard to imagine these movies without the music. When I'm driving along and I hear that song, it just pulls me right back into the movie."

"It was sort of a perfect marriage," Frank Marshall says. "People always want a song at the end of the movie by a pop star because it helps with marketing, but usually it doesn't fit organically. This was not the case here. We thought it would be great if we could go back to the early days of having singles written for the movie and weaving them into the picture."

With "The Power of Love" in the can, the band was approached to write another song for the end credits. This time, Zemeckis wanted something a bit more referential to the story. Lewis and fellow band member Sean Hopper spearheaded writing a song from the perspective of Marty, and the result was "Back in Time." While it was never released as a commercial single, the song reached number three on the Billboard Album Rock Tracks chart and has remained a staple of the band's live shows since the movie's release. Over the years, fans have debated about which of the band's two contributions to *Future* is superior, a discussion that those involved with the film are happy to watch from afar. "Why does there have to be a debate?" Bob Gale says. "They're both great songs, and I still love hearing them."

"Being that I wrote them both, I'm not allowed to make those choices," Lewis says. "It's like asking if I like my son or my daughter better. That's not fair. You know, you write songs, and you write them for different reasons. You never really know when they're going to connect. Sometimes they do, sometimes they don't, but those two really connected. We used them well."

With two wins with Huey Lewis in their column, Zemeckis and company decided to go for the trifecta. On March 29, the crew would be filming a scene where Marty and the Pinheads, his band, audition for the Hill Valley High Battle of the Bands. Once again, Zemeckis put a call in to the singer's manager, this time to see if Lewis would be interested in making a cameo. However, unlike the first two pitches, the director seemed about to strike out. "They came up with the idea that it'd be cool to have me in it, somehow," Lewis says. "I thought, *Nah*. The band was doing great. I was becoming a rock star. I was playing the role of my life, you know, and I was fine with that. I kind of resisted for a while."

After giving it some more consideration, Lewis agreed, providing his conditions were met. He didn't want his character to be listed in the credits or used in any promotional material in advance of the film's release, lest it damage his rock star image. In fact, it would be even better if he could be in some form of disguise. Zemeckis agreed and the deal was done. When the date came, the singer arrived at the McCambridge Park Recreation Center in Burbank, the day's shooting location, at 8:00 A.M. He was given a copy of his script pages, and then sent to wardrobe, where he was outfitted in a brown jacket and shoes—a marked departure from the white T-shirt and jeans he was accustomed to wearing onstage. When he put the clothes on and looked in the mirror, he laughed and shook his head at the familiar face staring back at him. It wasn't his own, but instead that of Jack Craigo, the president of Chrysalis Records, where Huey Lewis and the News were signed—a real pencil pusher type. The singer channeled the spirit of the record executive to get into character. The next time the two saw each other, after the movie's release, there was a subtle acknowledgment of Lewis's homage.

"Hey, Jack, how's it going?"

"I'm doing pretty good. I saw your little cameo in *Back to the Future*. I enjoyed it. I think you should win an Oscar." The executive paused for a moment and, without even the slightest bit of humor, added: "Or maybe I should."

Although he was proud of his contributions to the film, and undoubtedly pleased when he saw a poster for the band's *Sports* album prominently displayed in Marty's bedroom, Lewis was not surprised when the *Back to the Future* soundtrack failed to shoot to the top of the charts, even as the movie was doing well in theaters. With only ten tracks, the record was an odd one: two from Huey Lewis and the News, three from the (fictional) Starlighters, and three separate songs from Lindsey Buckingham, Eric Clapton, and Etta James. Alan Silvestri contributed two selections from his score, which omitted more than twenty instrumental music cues from the composer and his ninety-eight-piece orchestra. "I was very disappointed, as were myriad fans," Bob Gale says. "The corporate mentality back then was that orchestral scores didn't sell, and Universal wanted us to put those other eighties songs in the movie so they could put them on the album. They also had to pay a royalty to everyone in the orchestra based on how much music was used, so they limited it for that reason as well."

"That soundtrack record was just before *Dirty Dancing*—a year or so before soundtrack albums would become the thing,"

Huey Lewis says. "That soundtrack album sold nothing, because it was 'Back in Time,' 'The Power of Love,' and maybe a Phil Collins song, or something. It was kind of a crappy record. It didn't even go Gold at the time, while we were going platinum with our other records."

Though it took three months, the album did reach Gold status. While one can suspect Lewis was surprised, no one was more surprised than Harry Waters, Jr., who hadn't even expected to appear on the record in the first place. "We are invited to Amblin, and it's me, Huey Lewis, and Mark Campbell from Jack Mack and the Heart Attacks, and they're giving us a Gold record for *Back to the Future*," he says. "Huey, of course, was the reason that the album went Gold—thank you, Huey! It's hanging here on my wall. I got a twelfth of a cent for the half a million albums that were sold, so it wasn't a whole lot of money, but it is sort of legendary in the sense that there are all these different versions of 'Earth Angel' that show up when you google, and I get to be one of those."

Just as George and Lorraine remembered "Earth Angel" as being important to their relationship, *Back to the Future* audiences equally look back fondly at that moment in the film. While often overshadowed by the sheer exuberance of "Johnny B. Goode," the song is the perfect complement to the emotional climax in the film. "Music brings a lot of emotion in our lives," Neil Canton says. "You can hear a song and know where you were when you first heard that song. It's a very emotional connection."

"The music in *Back to the Future* transcends race, it transcends across social status, and it even goes across the world," Waters says. "When we did the *Back to the Future* reunion in 2010, there were people there from at least six different countries. I remember there was a couple from Canada, and he proposed to her in front of the stage after I sang 'Earth Angel.' I loved being a part of it."

But for all of the memorable experiences his performance in the film has brought him, Waters still has one bit of unfinished business with *Back to the Future*. Although it has been more than three decades since his scene was shot, the actor still hopes to have a chance to meet his fictional cousin, Chuck Berry. "I'd have to say, 'Excuse me, Mr. Berry, let me introduce myself to you,'" he says. "'My name is Harry Waters, Jr., and I was in that movie *Back to the Future*. I played your cousin Marvin. I'm sorry we never got to meet.' I'd have to wait and see what his reaction was, because I can't say, 'I'm sorry that we appropriated your song. I was just a willing participant.'"

5. TO BE CONTINUED

Friday, April 26, 1985

Michael J. Fox made his way to Stage 12, the 29,500-square-foot soundstage at Universal that was the largest on the lot and the eighth largest in the world. The expansive building was the ideal place for the crew to build several large sets required for filming, including Doc's 1985 garage and the inside of Doc's Packard, where Lorraine kisses Marty outside the Enchantment Under the Sea dance. Today marked the conclusion of a relatively easy and uneventful week for the otherwise jam-packed *Future* shoot. Monday of that week took production to Chino, about an hour eastbound down Interstate 210, to shoot the scene where Marty scares the elderly couple outside the Lyon Estates gates shortly after his arrival to 1955, but after that, the remaining weekdays were spent on the soundstage and backlot.

Even those who hadn't read the day's production call sheet could sense filming on *Back to the Future* was winding down. The heavy lifting was over, and as a result, fewer and fewer principal cast members were called to work. On this day, the 107th that the cameras rolled on the film, only Michael J. Fox and Tiger, the dog playing Einstein, were called so the crew could get some pickup process shots of them inside of the DeLorean. With *Family Ties* wrapped for the season, the actor was able to get a proper night's sleep and arrive on set at the comfortable and convenient time of 10:00 A.M. After just a few hours of work, the actor gave his thanks, said his good-byes, and made his way back home. As the crew disassembled the lights, Bob Gale took a final look at the call sheet. At the bottom, production manager Jack Grossberg, who took over the job for Dennis Jones for the final weeks of production, wrote in sprawling cursive, "That's all folks! Principal photography completed!"

Now the real work began. Arthur Schmidt and Harry Keramidas, along with the rest of the postproduction team, went into overdrive to complete the picture so it would be ready by its mid-August release date. "Artie and I often joke that we invented the 'speed-it-up' schedule and all the editors in Hollywood probably hate us now," Keramidas says. "It was the first time that we turned in a big movie that quickly after shooting." The duo rushed to complete what is known in the business as a "work-print," a rough cut of the movie that included some placeholders for the completed score, sound effects, and incomplete ILM shots. The editors put in long hours at night and on weekends in order to deliver the preview cut on time, which was screened in front of an audience at the Century 22 movie theater on Olsen Drive in San Jose in mid-May, just three weeks after the cameras stopped rolling on *Future*. For Zemeckis and company, the mood going into the test screening was a familiar mix of nervousness and excitement. The audience was completely in the dark in terms of what to expect, having only been informed that they were going to watch a movie starring Michael J. Fox and Christopher Lloyd.

"It was a very restless audience from the beginning," Arthur

Schmidt says. "They weren't with the movie during the first ten, fifteen, twenty minutes—maybe even the first half hour. I remember that some of the kids that were sitting in front of Harry and me were poking each other and talking. It was upsetting Harry a lot more than me, to the point where I finally asked him to go somewhere else in the theater."

As audiences have come to appreciate, *Back to the Future* is a movie that rewards patience. Early on, there are two sequences that set up a significant amount of exposition, which require a greater level of attention from the audience than your typical summer popcorn flick. The opening shot, with all of Doc Brown's clocks, was a late-breaking addition to the script, conceived in the transition out of the Stoltz era. Not only are viewers introduced to the motif and imagery of the importance of time, but careful observers might also notice a bit of clever foreshadowing—a clock with Harold Lloyd hanging off of it, harkening back to the iconic shot from the 1923 silent film *Safety Last!*, which mirrors the predicament Doc Brown will find himself in about an hour and a half later into the movie. The scene was devised to save money, as the set for Doc's garage was already built and the opening scene as scripted would have required the construction of another location, but it didn't make life any easier for the special effects team.

"The clocks had to all be set for the same time," Kevin Pike says. "Some of them worked, some of them didn't work. You had to stop them from going until they started the shot so they didn't get ahead of the time that it was supposed to be. We had twenty people behind the wall with strings, and wires, and buttons, and electric switches, just on the clocks. Then, take two, you had to reset everything. The camera does this very fluid pan, starting at a machine that drips hot coffee, ending where the dog food sort of flops into the bowl. The dog food that we originally had poured very comfortably into the bowl, but at the last minute they changed gears with branding, and we ended up with a different kind of food that had to be shaken out, and you couldn't do that in the shot. We actually had to have somebody underneath the camera with a blowtorch to heat up the dog food because it had to be an unopened, fresh can for each shot."

In total, the opening was filmed three times, as Zemeckis wanted to see all of the elements on-screen in one long take without any edits. The effect on the audience is strong, especially on repeat viewings, but at the San Jose preview, the viewers quickly grew anxious. Additionally, the first dinner scene at the McFly family home, with Lea Thompson and Crispin Glover in their old-age makeup, was another sequence that seemed to cause that first audience discomfort. While the growing seat-shifting during the test screening was a concern for the editors and some others in the crew, the Bobs never lost faith in their original concept to front-load the movie with information that would be valuable for the audience once Marty's adventure kicked into high gear at the Twin Pines Mall. "No one ever sees a movie in a vacuum," Bob Gale says. "They know at least a little something about it when they buy their ticket. That's the reason we were never worried about the long exposition at the beginning. We always will opt for taking a little more time to present exposition if there's a worthwhile payoff later. We believe in what I call the 'twenty-five-minute rule.' An audience will sit still for twenty-five minutes before their attention goes south—but you still should give them the sense that something is going on, that the filmmakers have a plan and know what they're doing, even if the audience isn't sure what it is. Show them interesting things, get them invested in the characters. It's different from writing a

TV show, where you have to make sure the viewer won't change the channel. In a movie theater, it's rare for people to walk out, and especially rare that they walk out in the first thirty minutes."

"I remember worrying that there was too much exposition, too much portent, and that it might not pay off," Clyde E. Bryan says. "But of course, then it did, so you're exhilarated when it works." The Bobs' faith in the audience was proven right. When the DeLorean was revealed, Zemeckis and company could tell their viewers were regaining their focus. Once Doc put Einstein in the car and began his experiment, they were captivated. When the DeLorean disappeared, they were uneasy and confused—perhaps believing the dog had been killed, and certainly unsure as to what to make of Christopher Lloyd's character and invention. However, once the time machine made its way back and Doc explained what had happened, they were buckled in and ready to go eighty-eight miles per hour with the characters. "It was still a work in progress at the time of that screening," Neil Canton says. "The ILM visual effect shots weren't done, and the music wasn't done, but the audience was just so into the story. You go, 'Holy smokes, remember this moment because it might never happen again. We won't have a time machine to come back when we wake up some morning and feel depressed. We won't be able to go back to San Jose and experience that moment again.'"

"It absolutely exceeded our expectations," Bob Gale says. "There were several moments throughout where the audience erupted in applause. It was amazing. The very last shot in the movie, with the flying car, was in black and white, but the audience didn't care—they went nuts for it. Bob and I, and the editors, were particularly worried about the 'Johnny B. Goode' scene because we actually stopped the movie to do a musical number. It's the only scene that doesn't advance story or character, and we didn't know how that was going to play. We always knew we could cut it out, but our concerns were totally unfounded."

The overwhelming audience reaction wasn't just restricted to jubilation during the screening. After the movie ended, the response cards that were returned to the production team indicated that around 90 percent of those who had seen the movie thought it was "excellent" or "very good." While the filmmakers were excited about their numbers, they remained cautious, carefully considering the pacing of the film. They continued to tighten the edit. Overall, about seven minutes were removed from the movie following San Jose: The Darth Vader scene was trimmed substantially, creating an accidental continuity error wherein the hair dryer Marty is holding jumps from his belt to his hand after a cutaway shot to George McFly; a scene before the problematic McFly dinner scene, where a neighbor sells George an abundance of peanut brittle, was cut; a scene was removed where Dixon, the redheaded kid with braces who cuts in during George and Lorraine's dance during "Earth Angel," locks George in a phone booth at the Enchantment Under the Sea dance; and a few seconds were taken out of the sequence where Marty first walks around the Hill Valley town square in 1955. "There were various other internal cuts in other scenes we made just to keep the pace moving along," Bob Gale says. "None of the cuts were made as a result of any specific critique or comment. We could just feel it in the audience when scenes went on too long."

Following the edits, there was another test screening in the Hitchcock Theatre on the Universal lot, with all the studio executives on the invite list. Hollywood lore had it that the venue was cursed, because the majority of films that had been tested there since its 1980 opening had underperformed with the public. To an extent, Zemeckis believed in the superstition surrounding the venue. He didn't think the venue was haunted per se, but he believed that it was impossible to get a good score from an audience that is going to see a Universal movie on studio property with a bunch of suits in the back. When the film started to roll, the director couldn't have been happier to be wrong, as *Back to the Future* continued to rewrite history. It was another smash, and this time there would only be one change made. Sid Sheinberg was pleased with what he saw on-screen and elated by what he read on the response cards. Now he was seeing green, not only for money, but also for go—and fast. His feedback: Don't touch a frame, and do what needs to be done to get the film in theaters ahead of its mid-August release date, in time for the Fourth of July holiday weekend. The more weeks a film plays during the summer, the better its chances for fiscal success are, and Sheinberg was willing to spare no expense to make sure the movie was released as early as possible. The team at ILM, the editors, sound mixers, and Alan Silvestri all made their contributions in record time, turning in a completed print on June 23. As an acknowledgment of the demands on their schedules, Universal took out an ad in *Variety* listing the name of each postproduction crew member, thanking them for an expedient job well done.

The race to complete the film under the new truncated timeline wasn't the first time a Sid Sheinberg note created agita among the production team. The executive loved the story for *Back to the Future*, but hated its paradoxical title. The story goes that while filming was under way, he wrote a memo stating that he wanted the movie renamed to something slightly less nuanced and more direct: *Spaceman from Pluto*, a title the exec hoped the audience would identify as a reference to a prop seen briefly in the film. As soon as Marty arrives in 1955, he crashes into Old

Man Peabody's barn and the family comes down from their house to inspect. Sherman, the young boy with a name inspired by the popular *Rocky & Bullwinkle* characters, holds up a comic book with striking artwork on its cover, designed by production illustrator Andrew Probert and styled after the old EC Comics from the era. Alongside a spaceship and an alien wearing a one-piece getup, there is a prominently displayed red box with the text "Space Zombies from Pluto" visible. Since Marty is initially mistaken as an extraterrestrial and spends some time in a radiation suit, the executive thought his suggested title would be a better fit for the film. Not only that, but Sheinberg failed to understand what the title was supposed to mean. How exactly could someone go *back* to the *future*?

Eventually the Bobs would find the memorandum that was sent down from the studio head's office funny, but at the time it was gravely serious. They didn't want to risk offending Sheinberg, whom they felt had been incredibly accommodating despite the production hurdles, but they felt even more strongly about not wanting to concede their title, which Zemeckis and company knew to be one of their strongest assets. "A good title is crucial," Leonard Maltin says. "And *Back to the Future* is a great title. It's entered the vernacular. It's clever without being off-puttingly so, and it evokes the film. It's not just a nice play on words; it essentially tells you what the film is about—time travel in both directions."

As the well-circulated story goes, Zemeckis went for assistance to Spielberg, who, once again, swiftly came up with the perfect idea. He drafted a carefully couched response to the studio head thanking him for his note. He wrote that the production staff all got a good laugh out of it and appreciated Sheinberg's sense of humor. Spielberg knew the executive would be too embarrassed to explain that he was serious. Crucial crisis averted. While this version of the story has been shared repeatedly over the past three decades, not everyone agrees with this version of events.

"That is absolute bullshit," Sheinberg says. "I don't know why they say that. It is true that I was, I don't want to say 'hostile,' but I didn't think that *Back to the Future* made any sense as the title. Of course, with the wisdom of hindsight, it was the perfect title exactly because it made no sense. But no, I never in a sober moment advocated *Spaceman from Pluto* as the title."

While the San Jose screening was a special event, it may have paled in comparison to the impact of screening the movie for the cast and crew after the final cut was locked. The false start with Eric Stoltz created an emotional roller coaster for many involved, and after a seemingly incessant shoot, which caused Zemeckis to dub his picture "the film that wouldn't wrap," the experience of watching the finished movie was a collectively cathartic and exciting one. "I've been to a lot of premieres, and sometimes you just get polite applause," Marc McClure, who plays Marty's brother Dave McFly, says. "This was real applause because I don't think anybody working on that film realized how it was going to turn out. Nobody understood how they were going to put this story together. Everybody got on their feet, cheering and screaming and yelling. It was a very honest reaction. It wasn't a Hollywood clap."

"I was excited because Dennis Quaid was there, and I'd always had a crush on him," Claudia Wells says. "I think I was more nervous than anything else because I was going to be on a big screen, and that was my very first movie. I went with my best friend, Patrick Labyorteaux, who was the kid actor on *Little House on the Prairie*. I was squeezing him so tight because I was so nervous. The biggest surprise to me was when they show the clock tower flyer with my handwriting on it. I thought, *Oh, my goodness, my handwriting is filling up the entire screen.* To me, for some reason, that was more exciting than my face. The assistant director or script supervisor had come up to me with a piece of paper while we were filming and said, 'Write this down,' so I wrote, 'I love you. 555-4823.' I didn't ask her why. I didn't realize that what I jotted down was going to be the draft that they showed on-screen."

"I was pretty impressed," Christopher Lloyd says. "It was just such a great story, so well written. Bob Zemeckis did such a superb job of directing it. Seeing it all come together, and the life and excitement of it—I still get off on it. If I am channel-surfing and I come to *Back to the Future*, I am very likely to watch the entire film. I still find it fun to watch."

However, for all the revelry that was to be had, the film was not perfect. Moviemaking is about compromising, and due to the tight turnaround time from the end of shooting to when the completed print was due, there were some visual effects shots that the team at ILM didn't have time to get right. "When the DeLorean goes back to contemporary time after getting struck by the bolt of lightning, we had to do that really quickly," Wes Takahashi says. "I always felt that we didn't have enough time in the optical process to match the look from the hand-animated flames to the real flames. If you look at it closely, there is way too much diffusion in the animated flames. These days there's all sorts of dynamic digital programming that can create realistic-looking fire, but it took a long time to get there."

"There was one kind of casualty, in that we had such a short time for some of the visual effects and Bob was never happy with some of them," Harry Keramidas says. "One in particular is when Marty sees through his hand when he's playing guitar. Bob never really liked that effect. It isn't very good. We were still trying to get that right, and finally just had to cut in what their final version was at the last moment. We didn't have any more time to work on it. It never really looked good to me. Nobody cared much except Bob or me, who actually knew what it was supposed to be like."

Before the movie sped into cinemas, Zemeckis and company were feeling confident about their chances of not only making more than just a small profit—something their first two films together failed to do—but even seeing the movie become a hit. Perhaps it was because of the volcanic response at the San Jose screening and the breaking of the Hitchcock curse. Maybe it was a subconscious feeling that unlike *I Wanna Hold Your Hand* and *Used Cars*, their latest film was more commercially viable. Or possibly there was another reason: "I vividly remember shooting with Michael J. Fox at Whittier High School, the night exterior stuff for the dance," Bob Gale says. "Word got out that he was in the movie, and we had a ton of local kids show up to watch us shoot. There was probably a ratio of girls to boys of at least two to one. They were standing seven-deep to get a glimpse of Michael. This never happened when we were shooting with Eric. Bob Z and I were amazed. We'd had no idea Michael J. Fox was such a big star—it was from *Family Ties*, of course—and that's when we thought maybe this time people would show up to see our movie."

But as the movie neared its theatrical debut, the Bobs' ace in the hole was nowhere to be found. Gary David Goldberg came up with the idea of sending his sitcom family to London to visit Oxford University, which resulted in *Family Ties Vacation*, a made-for-TV movie that was scheduled to air at the end of September, right before the beginning of the show's fourth season. Much to the frustration of the suits at Universal, Michael J. Fox was overseas when *Future* opened, and thus unable to make the usual sit-downs with Johnny Carson or David Letterman. As per their deal, *Family Ties* was coming first, and the financial stakeholders in the film were hoping that they weren't going to regret making that concession when the weekend's numbers were released.

For his first several months working on the film, Fox continued to prove his physical mettle as a young twentysomething—*Family Ties* by day, *Back to the Future* by night—while trying not to lose his footing as the hamster wheel maintained its grueling pace. While on the set of his television series, he once went searching for his JVC camcorder he thought he had misplaced, only to remember that that was a prop he needed for the movie, not the sitcom. As an actor who primarily worked on television, he didn't bother to memorize his movie lines in advance, which occasionally led to spontaneous ad-libs—like, "Rock and roll," one of the first lines Marty speaks in the film—but also led to a sense of delirium. He didn't know if he was coming or going half the time, and certainly had no clue whether or not what he was doing in front of the camera was working. When the film opened and Fox's agent attended a Los Angeles screening, he phoned his client right away. The actor was apologetic, acknowledging that he hadn't worked his hardest and promising to do a better job next time. Then he stopped speaking long enough to hear why he had been called. The picture, the agent said, was fantastic and was going to be the biggest movie of the summer.

Of course, Michael J. Fox's agent was only partially correct; in 1985, Zemeckis's film wasn't only the highest-grossing film of the summer; it was the highest-grossing film of the year worldwide. On September 29, *Back to the Future* ended a run of twelve nonconsecutive weeks atop the box office charts in America and surpassed *Rambo: First Blood Part II* to become the top-earning film of the year in the United States. By this time, critics had unanimously rallied behind the film, the soundtrack had gone Gold, and there was even Oscar buzz.

Universal Pictures never expected *Future* to be the unstoppable juggernaut that it was at the multiplexes throughout the summer of 1985, but then again, no one did. By the time its theatrical run ended, *Back to the Future* had earned $210.6 million in the United States. Internationally, the film performed almost as well. Before the end of the year, the movie arrived in well over a dozen countries, including Italy, France, West Germany, and the United Kingdom. In Japan, *Future* became the sixth-highest-grossing film in the country's history. All told, an additional $170.5 million was earned overseas. Only two other films made more money internationally that year—*Out of Africa* and *Rocky IV*, which earned $179.1 million and $172.6 million, respectively. Critics and audiences alike applauded the movie, with Gene Siskel and Roger Ebert giving the movie two thumbs up, while journalists from major publications such as the *New York Times* and *People* praised the story, direction, and performances. There were the occasional detractors (such as Sheila Benson of the *Los Angeles Times*, who found the film to be "big, cartoonish, and empty," with a premise "underdeveloped and overproduced"), but they were few and far between. Fourteen years after they'd met, the Bobs finally had a bona fide hit together. "Every week we had the same 'I can't believe it' conversation," Bob Gale says. "We were displaced from the number one spot by *National Lampoon's European Vacation* for one weekend, but then we returned to the top spot the weekend after and had that conversation once again. Actually, we still have that conversation as we marvel over the film's longevity and how it continues to capture the public imagination."

The conventional wisdom was that time-travel movies were destined to bomb at the box office, but Zemeckis and company proved that there were still innovative science fiction stories to tell. And that was only the first convention the *Future* team upended. While it has since become commonplace for actors to bounce back and forth between television and films, in 1985 that was not so. *Back to the Future* broke new ground by not only illustrating the ease with which a sitcom actor could cross over, but how insanely profitable that transition could be for all parties involved. "It was interesting how Zemeckis and Spielberg and Bob Gale pulled it off," Courtney Gains, who played Dixon, says. "Their decision to cast Michael J. Fox was completely outside the box. That wasn't how you were supposed to do it. But obviously it worked and you got to see Fox is a really excellent comedic actor."

"Those of us who went to law school remember the phrase '*res ipsa loquitur*,' which means 'the thing speaks for itself,'" Sid Sheinberg says. "People who saw *Back to the Future* realized that it was like somebody had invented a precision Swiss watch and had it made with wonderful components. Michael J. Fox, Chris Lloyd, they were really perfectly cast. Bob had made a superb picture."

As dollars, marks, pounds, and yen poured in from all parts of the world, Zemeckis and company were additionally pleased to find their movie bestowed with honors from those within the international film community. In Italy, the movie won Best Foreign Producer (Steven Spielberg) and Best Foreign Screenplay at the David di Donatello Awards. In Germany, *Future* was honored with a Goldene Leinwand (Golden Screen) for having sold more than three million box office tickets in its first eighteen months of release. In Japan, the movie won the award for Best Foreign Language Film by the Japanese Academy. In the United Kingdom, the movie was nominated for five BAFTAs, awarded by the British Academy of Film and Television Awards.

Stateside, the support from the industry was similarly strong. There were six nominations and three wins at the Academy of Science Fiction, Fantasy, and Horror Films' Saturn Awards; a nomination for Best Casting in a Feature Film—Comedy category from the Casting Society of America; a Grammy nomination for Best Album of an Original Score Written for a Motion Picture or Television Special; and a nomination for Best Screenplay by the Writers Guild of America. The movie struck out four times at the Golden Globes, and at the Academy Awards fared only slightly better, winning an Oscar for Best Sound Effects Editing, while losing in three other categories (Best Original Screenplay, Best Sound Mixing, and Best Original Song—"The Power of Love").

"We were nominated for a Golden Globe that we didn't win, and we were nominated for an Oscar that we didn't win, for the song," Huey Lewis says. "Which was really kind of a crime. I think Lionel Richie got the Oscar for 'Say You, Say Me' because he had done USA for Africa that year. It was basically a political thing. When we went to the Oscars, I sat down, and Marvin Hamlisch was in front of me. He turned around, and he said, 'Uh-oh.' I said, 'What is it?' and he said, 'Lionel's on the aisle.'"

Their imperfect record at awards shows was disappointing, sure, but the best prize of all came when, on February 4, 1986, President Ronald Reagan name-checked and quoted directly from the movie—*where we're going, we don't need roads*—in his State of the Union address. Overnight, a sequel became inevitable. "We all bought Universal stock, a hundred shares each. We thought we were going to get rich because the movie was doing well," Frank Marshall says. "The studio was supporting the idea of a sequel because the movie had been so successful, but it was kind of up to Bob and Bob. Steven said to them, 'If you think you can do it, great, but if you want to leave it where it is, it's fantastic.'"

"It's in the nature of this business that as soon as one has the inkling that something is going to work, he or she immediately begins to think of a sequel or a prequel," Sid Sheinberg says. "That's not an act of any great brilliance or originality. I'm sure everyone connected with the picture began to think about where else we could go once they saw the first one."

Zemeckis was open to the conversation, but far from eager to move back to Hill Valley. His reluctance wasn't because of the difficulties encountered while making the first film. Bringing *Future* to the screen was hard work, but both Bobs were unspeakably proud of how the film turned out and was received. Although it was stipulated in their initial agreement that no sequel or remake could be made without the studio discussing it with the Bobs first, essentially giving the two creators veto power over any future installments with their characters, Zemeckis once again felt the pressure from Sid Sheinberg's office. In Bob Z's mind, Universal's stance was very clear: "You could either be part of this or not, but we're making a sequel anyway."

The director describes his reluctance as being "stuck by Sophie's Choice," the ultimate no-win situation. Either Universal would find a way to move forward with the project without the Bobs, potentially not doing justice to their original vision, or the duo would sign back on, and risk alienating their biggest fans. "Audiences have a love-hate relationship with sequels," Zemeckis says. "What do you really want? You want the same movie, but different. 'But wait a minute, not too different, because then it'll piss me off.' Everyone in the world who loves your movie has an opinion, and you can't win as a filmmaker. You can't please everybody with a sequel."

Besides the fear that audiences wouldn't accept a *Future* follow-up, Bob Z believed that sequels were the antithesis of films. The interest was flattering and exciting, and they understood the desire to make another *Future* film from a commercial sense, but for Zemeckis, it was further proof that, for movie studios, making a sequel was not about art, but about the bottom line. "The only reason why we make sequels in Hollywood is because it's the only sure thing that anyone knows about in the movie business—that you can open a sequel to a successful movie," he says. "That's the only reason." Further complicating their decision, the Bobs didn't have a story in mind for another *Future* installment and, in fact, had committed to other projects— Gale signed on to a film adaptation of Marvel Comics' *Dr. Strange*, which ended up stalling in development, while Zemeckis was in preproduction on the highly demanding *Who Framed Roger Rabbit* for Walt Disney Studios' Touchstone Pictures, a gig he was offered once Steven Spielberg and the rest of the Amblin Trio signed on as coproducers of that project.

But even with the director's doubts, there were realities both he and his partner had to deal with. Even if Universal made half as much money on a sequel, it would still be a huge hit. Sheinberg would give them carte blanche on creative decisions. After all, who could know more about how to make a *Future* film successful than the two people, along with Steven Spielberg and the rest of the production team, who had caught lightning in a bottle the first time around? Perhaps it would be selling out, but they knew that selling out and making a bad film were not mutually exclusive. What if they shocked everyone by not only doing a sequel, but also one that was pretty damned impressive in its own right?

"At first there's always the question: Is it going to be as

good?" Dean Cundey says. "Is there the kind of material in the original film that lends itself to a sequel without it just being a repetition? I think that *Back to the Future* was such a great complete story that you have to say to yourself, 'Well, I wonder if we can do anything new and different and take the story further down the path.' At the end of the film, when Marty is challenged to get involved again because there's something personal—a problem with his kids—a sequel lent itself immediately to being a logical extension of the story. We certainly felt that the potential was there, based on the fact that the story could be continued."

"We all were optimistic about the sequel because the first movie left you with so many places to go," Frank Marshall says. "Whereas *E.T.* didn't. We never thought about a sequel for *E.T.* With *Raiders of the Lost Ark*, we actually committed to three movies at the start. *Back to the Future* kind of fell in the middle. We were open to it. As long as you don't make the same movie over, then I think you're okay. You don't want to make a sequel just because you can."

The Bobs agreed to spearhead a second installment if Michael J. Fox and Christopher Lloyd returned. If the stars declined, the creators were willing to walk away, leaving Universal to move forward on producing a follow-up without their involvement. Their decision wasn't simply an issue of loyalty or stubbornness, but one of what they perceived to be necessity. *Back to the Future*'s ending, with the two protagonists and Jennifer taking to the sky in Doc's time machine, was designed to be a tongue-in-cheek, here-we-go-again moment for our hero, who, having spent the length of the movie trying to solve a problem between his parents in the past, now had to go into the future to fix a problem for the next generation of McFlys. The Bobs conceived the ending as homage to a familiar cliché. Adventure films typically conclude with the hero heading toward his or her next journey—the cowboy rides off into the sunset toward a destination unknown, the superhero races on to the next mission. *Future* was no different.

As they began flirting with the idea of continuing Marty and Doc's story, the Bobs knew it would be impossible to meet the expectations of the fans without the leads on board. During the summer of 1985, Michael J. Fox's face was inescapable on television sets, in movie theaters, and on magazine covers around the world. The actor had concurrent cinematic hits with *Back to the Future* and *Teen Wolf*, which was aided in large part by a promotional campaign that reminded the public that *Teen Wolf* also starred the actor from that time-travel movie everyone was buzzing about. Fox continued to print money for the advertisers of *Family Ties*, which took over the runner-up spot in the Nielsen ratings in its 1985–1986 season, surpassed only by *The Cosby Show*, and he signed on to star in *Light of Day*, a drama directed by Paul Schrader, and *The Secret to My Success*, Herbert Ross's comedy, which would go on to be another hit for Universal. If he didn't return, it was unanimously thought that fans would join him in sitting out the next installment. Happily, when he was approached about a sequel to *Future*, the actor readily agreed to sign on. Christopher Lloyd, who had moved on to appear in featured roles in a number of films, including *Clue* and Zemeckis's *Who Framed Roger Rabbit*, was also on board. Both actors enjoyed their time working with Zemeckis and, in a way, felt they owed him for infusing a jolt of electricity into their careers. With Fox and Lloyd willing to continue telling Marty and Doc's story, Zemeckis and Gale were confident that a suitable narrative could be concocted that would be satisfying to the fans, studio, and, perhaps most important, themselves.

Sid Sheinberg took to the phones and brokered a deal with the two leads. Thinking ahead, the studio head included a clause in each of their contracts that the actors would appear in a third install-ment in the series, just in case, even though none was planned at that moment. With the actors in agreement to the terms, preproduc-tion unofficially began on the sequel. When Universal released *Back to the Future* on VHS and Beta on May 22, 1986, a new title card appeared in that familiar red and yellow italicized font before the end credits began: *"TO BE CONTINUED . . ."*

"I don't recall who came up with the idea, but we were abso-lutely on board with it," Bob Gale says. "I know we approved the typeface and placement of it. It's possible I was involved in how it was going to work creatively. And similarly, we were the ones who had it removed for the 2002 DVD release, because we wanted the DVD to represent the movie as it was seen theatri-cally. I still get people swearing to me that they remember seeing 'To Be Continued' in the theater back in 1985."

The writing process began immediately on *Number Two*, the first working title for the sequel, and was more challenging than the Bobs had anticipated. The expectations of the public weighed heavily on the screenwriting process, long before the first word of *Number Two* was written. Although *Future* was ini-tially considered to be a strong launchpad for a second chapter, the ending proved to be too cute by half, and inadvertently dic-tated the parameters for the beginning of Marty and Doc's next adventure. Zemeckis and Gale felt the best sequels in terms of storytelling were a direct continuation of the first film's narrative and character development, but knew that, generally speaking, those were bigger financial risks, as audiences were more accus-tomed to serials.

"The most successful sequels are the ones where the lead

character never changes and never has character growth, like James Bond or Indiana Jones, or all these comic book things," Zemeckis says. "They just go on different adventures, and the most fun part of those movies is always the villain. Batman fights a different villain, but Batman is always the same guy. Those work because the main character is not different when the movie ends, so the next movie just picks up because there's a new problem. You can't make a sequel to *Forrest Gump*, for example, because he's changed by the end of the film. You can't undo him."

Before they drafted the script, the Bobs wanted to find out who else from *Future* would be interested in coming back. Bob Z had taken a number of his crew members along with him to work on *Roger Rabbit*, which made the pitch easy when he asked for them to return to the Universal backlot. Among the cast, the first telephone call went to Lea Thompson. She wanted in. Tom Wilson? Absolutely. Crispin Glover? Well, every *Titanic* hits its iceberg sooner or later.

Exactly what transpired between the actor and the film's producers during negotiations remains a mystery. Each party has their own version of the events that they have held on to tightly for the past three decades. According to Glover, the Bobs were unwilling to negotiate fairly with his agent because they were angry with him over a dustup filming the first movie. When he was offered the role in *Future*, the actor hadn't received the entire script, but instead only a treatment and a copy of the scene he had auditioned with. Based on the strength of the writing he had seen, he signed on. The actor claims that the film's ending was rewritten several times throughout production and that when the final pages arrived shortly before they would have to be shot, the actor read the movie's denouement, where Marty returns to 1985 and his family's life has improved financially, and logged a complaint.

The sequence in question remains a source of disagreement between the Bobs. Zemeckis feels the scene is very much of its time, a resolution that was appropriate for the Generation X viewing audience. According to the director, overseas audiences were critical of the film's seemingly materialistic moral during the film's initial run. For the most part, American audiences found little wrong with the ending, although some journalists in the States did critique the conclusion as being overly idealistic. Zemeckis has suggested that if the film were made today, the ending would likely be different. Bob Gale, however, disagrees. "I have no problem with, nor apologies for, the scene," he says. "The scene shows the result of George McFly being a successful and confident person. This is reflected in how the characters behave and interact with one another, and in the physical environment of the home, all as a contrast to the family scenes in the early part of the film. The home furnishings and décor show that George is doing better financially, because when people do better financially, they usually try to provide a better life for their family. We also see this in the fact that Dave no longer works at Burger King, Linda is a social butterfly, and Lorraine is happy, in better shape, and no longer drinks and smokes. Yes, George has a BMW. It's a contrast to the beat-up car he has at the beginning and again shows that he's better off financially."

Glover addressed his concern with the film's ending in an extremely unorthodox way. "Crispin had a real problem with his wardrobe in that scene," Gale continues. "He wanted George to be bohemian and look like an eccentric college professor. In fact, if you look at the film, the author photo on the back cover of his novel shows how Crispin wanted the character to look. But the image didn't tell the story. It could have easily been interpreted that George was still a nerd, and it would have required dialogue to explain it. We wanted to get the point across visually, and the polo shirt, sunglasses, and tennis racket did all that. Crispin actually went around the set in the wardrobe he preferred and took a survey of the crew regarding it, but he got unanimous thumbs down. My recollection is that Neil Canton read him the riot act to get him to behave and do what Bob Z wanted. It was a challenge to get him to just behave like a normal, together guy."

On another occasion, when reshooting a scene in George McFly's backyard that was originally done during the Stoltz era, the actor was either unable or unwilling to stay within the parameters of the frame. For take after take, Glover delivered his lines while making broad movements with his legs, sauntering in and out of the shot. In order to get the shot, a brief hiatus was called and the grips quickly constructed a barrier made of plywood in order to box him in. "It was just about dealing with him, the craziness of the world of Crispin, and trying to contain that into a day's work," Neil Canton adds. "He was kind of a wild man. He wasn't the consummate professional. It was sort of like, how do we deal with that?"

By all accounts, Crispin Glover was an incredibly polarizing figure on the set. Those who worked behind the scenes found him to be annoying and quirky in the worst way, while his compatriots in front of the camera thought he exuberated a creative brilliance and healthy eccentricity. In reality, it appears the actor was a mixture of both—an odd duck who was uniquely suited for the offbeat sensibilities of the role he was cast to bring to life. "I've always loved to say that the character of George McFly is Crispin, but that he's the *controlled* version of Crispin," Clyde E. Bryan says. "He's not as wacky as the real Crispin. Crispin was cute and funny to us, but he was just so much extra work."

"Crispin was a real interesting worker," Marc McClure says.

"Very focused on what to do in a scene, and he pretty much stuck to it. So anytime he would do a take, he wouldn't veer too far away from his very first time. He would just keep giving you very good, very unique stuff."

"I certainly know Crispin was a bit of a handful, but you definitely got your money's worth out of him," Lea Thompson says. "He's just a great actor. Crispin did this funny thing in the scene where we were watching *The Honeymooners* in the beginning of the film where he was laughing at the TV. We couldn't stop laughing. We blew like twenty takes and nobody even cared. We were just laughing at Crispin because he was being so ridiculous. I had to try not to laugh, though, because if you laughed too much, you would break the seams of the makeup on the sides of your face. It was a really happy moment on set."

Like the majority of the rest of the cast, Courtney Gains, who played Dixon, found Glover easy to work with. The two were previously acquainted while working with director Trent Harris on *The Orkly Kid*, a 1985 short that was eventually released as a part of *The Beaver Trilogy* in 2001. In the vignette, Glover played Gary, a man obsessed with Olivia Newton-John who took to performing as her in talent shows. "I started doing my lines, and then this bathroom stall opens and Crispin Glover is dressed in the black outfit that she wore in *Grease*, with the wig and everything," Gains says. "I was watching this guy, thinking, *This is surreal*. As an artist, the guy is brilliant. I don't use that word a lot, but Crispin is a fucking interesting actor. That's one thing you can't say about Crispin, that he's ever not interesting. Whatever he does, you've got to watch him. As actors, that's what we recognize, that artistic genius. That being said, he's definitely a bit of an eccentric. For the crew, who are not as interested in his acting chops, maybe he comes off a little crazy."

Although not a household name at the time of *Future*'s filming, the actor is the only child of two actor parents and had several significant credits of his own prior to *Back to the Future*, including guest appearances on *Happy Days* and *The Facts of Life*. While some have chalked up his behavior to quirks, at least one of his peers feels Glover's vocal unhappiness with the film's ending was the result of something else—entitlement. "Crispin was privileged, and because of it, he was able to live through his politics," Harry Waters, Jr., says. "That was his choice, but some of us, and especially as artists, were not even thinking politics—we were thinking survival."

Despite his unhappiness with the script, Glover claims that he continued to play nice during the duration of the shoot, primarily out of fear. The memory of Eric Stoltz's abrupt firing, with no clear explanation given to the actors as to the reason why, was stronger than his moral outrage. Glover tempered the theatrics for the remainder of the shooting, and despite their occasional differences on set, the Bobs were willing to cast their personal disagreements with the actor aside in order to have him reprise his role in the sequel. "Crispin gave a terrific performance in *Part I*, and it's still a pleasure to watch," Bob Gale says. "And I got along with him fairly well. It's unfortunate that he has chosen to blame me for the decision he made in repeatedly turning down the several opportunities we gave him to return in the sequels, solely over money."

In the decades following the first film's release, Gale has received the brunt of Glover's ire, with the actor frequently mentioning in interviews that the producer has been giving misinformation about the details of the sequel negotiations. For his part, Gale is undeterred by what he considers to be the actor's self-serving revisionist history. "I don't waste my time with Crispin's versions of events," he says. "We asked him to be involved before we even conceived the sequel story, as we did with Lea and Tom. This would have been in 1986 or 1987. Crispin, via his agent, Elaine Goldsmith, asked for the same money that Michael J. Fox was receiving, as well as script approval and director approval."

Court documents from a 1990 suit state the amount requested as $1 million. With the actor having received less than $60,000 for his work on the first film, an increase of over ten times that, plus perks, was a nonstarter as far as Gale and the other producers were concerned. "I told Elaine that this was so far out of line that I wouldn't respond with a counteroffer," he continues. "She knew it was out of line too, but she was legally obligated to convey her client's terms. I told her to try to talk some sense into him and come back with a reasonable offer within two weeks or we'd write him out of the sequel." But threatening to make the sequel without Glover didn't mean writing the movie without the character of George. At least partially because Gale was exasperated with the actor's behavior on the first film, as well as the anemic state of contract negotiations, the first draft of *Number Two*, which Gale wrote almost entirely alone due to Zemeckis's other commitments, saw George's role drastically reduced from the original film.

The first draft of the sequel script began very similarly to how the film materialized on-screen: Marty and Doc go to the future, Biff steals *Grays Sports Almanac*, the present timeline is altered, and our heroes have to fix it. Where it differed significantly was in the third act. Instead of going back to 1955, Biff thought it would be cool to see the sixties, and gave himself the book in 1967. The adventure takes place there, with George McFly as a college professor, away giving a lecture at the University of California at Berkeley and, thus, absent from the majority of the script, and Lorraine as a flower child. As one more needle in Glover's side, his character's birthday was changed from August 18, as it appeared in the first film's novelization, to April 1. While it was uncertain whether or not Crispin Glover would return—the Bobs knew it was unlikely, but the door was left open for negotiations to continue if the actor and his representatives wanted to operate in good faith—one thing was now guaranteed: If the actor were to return, it would be as April's fool.

"Bob and I had decided we would devise the story around the cast that we would have," Gale says. "Because Crispin chose not to be in the sequel, but Lea and Tom had agreed, that motivated our creating the alternate Biffhorrific 1985 story in which George was a tombstone. *Number Two* had George making a brief appearance only because I thought Crispin might change his mind."

Zemeckis liked Gale's script, but realizing they might be missing a unique opportunity, he suggested the two continue to think of a better way to continue their story. They remembered their governing rules: Check your ego at the door, write a film that both of them would want to see, and if someone thinks they can improve upon an idea, it must mean there's a better one out there. The two gave it some thought and, in almost no time, decided to make a sharp move in a paradoxically different, yet familiar, direction.

"Bob and I looked at each other and said, 'You know what? We have a very, very unique situation here,'" Zemeckis says. "'We have the potential to make a sequel of a story where the inherent device is time travel and we could actually do what the audience really, really wants, which is go back and revisit the movie they just saw.' That is the thing that excited me the most, this idea of seeing the same movie from a different angle. It was a very unique situation that will never happen again because I'll probably never make another movie about time travel where the character can actually go back into the first movie."

"The idea of revisiting the first movie and creating an additional story taking place within it is the single best idea of *Part II*," Gale says. "That's what makes it unique, and Bob Zemeckis deserves the credit for coming up with it. When you're working with a great idea, it makes the writing process easier because you know you're working toward something special."

A second draft was written under what became the official working title for the sequel—*Paradox*. The 165-page screenplay began in a fashion similar to that of the first draft, but the second act was a large-scale return to the first film. The third section, which began a little past the hundred-page mark, introduced a number of brand-new characters, as Doc Brown was accidentally sent from 1955 to the Old West by a lightning strike to the DeLorean. There was a new love interest, this time for the Doc, a schoolteacher named Clara Clayton, as well as a new antagonist in Buford Tannen, who at the time was nicknamed "Black Biff" instead of the finished film's "Mad Dog," the somewhat distant relative of Tom Wilson's character from the first film. Bob Gale loved what he had written, in concept, but was displeased with how it was coalescing on the page. It was too rushed, and more important, he felt it was too jarring to introduce so many new characters into Marty's world that late in the film. While looking for a place to start making cuts, Bob G had a nagging feeling that while he was tasked to write one sequel, he had actually been developing a comprehensively fleshed-out treatment for two.

He spoke with Zemeckis, whose *Roger Rabbit* was now in postproduction in London, and expressed his concern. Gale was sabotaging his own film—and their hard work—by making edits that would damage the story. He wanted to write the sequel script the way he wanted to see it on-screen, and he wanted his partner's blessing to do so. Bob Z agreed, and the portion of the screenplay that took place in 1885 was fleshed out. The result was an epic clocking in at more than 220 pages, which Gale shared with Zemeckis and his coproducer.

"That script," Neil Canton says. "The first time I read it, when I put it down I was like, 'Holy smokes! This could be the greatest movie ever made.' There was so much in the movie. No one was going to believe it. We're in the future, we come back to the present, we're in the alternative timeline, and now somehow Doc disappeared and Marty's in the West. I just thought—wow. It was like if you took every fan's letter who wrote in saying, 'This is what it should be,' and sort of put them into a blender, it wouldn't have been as great as this could have been."

However, *Paradox* would never see the light of day. From the moment Gale first admitted his desire to free himself from the standard motion picture format, he knew that he might be sabotaging himself in a different way: What if Universal refused to approve of the script as presented? The movie would have been more than three hours long, well past the first film's running time. As a preemptive measure, he began lobbying Zemeckis and the rest of his production team to push for not just one sequel, but two. "Sheinberg was resistant, although he denies it now," Gale says. "So I asked our production manager, Joan Bradshaw, to budget the new long version as two separate films." Within short time, the numbers were in: $50 million for one film, $70 million for two.

Nowadays, it's not unusual for a major motion picture to have a budget of well over that figure, but in the mid-1980s, spending that amount of money on a film—even one almost guaranteed to have a successful opening weekend—was risky business. The first *Back to the Future* had a final price tag close to $19 million. By comparison, if you added the expenditures for the two original *Star Wars* sequels, they would have cost less than *Paradox* would have, and just slightly more if you adjust for inflation. The sequel would have been tied with 1978's *Superman* for the third most expensive film ever made to date, behind 1988's *Rocky III* and Zemeckis's own *Roger Rabbit*. Sure, the *Back to the Future* sequel—or sequels—would be nearly certain to make money, but there is no such thing in Hollywood as a guarantee.

With the numbers crunched, Steven Spielberg took the spreadsheets to Sheinberg's office and gave him the pitch. Weren't Michael J. Fox and Christopher Lloyd contracted for two more sequels? Lea Thompson and Tom Wilson were so amenable to working with the Bobs again, they would likely welcome an opportunity to extend their time spent as Lorraine and Biff, respectively. If the second film was successful, wouldn't it be better to already have another film in the pipeline instead of having to round up all the actors again two or three years down the line for a third volume? No one knew exactly how things would shake out with Crispin Glover yet, but it would be no more difficult for him to return for one sequel than two. Both films could be shot consecutively, with editing on the third installment being wrapped while the second was in theaters. Sheinberg too saw the potential.

By the time the decision was made to split *Paradox* into two, it was the end of January 1989. The majority of the cast and crew were waiting for their start date, unaware that, as with work on the first film, their tenure with Zemeckis and company was soon going to be extended far beyond what they had originally bargained for. And once again, Michael J. Fox would have to make significant sacrifices. The 1988–1989 season would be *Family Ties'* last, meaning that for a significant portion of work on *Paradox*, Fox would be up to his old moonlighting tricks. But now there were additional considerations. The actor was a newlywed and his wife was pregnant with their first child. Agreeing to go back to the future, he would soon find out, was just the beginning of what was to be a very draining year and change for all involved.

6. WE'RE BACK

Wednesday, February 8, 1989

Bob Gale thumbed through the inches of white, canary, pink, blue, green, and golden pages on his desk that were bound together by a trio of brass fasteners. The multicolored tome was a testament to the several rewrites completed in the preceding three months, all in preparation for the impending *Paradox* shoot, which was scheduled to start in just a few weeks. With Sid Sheinberg having given the okay to two sequels, the crew was notified to plan on sticking around for a bit longer than they originally expected. The screenwriter turned to a page in the middle of his book, where he had inserted an important revision on colored paper—*As Marty bends down to attempt to revive the unconscious Doc, we CRANE BACK. Superimpose title: "TO BE CONCLUDED NEXT SUMMER IN BACK TO THE FUTURE 3!"* He wasn't sure that would be enough to do the trick, but he hoped it just might be.

Gale's screenplay was ambitious, and not only because of the number of pages that passed through his typewriter. Partially because of the way the original film concluded, and partially because of letters the filmmakers received from the public pitching ideas of how to best reconcile the original film's cliff-hanger ending, *Paradox* started off just a few moments before Doc arrives back from his first trip to the future, directly revisiting the last few minutes of the first movie. The Enchantment Under the Sea dance, along with several other moments, were also revisited and looked at from another perspective. For the lead actors, visiting more time periods meant embodying even more iterations of their characters, making it crucial that the principal performers were okay with the new game plan before filming began. Once the decision was made at the beginning of the year to split and expand *Paradox* into two, Sheinberg made deals with Lea Thompson's and Tom Wilson's agents for a third installment. This was as easy as the producers thought it would be, as the two were happy to renew their membership in the Zemeckis club. "I just thought the story was great," Thompson says. "And I loved all the weird stuff I got to do, like being eighty-year-old Lorraine."

In the return to Hill Valley, the more that things would change, the more they would stay the same. In the interest of maintaining a consistency of vision, Zemeckis and company sought out as many members of the original team as possible to return for *Paradox*. A number of people, like Dean Cundey, Clyde E. Bryan, Arthur Schmidt, and Alan Silvestri, made the journey over to England to help the director on *Roger Rabbit* and were happy to continue their working relationship with Bob Z. And as with Thompson and Wilson, there was little or no opposition to the change in production schedule and additional film among the cast and crew. The first half of the *Paradox* script, what would become *Back to the Future Part II*, would be filmed first. The crew would then break for a few weeks, and start working on what would become the third film. "The feeling was that it was going to be an economies-of-scale situation because we would all be just continuously making sets and shooting," Dean Cundey says. "And the studio didn't know if anybody would sit for three hours of Marty McFly. It turned into being a great thing, which everybody loved. Outside of the fact that it was so much fun working on the films, people would be employed for a longer period of time. I was working for a year and two weeks doing the two films back to back, with very little time off in between. It was great because you were working on one large project, with intricacies and story points that were related. Props from this film could work in that film. There was not a single moment where anybody said, 'Oh, no, this is going to be tedious.' Everybody agreed it was going to be a great adventure, which it was."

In order to make good on the story the Bobs had constructed, as well as deliver on audience expectations, it was decided early on that as many of the original actors as possible should be invited back. Harry Waters, Jr., who had landed a number of guest appearances on television shows like *What's Happening Now!!* and *227* since the first film, was among the featured actors eager to return. "It was 1989, so we were all older and more evolved," he says. "I had more experience working in the industry. When we got the call, I was actually able to tell my agent, 'Here is what we should ask for,' and it wasn't because I thought they had to have me. It was like, 'Wow, I get to do the next version of this. How cool,' but I wanted to get compensated."

As for most of the actors, Waters's salary was adjusted for inflation. "I was able to get a nice deal because I had also done another TV series. I had a little bit more pull," Waters says. "You know how they have all those things in billing? I got to be top of the card. It was amazing getting on the set with the Starlighters because they were able to find the same guys again. I couldn't believe they were able to pull them back together."

Despite the producers' best efforts, some of the audience's favorite featured characters would be absent from the second installment. Although the Enchantment Under the Sea dance would be heavily revisited in the sequel, and re-created using the same costumes, set pieces, and even some of the same dancers, the character of Dixon was omitted from the sequel, a disappointment to Courtney Gains. Additionally, two scenes were shot and removed from the movie before its release, leaving two more characters on the floor of the cutting room. During the Biffhorrific sequence, Marty was supposed to stumble upon his brother, who was now a down-and-out alcoholic. "That was pretty fun," Marc McClure says. "It was a pretty wild night. Spielberg was on set during that particular sequence. There was fire and a bunch of people there. It was a big night for the extras." However, when the film was shown to test audiences, viewers wondered what had happened to Linda, Marty's sister, and why she wasn't in the film. Wendie Jo Sperber, who played the role, was pregnant at the time of filming and unable to reprise her character. In the interest of clarity, it was easier to remove the scene altogether. Bob Gale called McClure to give him the word shortly before the theatrical release. There was also a scene removed with Will Hare, who played Old Man Peabody, in the portion of the film where Marty and Doc return back to 1955, because the filmmakers didn't think the character had made a strong enough impression in the first film to have been remembered.

Due to her mother's battle with cancer, Claudia Wells relinquished the part of Jennifer. "I knew that I couldn't do it at that point," she says. "There was so much going on at home. It's such a stressful experience in the family dynamic to have your mom die. There was no choice for me." Instead, Elisabeth Shue, who starred in 1984's *The Karate Kid* opposite Ralph Macchio and

1987's *Adventures in Babysitting*, was hired to pinch-hit. Although she isn't a dead ringer for Wells, she did meet regulation Jennifer height. At five foot two, she was okay to play opposite Michael J. Fox by the metric the Bobs had set on the first film. The actress was outfitted in the same costume, and her hair was treated to match Wells's as best as it could. It wasn't the perfect solution, but it would have to do.

The first few pages of the *Paradox* script called for Zemeckis to re-create the last moments of *Back to the Future*, with a few new lines of dialogue for Biff, once again clueing the audience in to the fact that they would be revisiting some material from the first installment from a new perspective. With the first film four years removed, the hope was that the scene re-creation would have the added benefit of helping mask that the role of Jennifer had been recast. "I actually thought it was really smart the way they did that," Claudia Wells says. "I was more impressed than thinking it was odd. I've always admired Elisabeth Shue's acting, so to have her be cast in my part was a compliment to me. That's how I took it. I mean, *Leaving Las Vegas* and all the other films she's done? She's an incredible actress, so it was flattering."

For the rest of the cast, news that Wells's role was being recast stirred mixed emotions. Lea Thompson and Claudia Wells didn't work together much on the first movie, since their only shared scene was the film's final one, where Doc returns back from 2015. Though she was empathetic for Wells's family situation, Thompson was pleasantly surprised to have another opportunity to appear on-screen with Elisabeth Shue. The two were well acquainted after having appeared in a number of Burger King commercials several years earlier, and although they too only worked together briefly—on the scene in the 2015 McFly home in Hilldale—the two actresses were happy to reconnect.

For Christopher Lloyd, the change required a larger adjustment. "Claudia Wells not coming back was very disappointing," Lloyd says. "But it had to happen. It was wonderful working with Elisabeth Shue, but I was very comfortable with Claudia."

While Wells was handling family issues, Shue was engaging in similar struggles. The actress's experience filming the *Back to the Future* sequels was not a happy one. In August 1988, the actress met up with her brothers at their parents' summer home in Maine. One of her brothers, William, was on a tire swing and the rope broke above him. He landed on a broken tree branch, which impaled him upon impact. It was a fatal freak accident. In recent years, she has described the experience filming both movies as one she barely remembers. She wasn't really in a proper headspace to enjoy it like most of the other actors did.

There were also some significant changes to the creative team. While in London, Zemeckis met and worked with a number of people whom he wanted to bring into his regular repertoire of collaborators, including a young England-born costumer named Joanna Johnston.

Johnston, who had worked on Steven Spielberg's *Indiana Jones and the Temple of Doom* and *The Color Purple*, recalls getting a long-distance call from Zemeckis in Los Angeles. She was more than five thousand miles away, in London, where the two had met when she served an assistant costumer on *Roger Rabbit*. "Jo, I'd like for you to come and do the next *Back to the Future*. You'll be okay coming to Los Angeles and doing that, won't you?"

"I was pretty young and quite green," she says. "But I was absolutely in awe of him as a filmmaker. We got on really well, so I went quite blindly to work in L.A. on an entirely American project. The only people I knew were Bob and Steve Starkey."

Steve Starkey made his start in the business serving as an

Back to the Future cocreators Bob Gale and Robert Zemeckis, or "the Bobs," on the set of *I Wanna Hold Your Hand*, their first feature-film collaboration.

With Michael J. Fox originally unavailable to play Marty McFly, Eric Stoltz was cast and shot for six weeks. "Although he was doing the part well, he was not bringing that element of comedy to the screen," Christopher Lloyd says.

"Eric really understood how to skateboard," Stoltz's double Bob Schmelzer says. "He added a bit of punk to the character."

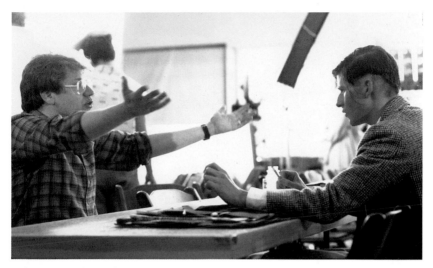

Robert Zemeckis with Crispin Glover. The actor proved to be a polarizing figure on the set, beloved by the cast and irksome to the crew.

© Universal City Studios, Inc., 1985

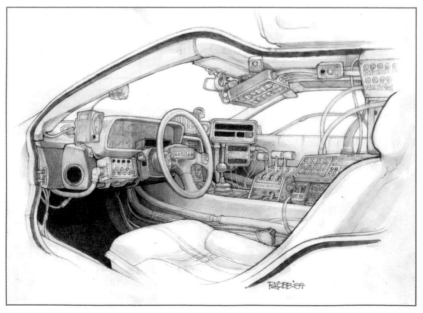

Ron Cobb's interior design for the DMC-12 time machine. "A movie car should tell you instantly how it works, just by looking at it," he says. "I wanted that sense for the DeLorean."   © Ron Cobb, 1984

Bob Z (Robert Zemeckis) directing the dinner scene in the 1985 McFly home. Many on the production team feared there was too much exposition in this sequence, but the Bobs remained confident audiences would remain interested.

© Universal City Studios, Inc., 1985

From left, Robert Zemeckis, Huey Lewis, Bob Gale, Neil Canton, Frank Marshall, and Bob Brown, manager for Huey Lewis and the News.

© Universal City Studios, Inc., 1985

"His memory was so good," Michael J. Fox's guitar coach Paul Hanson says. "I attributed it to the fact that he had to memorize lines all the time being an actor. He could have actually had a career as a guitar player."

"They came up with the idea that it'd be cool to have me in it," Huey Lewis says. "I thought, *Nah.* The band was doing great. I was becoming a rock star. I kind of resisted for a while."   © Universal City Studios, Inc., 1985

Drew Struzan illustrated dozens of concepts, including the one shown here, before settling on the iconic one-sheet for *Back to the Future* of Marty staring at his watch in disbelief.

© Drew Struzan, 1985

Tom Wilson gets his old-age makeup touched up during the *Back to the Future Part II* shoot.

© Universal City Studios, Inc., 1989

Jason Scott Lee, whose face is not visible, along with Ricky Dean Logan and Darlene Vogel shooting the hoverboard stunt sequence on the futuristic Hill Valley courthouse square.   © Universal City Studios, Inc., 1989

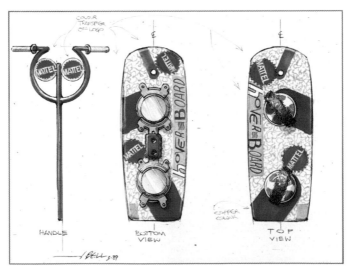

John Bell's concept art for the Mattel hoverboard. "It just kept getting whittled down because . . . they didn't want to blow a lot of money reproducing intricate designs," he says.   © John Bell, 1989

A number of different techniques were used to create the illusion of functional hoverboards. When the actors' feet were obscured, they were often put on actual skateboards.   © Universal City Studios, Inc., 1989

Neil Canton and the Bobs. © Universal City Studios, Inc., 1989

From left, Robert Zemeckis, George Lucas, Steven Spielberg, and Neil Canton on the *Part II* set. Lucas also visited while *Back to the Future Part III* was in production in Sonora. © Universal City Studios, Inc., 1989

Dean Cundey and Bob Z set up a shot on the 1955 set of *Part II*.

Tom Wilson, Lea Thompson, and Lisa Freeman.

From left, Tom Wilson, Robert Zemeckis, Charles Fleischer, Michael J. Fox, Dean Cundey, and Neil Canton. © Universal City Studios, Inc., 1989

Tom Wilson and Jeffrey Weissman, who replaced Crispin Glover for the *Future* sequels. When Michael J. Fox first saw Weissman as George McFly, the star made the prophetic declaration, "Oh, Crispin ain't going to like this."

© Universal City Studios, Inc., 1989

"I was kind of annoyed that Jeffrey Weissman was doing those scenes with me," Lea Thompson says. "Crispin . . . was a genius in *Back to the Future*, so it was hard that he wasn't there. It gave a real bittersweet feeling to revisiting those scenes."   © Universal City Studios, Inc., 1989

From left, Christopher Lloyd, Robert Zemeckis, Neil Canton, Michael J. Fox, and Steve Starkey.   © Universal City Studios, Inc., 1990

One of Joanna Johnston's costume designs for Doc Brown in *Back to the Future Part III*. Artwork by John Bell.   © Joanna Johnston, 1989

"I confess to having been infatuated with her, and I think it was mutual. We never got involved at all in any kind of relationship, other than being on the set and enjoying each other's company," Christopher Lloyd says about working with Mary Steenburgen. © Universal City Studios, Inc., 1990

Robert Zemeckis and Steven Spielberg at the premiere of *Back to the Future Part III* at the Cineplex Odeon in Los Angeles. Ron Gallela, Ltd./Ron Gallela Collection/Getty Images

From left, Bob Gale, Robert Zemeckis, Lea Thompson, Michael J. Fox, Christopher Lloyd, Mary Steenburgen, and Huey Lewis at the *Back to the Future* 25th Anniversary Trilogy Blu-ray/DVD reunion and launch party in New York City.

assistant editor on George Lucas's special-effects-heavy original *Star Wars* sequels. By 1985, he was working on *Amazing Stories*, a half-hour television series produced by Amblin for Universal's NBC network. He had caught wind of the company's newfound attachment to *Roger Rabbit* and made it known that he was interested in working on the project. Robert Watts, the head of postproduction at Amblin, was looking for someone to supervise the visual effects and additional components of postproduction for the film, and Starkey got the job. The *Roger Rabbit* shoot was a long one, nearly as long as the first *Future* film's, and the postproduction period was even longer. For slightly over a year, all of the animation and live-action components were painstakingly blended together, along with sound and score, to make a revolutionary and visually realistic spectacle. The picture went on to win a number of awards, including Oscars in the postproduction categories of Film Editing (Arthur Schmidt), Sound Effects Editing (Charles L. Campbell and Louis L. Edemann), and Visual Effects (Ken Ralston, Richard Williams, Ed Jones, and George Gibbs). Williams also took home a special award for his animation direction and creation of the cartoon characters for the film. While the special and visual effects of *Back to the Future* were applauded, Zemeckis knew *Paradox* would require even more attention. To that end, he wanted Steve Starkey on board to help make sure everything remained on track, as he had done to such success in their first collaboration.

While Zemeckis was assembling his dream team, some *Future* veterans were asked to sit out. Although the aesthetic of Hill Valley, in both its past and present-day iterations, was an integral component of the first film, production designer Larry Paull was not rehired for *Paradox*. In their depiction of the future, the Bobs knew they wanted to avoid what they felt had become commonplace cinematically—presenting a bleak and desolate Orwellian world. Before working with Zemeckis, Paull had helped create the iconic look of Ridley Scott's futuristic world in *Blade Runner,* which had earned him an Oscar nomination. There likely would have been differing opinions between Zemeckis and Paull about how to best realize the future in *Paradox,* just as there were differing opinions while making the original movie.

In his concept for the first film, Paull sought to create a saccharine look for the 1955 set, which was then altered for the modern-day scenes. Remnants of consistency remained, such as the Essex Theater, but there was an obvious deterioration in terms of the quality of life for Hill Valley's 1985 residents. Instead of *Cattle Queen of Montana* being shown, which starred Ronald Reagan decades before his presidency, the pornographic *Orgy American Style* is the prominent title on the marquee. The design, in effect, highlighted a subtle, understated critique the Bobs' script made about the 1980s. Maybe Marty and other teenagers believed their current decade was great, but there was an innocence and naïveté lost between the 1950s and the 1980s. Maybe "the good old days" wasn't just an expression, but a distinct period in time that would be foreign to the McFly-aged viewers showing up to movie theaters on the Fourth of July weekend.

"I wanted the present-day Hill Valley in *Part I* to be representative of the eighties, in how it was dressed," Paull says. "It was really run-down and funky. It was what happened to small towns ten, twenty, or even thirty years ago. The towns were dying and the stores were going out of business. We see this in documentaries and on the news all the time. Various towns or cities are just falling apart at the seams because no one shops there anymore. That's why Hill Valley in 1985 was so much different from Hill Valley of 1955. What we needed to do, for story purposes, was introduce elements into 1985 that were not there in 1955. In the beginning of the first movie, you can see that Dr. Brown's garage was right next door to a Burger King, right? That's because his house is torn down. All that's left is the garage."

In order to achieve this vision, Paull was adamant that the scenes in and around the Hill Valley town square not be shot on location, which was what Zemeckis and company had originally planned on doing. "We scouted Petaluma, in the Bay Area, as Hill Valley, but the expense of taking out modern streetlights and the basic cost of buying out a lot of businesses who would have been impacted made it out of the question," Bob Gale says. "After that scouting trip, Bob Z realized that Larry was right, and that our money would go further on the Universal Town Square."

"We were going to shoot in November into December, in the height of the Christmas season, when all these real stores are out there trying to make their year-end money," Paull says. "I said that we should be conscious of money too, but we should be doing it in a way that we're used to, by incorporating the backlot. I'd explored the backlot and laid it out in my head—what were going to be the key stores in the film. Then it became just reaching into the past or into *Look* and *Life* magazines, finding these places that really existed in the fifties. I could put them all together and make the backlot representative of 1955 California."

Having won that battle, Paull was less successful in fending off the invasion of product placement the producers demanded he integrate into the set. The production designer thought it was an unfortunate restriction to dictate which companies would and would not appear in the film depending on how many dollars they threw at the producers, but since it was a mandate, he played ball. When possible, he was insistent on including certain brands over others, in order to keep Hill Valley a familiar-seeming place for the audience. For example, an undisclosed gas company was willing to give a significant chunk of change to have their logo on the gas station in Marty's town, but Paull insisted on using Texaco, primarily because it reminded him of a gag from *The Milton Berle Show*. In the end, the filmmakers were able to make the product placement work out to their advantage, creating some very memorable sequences in the film by juxtaposing the differences between products Americans used in the 1950s and 1980s. During filming, Deborah Lynn Scott costumed one of the extras in a vintage gas attendant costume for the Texaco scene. When Zemeckis saw this, he came up with an idea. Scott took her directive, returned with three more extras in matching costumes, and the director shot a quick gag where a driver pulls into the station and is swarmed by attendants eager to help by checking the tire pressure and oil, cleaning the windshield, and filling the gas tank, all in a few seconds. These seemingly inconsequential visual jokes create a more realistic mise-en-scène, a cinematic term used to describe all the elements that appear before a camera, and also allowed the filmmakers opportunities to use shorthand to compare the different time periods in the film.

These were the occasional straws Paull put on the camel's back while in production, and before hiring was started on *Paradox*, it appears one of those had broken it. "I wanted to come back," he says. "But Bob and I had a . . . what we call a 'creative difference' over something that happened on the original, and I was not asked back." Instead, the job was offered to Rick Carter, another veteran of *Amazing Stories*. The two met when Zemeckis was hired to direct an hour-long episode of the series, "Go to the Head of the Class," which starred Christopher Lloyd and included music from Alan Silvestri. The two hit it off, and when someone was needed to fill the vacancy left by Paull, the director sent a copy of the script to his former colleague. "That story, pleasantly, fried my brain," Carter says. "And I enjoyed the sensation. We had so much to think about and so much to visualize. It was fun to imagine jumping into that world, especially after having seen the first *Back to the Future*."

The first order of business, of course, was designing what the Hill Valley landscape would look like in the four time periods the film is set in: 1955, 1985, 1985-A—the alternate version of the present day, where Biff has taken over the town—and 2015. Rick Carter began by looking at the first film for clues not only about how to re-create the visuals of the original picture, but also how to extend and expand upon those visual themes to create an original, yet coherent, vision for the series. "It was different than any other movie, where you could actually go film at a place that really existed," Carter says. "In this case, it certainly existed in everybody's minds because the first production was so good, and the movie was so successful, and that town square was so iconic. It was about knowing that Hill Valley was the heart and soul of the movie on a visual level.

"Re-creating 1955 was a lot of fun in the sense that we got to reimagine something that you knew everybody had already responded to," he continues. "The challenge, of course, was to project that not only forward in the future, but also in the alternate version of the present for Biffhorrific, as it was labeled by Bob and called at the time. On the first *Back to the Future*, they really seemed to exude a kind of warmth toward the time periods they were expressing, so I wanted to do that. We created this terrific alternate version of 1985, a 'Las Vegas meets Bangkok meets some derelict New York,' early seventies version of a run-down city. Sex and pollution were dominant in those scenes, and there was an exaggeration of the value of money. There was a lot to play with there, and a lot to express with all the signage and lighting. It was really fun."

Joanna Johnston also found it a healthy challenge to continue the work someone else began. Deborah Lynn Scott's contributions to the first film were just as memorable as Larry Paull's production design, and her successor was determined to preserve the integrity of the original design, while also adding her own personal touches. "Scott's stuff was really quite challenging," she says. "The style of it was really interesting to me because I'm not American, and I had not lived in America at all at this point, so I was going in and looking at the cultural stuff of American clothing. It was just totally different from what was going on in London at the time, but I had to do it. There was not even the possibility of shifting off it, because you're picking up somebody else's baton. You need to honor that."

This was less of a challenge when it came to the more fantastic time periods in the picture, like 1985-A and 2015. "Biffhorrific, well, it was just that," Johnston says. "It was everything going wrong. Bob wanted Lea Thompson to look really tacky and sleazy, so we put a fake full chest on her with this enormous cleavage. All of her clothes are completely revolting, and so are Biff's. It's easy, that stuff, because you just go to the wrong side. I suppose there was a counterbalance to what the rest of the film was doing with the optimistic Hill Valley future."

In designing the future, the team was able to flex their creative muscles. It's true that "not *Blade Runner*" can only be carried so far as an edict, but Bob Gale's screenplay provided valuable clues as to how the Bobs wanted the twenty-first century to appear on-screen. Technology would be more ubiquitous, but in a helpfully efficient way, not an oppressive one. Instead of trying to predict where technology was headed in the real world and forecast those guesses on-screen, Gale went for humor, expanding upon some of the gags from the first film, like Marty inventing the first skateboard, and including some in-jokes to mock 1980s popular culture, like the seemingly endless *Jaws* sequels and even the momentous appeal of Zemeckis's own *Roger Rabbit*.

However, even without trying, the filmmakers did make some accurate prognoses. For example, the residents of Hill Valley have thumb pads that enable them to make quick payments, as Old Biff does after exiting the taxicab. In fact, thumbprint technology is completely integrated into Zemeckis and Gale's future, with its uses including, but not limited to, the ability to unlock doors, just as it has become a popular means of punching in at workplace time clocks and unlocking telephones in recent years. "The big crime was going to be people's fingers being cut off," the director told his team before filming. "People will cut off fingers, and they'll run the tissue to the bank, the ATM, and get your money out." Much has been made of the film's prophetic inclusion of videoconferencing, multichannel television viewing, and flat screens. In Hill Valley's future, cosmetic surgery has become easy and commonplace. Doc Brown's face is made more youthful by visiting a "rejuvenation clinic," and careful observers will notice the presence of Bottoms Up, a breast enhancement company, which advertises on the McFly television and can be seen in the background of some future scenes. There is instantaneous written correspondence, although the film inaccurately thought there would be an expansion of fax technology, which, of course, was superseded in the real world by email and text messaging. In both the fictional and real 2015, televised advertising is virtually omniscient, like Goldie Wilson III's hover conversion commercial that broadcasts over the square, and personally targeted ads are indeed part of everyday life now—just not often in the form of a large digital shark projecting from movie theater marquees.

Perhaps the best, and most underrated, example of one of Gale's jokes turning into a reality can be found in the *Number Two* draft of the script. Marty inadvertently stumbles upon a Huey Lewis and the News concert, but realizes in short time that the band isn't actually there. Instead, it's a realistic hologram on a theater stage, eternally preserving his idols in their best physical condition. In the real world, holographic concert technology has been on display at least since 2012, with deceased music artists like Michael Jackson, Tupac Shakur, and Lisa "Left-Eye" Lopes "performing" in front of audiences of thousands.

Animator John Bell, who proved to be an invaluable addition to the creative team, designed many of the ancillary aspects of the future set. Even in its earliest version, specific elements, like flying cars, were written into the 2015 portion of the film. Years before Gale submitted his first draft to Universal, during that "unofficial preproduction" period, Amblin and ILM took baby steps toward pushing the sequel toward the green light, which included coming up with elements of Hill Valley's future landscape. "I was less than a year into my employment at ILM at the time," Bell says. "I had just finished working on *Star Trek IV* and was in between projects. Back then, there were just two other people in the art department with myself. One of the producers at ILM, Patty Blau, came into the art department, knowing there wasn't a lot going on, and told me about the project. At that point, all we knew was that Bob was going thirty years into the future and there was something called a 'hoverboard.' They asked me to just come up with some ideas."

Over the course of the next six weeks, Bell completed dozens of detailed images: a vibrant town square, the interior of Doc's laboratory, and the Hill Valley courthouse with large glass windowpanes above the clock and a monorail nearby. The artwork was sent to the director, who left them to languish in storage as filming began on *Roger Rabbit* in December 1986. Bell started working on Ron Howard's 1988 film *Willow* without giving *Future* too much of a second thought, until a phone call came from Rick Carter that August. "The film has been green-lighted and we're getting ready to start," he said. "We have a script now. Can you come down to Los Angeles and come up with some designs for some specific vehicles and moments?" Bell's planned three-week journey to L.A. ended up lasting months.

Bell and Johnston collaborated on concepts for some of the futuristic costumes, particularly the look of Biff's grandson, Griff, and his gang. Harkening back yet again to the original film, the antagonistic Tannens were given a band of bullies to parade around with in every time period. The costumes for the gang of 2015 would have to appear not only intimidating and distinctive, but congruous with the palette created by the art department. This was an assignment that required a lot of attention, with work beginning almost as soon as both the animator and costume designer were hired. "Designing for the future was easy. You just use certain fabrics and leathers and bits and accessorize. They were pretty much all monochromatic, just with a few highlights," Johnston says. "For the girl, she was in the same vein, but I kept her quite girlie. She was really pretty, kind of androgynous. She was edgy—sexy and tough all at the same time.

"The strongest thing about Bob is that he has no fear about where to go," she continues. "That's why he gathers like-minded people around him. Although I was quite apprehensive about the job, because I was so new to the game, I knew I could just spin off into crazy places and he'd be happy with all of that, whereas a lot of directors would want to rope you in."

Zemeckis's vision of the future, and the need for increased functionality of technology, also extended to the clothing. Not only did he want the designs to be original, but also practical. One of his ideas was that, in the future, clothing stores would no longer carry multiple sizes of the same item. If people outgrew a particular size, why should they have to throw out their old garments? Instead, all clothing would be one-size-fits-all and adjustable to a person's body. The result was Marty's retractable jacket and self-lacing Nike Mag sneakers. Johnston made the jacket out of rubber because of another Zemeckis idea: "Make it so that you wouldn't have to take it to the dry cleaner's or Laundromat. You could just hose it down."

When Johnston was hired, Frank Marshall told her that a component of her job would involve working with Nike on product placement for the film. The executive producer grew close with Pamela McConnell at the footwear company back when Michael J. Fox was hired for the first movie. Deborah Lynn Scott outfitted him in wardrobe and brought him out to show Zemeckis, his producers, and the Amblin Trio, but she had neglected to put him in Marty-specific shoes. The actor wore a pair of white low-top Nike Bruins with a red swoosh to the costume fitting, and Zemeckis instructed the actor to just wear what he came in with. They were perfect. The next day, Scott called Marshall, frantic. She had tried to go out that morning and buy ten pairs to use for filming, but none of the local shops were still carrying the sneaker. The shoes Fox had worn had been discontinued. Marshall called some friends who worked for Nike, who directed him to McConnell. He explained the situation and she was happy to assist. It might be because product placement wasn't as prevalent in the mid-1980s, but Nike didn't charge Universal a dime. They sent ten pairs of sneakers, and a beautiful relationship between the producers and the company was started, which maintains its strength to this day.

Initially, Joanna Johnston couldn't care less about the attractiveness of this partnership. The costumer felt she was in no place to really put her foot down, but she was less than enthusiastic about being forced to work with a brand. Product placement, she felt, was hokey, and furthermore, she could not understand the American obsession with sneakers. In her first few weeks here, Johnston was overwhelmed by the pervasiveness of sneaker culture in the United States. On the set, Zemeckis would wear sneakers daily, and to her surprise, even Mr. Steven Spielberg himself wore his casual kicks when he visited the backlot. She was used to working with English directors who would put on a jacket and loafers when coming to set, not adults who showed up to work wearing the same clothes as teenagers at the local mall. She thought the whole thing not only distinctly American, but Californian, and in the worst way. Her opinion changed once Zemeckis hit her with another conceptual idea. He told her that sneakers weren't going to go out of style and, in fact, would become more feminine in time so they could be better marketed to women, even foreseeing a trend of high-heeled sneakers in the future. Inspiration was sparked—she didn't have to work within the confines of existing designs. Perhaps there were creative things the sneaker company could bring to the table. She held a meeting with Nike and, together, they came up with the self-lacing shoes, among other futuristic footwear.

With some of the costume designs in place, John Bell continued working on the incidental background elements of the futuristic Hill Valley. While he wanted to push the look of the film decades ahead of the present day, the illustrator was cautious not to move too far beyond the familiar. He implemented a

"15:85 rule," a ratio of unrecognizable to recognizable elements used in the design process. For example, consider Bell's concept for a Federal Express mailbox. In his original sketch, it appears much like a standard U.S. Postal Service receptacle one might find on any street corner in America, but there is a red digital monitor attached where a person could input their address and other shipping information. Someone looking at the sketch can easily identify the object and its purpose, but there are elements that make it appear a little foreign.

On *Back to the Future*, Steve Gawley, the supervising model maker at ILM, oversaw the construction of the miniature DeLorean used for the visual effect at the end of the film when Marty, Doc, and Jennifer take to the sky. The small-scale model was shot against a blue screen, with the miniature's movements controlled by a computer that would send information to a servomotor, a small device that allows for precision of acceleration, angular position, and velocity of the object to which it is assigned. Because the flying time machine would have greater importance in the sequel, the team at ILM created a new 1:5 scale model, but this time the device was far more intricate. There were turn signals, an opening door, and fully functioning lights, including a blinking flux capacitor. In total, there were more than twenty working components that would allow Zemeckis to seamlessly intercut between footage of the actual car and the model. To complete the illusion, there were also two fifteen-inch servo-powered puppets made in the images of Marty and Doc, the same technology used to make Elliott and E.T. ride their bicycle over the moon.

Car customizer Gene Winfield built a full-scale model DeLorean out of fiberglass that could be used for practical shots for special effects supervisor Michael Lantieri, who took over the job from Kevin Pike on the first film. The faux car could then be lowered down into the frame via a crane to give the appearance of a smooth landing. For the remainder of the futuristic vehicles, some were models, while others, like the police motorcycles designed by Tim Flattery, were built upon previously functional machinery. Because of budgetary considerations, the motorcycles were made out of two Kawasaki 250 Ninjas. The wheelbase of the used bikes did not match Flattery's sketches, so compromises had to be made when constructing the props. Anyone who walked past them as they were idling on set would be able to see two extra sets of wheels peeking out from the bottom, as they were unable to be fully concealed.

With a script in place and cast and crew nearly finalized, it became increasingly important to deal with the issue of George McFly. Bob Gale had no greater indication that Crispin Glover would reconsider and accept the current offer on the table for him to appear in the film, forcing the production team to begin thinking of ways to replace him. As much as they didn't want to do it, substituting Elisabeth Shue for Claudia Wells was a relatively painless transaction. Sure, the two actresses looked different, but that was a nominal concern. Jennifer was a minor character in the first film, and even though she would have more screen time in the sequels, she would be unconscious for the majority of them and largely incidental to the plot. Conversely, with portions of *Paradox* revisiting moments from the first film, the necessity to cast an actor closely resembling Glover was paramount. As production neared, this became more and more prevalent in the producers' minds, until Sophie reared her head again to deliver another ugly choice—this time on how to solve the George McFly problem.

7. YOU'RE GEORGE McFLY

Monday, February 20, 1989

It was an all-too-familiar scene on the Universal backlot, which had been restored back to Hill Valley, 1955. Robert Zemeckis was reviewing the upcoming shot with Dean Cundey, Bob Gale and Neil Canton were double-checking that the crew had arrived, and elsewhere, in his trailer, Christopher Lloyd was filling with anxiety. The first day of shooting any film carries with it a normal and healthy bit of nerves, but what the actor was experiencing was beyond the standard amount of trepidation. As he waited to be called on set, Lloyd reviewed his pages. The scene being shot this day, the first for *Paradox*, was a revisit to a pivotal scene from *Back to the Future*, right after lightning strikes the clock tower and Marty I, the original Marty from the first film, is sent back to 1985. In the scene being shot this evening, Marty II, the one who returns to the fifties in an attempt to capture the sports almanac, grabs the Doc by his shoulders and causes him to faint. The actor now had the added burden of not only re-creating his character, but also expanding upon an exact scene from the first film.

While the mood on the set was characteristically light, the

actor knew a lot was riding on the sequel. *Back to the Future* was the ninth-highest-grossing film of all time in the United States, and although no one was saying it outright, the actor sensed that he wasn't the only one feeling concerned about the sequel's success. VHS copies of the first film could easily be found on the set, and when Zemeckis saw that the actor was jittery, the two sat down and watched the clock tower scene from the first film. Lloyd still felt nervous, but slightly more confident. He made his way to the familiar set, met Michael J. Fox—who had since traded in Marty's classic costume from the first film for "something inconspicuous," a black leather jacket over a maroon T-shirt—and shot the scene. Once the cameras started rolling, it all came flowing right back to him. For Christopher Lloyd, playing Doc Brown, it turned out, was a lot like riding a bike.

It was decided early on that the VHS of the first film would be one of the production team's most valuable players during the *Paradox* shoot. A few weeks before the start of principal photography, the cast and crew were invited to Amblin to view *Back to the Future*. The stated goal was to remind the actors of their performances in the first film, but there was an additional advantage. Rewatching the original movie reminded many of how special that picture was and the obligation they had to the public to do the best job possible. *Paradox*'s script was thought-provoking, challenging, and certainly not indicative of a cash grab on the part of the Bobs. It was obvious that the two creators cared about their characters, and as the team that would be working on *Paradox* watched Lorraine and George kiss on the big screen, they were reminded that they cared about those characters too. The sequel shoot was sure to be taxing and, with the extra technical demands, maybe even more complicated than the original film, but there was a silent understanding that everyone was going to grab an oar and help keep this boat afloat.

But while the Amblin screening was a welcome reunion for the *Future* returners, one cast member was noticeably absent—Crispin Glover. The back-and-forth of whether or not the actor would return continued well after the rest of the principal cast was in place, up until just a few weeks before filming began. "Once we were in preproduction, Elaine Goldsmith called back saying that Crispin now thought he had made a mistake in deciding to not return for the sequel," Bob Gale says. "I told her we'd consider using Crispin, but the role would be small, as we weren't going to rewrite the script for him. He came into the office, met with Bob Z, Bob talked him through the story, and Crispin seemed ready to participate. When Elaine called me, I told her that we would pay him the same weekly salary that Tom Wilson was getting, and not a penny more. I told her I would not negotiate; it was a take-it-or-leave-it offer.

"Crispin didn't like the money," he continues. "So he fired Elaine and hired new agents, John Gaines and Gerry Harrington, both of whom are now deceased. They called me, and I told them the exact same thing: Our budget was locked, we were already prepared to make the movie without Crispin, and we didn't care if he said yes or no. I also told them that if they came back and tried to negotiate for a higher salary, I would respond with a lower take-it-or-leave-it offer. Well, that's what happened. They asked for more money, so I lowered the offer by five thousand a week, and Crispin blew the deal."

The search was on for a new George McFly. However, replacing Glover was quickly proving to be easier said than done. Just as they had done when they ended the first film with Jennifer in the DeLorean with the two protagonists, the Bobs had painted themselves into a corner with the sequel storyline they came up with. Zemeckis's idea to revisit the first film was innovative, but even the most drastic reduction of the McFly patriarch's role in the movie would still require him to appear in the film—and look pretty damned close to the way he appeared in the series' first installment. While Claudia Wells was also not returning for the sequel, it was less important to the narrative that her physical appearance remain constant. Elisabeth Shue in an identical costume would do just fine, but because the Enchantment Under the Sea dance was so pivotal to the original film, as was George's role in it, the Bobs had to come up with a plan.

Coincidentally, the answer to their problem was virtually under their noses. While the Bobs were working out of Amblin, actor Jeffrey Weissman was working at Universal Studios, interacting with the patrons while performing look-alike impersonations of Groucho Marx, Stan Laurel, and Charlie Chaplin, a job he had held for several years. After a day of work, he received a call out of the blue from an agent friend of his.

"Do you know who Crispin Glover is?"

"Sure. I worked with him at the American Film Institute on a project a few years ago."

"And are you his height?"

"I think I'm a little bit shorter." He thought for a second. "Wait, is someone looking for a Crispin Glover double?"

"Yes."

"Is this for the *Back to the Future* sequel in the works?" He was finding it hard to contain his excitement. Like millions of others, Weissman had seen *Back to the Future* in theaters and was anticipating the new film's release. While he liked his current gig, it would obviously be more beneficial to work for a Universal picture than a Universal theme park.

"I'm not at liberty to say," his friend responded. "I've been sworn to secrecy."

A few days later, the actor was brought into an interview and formal audition with casting director Judy Taylor under the pretense that he was being considered for Glover's photo double. He read a scene from the first film, where George is hanging laundry and talking to Marty. As he exited, he saw other actors waiting to audition. None of them looked too much like Glover, but that, the actor accurately assumed, was a nonissue. They all appeared to be of similar height and the same complexion as each other, so perhaps they were all up for the double position too. Within a few days, he was invited to meet with makeup artist Ken Chase. Like the rest of the hopefuls, Weissman bears little resemblance to Glover, so latex prosthetics were added onto his face to help him appear less like himself and more like the George McFly audiences would be expecting to see in the sequel. Molds weren't taken of his face in advance, something that didn't immediately strike the actor as odd. Instead, the facial appliances, which had been used for Crispin Glover's old-age makeup in the first film, were readily available, having been pulled out of storage, where they had been kept for the past several years.

Once the transformation was complete, the actor was sent in to screen-test with Robert Zemeckis. "That was the first time I met Bob," Weissman says. "He didn't really say much to me. He just gave me direction, and most of the stuff went successfully, apparently."

In what could have been a red flag to the actor had he the benefit of hindsight, Zemeckis leaned over to Dean Cundey after the actor was finished with his scene. "What d'ya think?"

"I think we have Crispin," the cinematographer said. "Crispin without the trouble."

At the time, no one in the room could have foretold how

incorrect that statement could have been, especially Weissman. In his blissful ignorance, he thanked them, got out of makeup, and went home. He was hired, and right before filming began, he was offered the role of George, not to be a double or stand-in as he'd originally thought. Universal opened negotiations with the actor's theatrical agent and offered Weissman $20,000. The actor's agent couldn't believe their good fortune.

Once shooting on *Paradox* began, the returning cast worked on embodying their now-iconic roles—and the various iterations of them that appeared throughout the film—for the sequel. Lea Thompson was able to reassume Lorraine's mannerisms, but found her greatest challenge to be capturing the Biffhorrific version of the character, which she describes as the "diva-drunk, poor old alcoholic Lorraine." In addition to her having to portray that extreme version of the character, the makeup design, which was provided by Ken Chase before he left the production after the second week of filming over a financial dispute about his salary, left her straining to perform through the plastic.

"It was horrible," she says. "Old-age makeup feels horrible, especially back then. Now they use something different that's a little bit more malleable, but that makeup was so stiff. It was awful. You're gluing something to your face—I would get blisters on my neck. It's hard to complain as an actor, because we're really, really lucky, but anytime you see wigs and makeup and period costumes, imagine wearing that stuff for twelve hours. It's really painful."

As inhibiting as the makeup was, the physical appliances added for the Biffhorrific scenes did help the actress get into character. The prosthetic Thompson wore to make it appear as if she had gotten breast augmentation surgery provided a healthy dose of entertainment on set. On one occasion, Steven Spielberg came to visit, dropped his keys down in her fake cleavage, and picked them back out, much to her amusement. Other times, when the actress was only partially in her costume and sitting in the makeup chair, she would elicit gasps from onlookers who would have to take a moment to realize she wasn't really topless. "I just loved that character," she says. "I loved that sequence. I loved that set. I loved the shot of me coming out of the bedroom when Biff comes in. There's that huge crane shot that comes out into that incredible set that they built on the Universal soundstage. I just think that sequence is genius. It's one of my favorites that I've ever done. It was over-the-top, but I think that that whole part was fantastic. The fact that I got to play all these different aspects of one person under different circumstances, and such an interesting character, was so lucky for me. Now, on my reel, I put those parts, especially Lorraine in *Back to the Future Part II*. No one will give me that diva part, and I'm like, 'Dude, I did this when I was twenty-three! I can do it even better now.'"

Tom Wilson also found the makeup process for *Paradox* taxing, to say the least. For the vast majority of his shoot, he had to endure six hours of makeup application, and sometimes also a fat suit, in order to play the various versions of the Tannen family in the film. In order to make it to the set by ten, Wilson's days often started in the makeup chair at 3:30 A.M. He would shoot for seven or so hours, then begin the easier, but still time-consuming at an hour long, process of being undone and transformed back to his regular self. Sometimes the shooting schedule required that he begin the day in heavy prosthetics but end it with a clean face, like when the actor shot the scene where Old Biff gives Young Biff the sports almanac in the 1955 portion of the film. In addition to having to perform through the uncomfortable appliances, the actor had the unfortunate battle wounds of a severely irritated and blistered face and neck—a side effect of a slightly toxic chemical the makeup artists used to quickly remove the latex from the actors' faces—left after each day of shooting, which, if need be, would simply be covered over with makeup so Wilson could continue working.

Although it may seem like the obvious decision, using the same actors to play their older counterparts in the first film was a novel idea. The Bobs were fully committed to making it work, believing it would be more fulfilling for an audience to see the same actor when Marty goes back to 1955. During auditions, the actors reading for Lorraine, George, and Biff all endured a makeup test before being offered the part. For Thompson, being entrusted to stretch as an actress to portray someone so much older than she was made her confident in the project and in the filmmakers who were guiding her. "It's magical when you first see Lorraine in the past after seeing her so sad and beaten down in 1985," she says. "When you see her for the first time in the 1950s, she's so young and full of life. It added so much to the dimension of the character. It's one of the reasons people go to the movies. The fact that they had such faith in Crispin and I, and Tom Wilson, to pull it off was really great."

While the day-to-day operations of moviemaking were largely the same, the atmosphere on the set filming *Paradox* was slightly more pressured, partially because of the expectations of the audience and studio executives, but mostly because the sequel was more technically ambitious than its predecessor. The perfect case study is the scene where Reese and Foley, two police officers played by Mary Ellen Trainor, Zemeckis's wife at the time, and Stephanie E. Williams, bring Jennifer to her future home in Hilldale. The director had hoped to shoot the descent of the police car starting underneath the vehicle until the door opens, with the three exiting in one long take. There were a lot of nerves on set that night, with some on the crew on edge about the director's wife being involved in a minor stunt—she and the other two actresses would be in the car as it was lowered onto the ground. To further complicate matters, it was one of the last nights the production team had available to shoot at their location on the corner of Oakhurst Street and Somerset Avenue in El Monte. Light was disappearing as the sun set, and of course, the car wasn't working. In designing and building the car, Tim Flattery built a channel so an industrial-size forklift could be fed through the bottom and it could be raised. The result, in a perfect world, would be a clean shot without any special effects trickery visible. Since a similar technique was used for one of the flying DeLoreans, Michael Lantieri expected the operation of this effects car to be the same. About a half hour before the shot was going to start, one of the crew members got into the forklift and prepared for the test run. He threaded the police car with his machine, started to lift, and—

"It's bending! The forklift's bending!" The back end of the effects vehicle was in the air, its front still on the ground. The effects team wasn't using a machine with a proper gauge to suspend the car in midair. The man inside the forklift looked out his window and spit out a huge wad of chewing tobacco.

"I know it's fucking bending." Instead of stopping, he kept lifting, risking damage not only to his machinery, but to the custom car that had taken several months to design and construct. When he finally stopped, the back end was almost six feet in the air, with its nose facing downward, like a roller-coaster car before the first big drop. Audible disbelief started to crackle among the crew.

"Holy shit."

"How do we even get it down?"

"Bob. Where's Bob? Someone get Bob."

"Let me see it." Zemeckis was making his way to the scene of the incident, while crew members urgently walked ahead of him, like siblings trying to warn their older brother that Dad is on the way. Then he saw it. "How much fucking money did we spend on this car?"

"It was a long night," Tim Flattery says. "I'd never seen him ever blow up about anything. We were shooting nights all week and it was the last shot. All of sudden, this is his problem. He turned the corner and sees this car all hung up in the air. It was horrible."

The crew managed to get the car down, but now a second option was needed to get the car to function properly for the shoot. In the haste of the moment, it was difficult to see who made the decision, but it was clear that one had been made. Someone grabbed a hammer and knocked out the bottom of the car. Since the forklift could no longer be threaded underneath the vehicle, it was chained to the car's chassis, its main frame, which covered the entire rear half of the vehicle. The shot as originally conceived was now impossible, as only the front of the car would now be suitable for filming. The rest of the car was now covered in the chains required to allow it to safely and smoothly be lifted from the ground and back down again. With the sun setting at a rapid rate, there was a chance that the entire setup might go to waste. There was a test run of the newly modified arrangement, and despite the crew members' crisis of confidence in the jerry-rigging of the vehicle, all went well. The three actors got into the car, the operator lifted it up, the director called the shot into action, and the crane lowered. Before the end of the night, they got the shot, even if it wasn't exactly to Zemeckis's liking.

"As a concept designer and somebody who's seeing these things through to completion, your job is to give the director his vision," Flattery says. "Whether it's the shot or the aesthetic, that's what you're hired for. If something goes wrong and he's had this vision all the way through preproduction, you feel terrible. You feel like you let him down. That was a great learning experience for me as far as how I went about my construction from then on in movies, and how I went about testing processes. I now maintain constant communication with directors as far as, 'What exactly are you planning on doing on the day with this?' Then I can have everything ready."

While *Back to the Future* was an unknown quantity while the cast and crew were filming years earlier, this time they all were aware of the expectations—and felt the pressure on a daily basis. "It was much harder," Neil Canton says. "First of all, wherever you went, people said, 'What movie are you working on?' You'd tell them it was *Back to the Future Part II* or *Part III* and they'd go, 'Oh, wow, we love *Back to the Future*. What happens to Doc? What happens to Marty?' There was much more pressure on us to make something that would be as good. We all felt it. Bob obviously felt it, because he was the director of a movie, a very successful movie. We always felt like we had to do a little bit more so that we could bring some kind of freshness or originality to *II* and *III*. We shot more, and it was hard on the actors. I know Chris was worried about whether he could get back into the place where Doc Brown was in the first movie. Could he do that again? Could he duplicate that performance? Michael was worried about that too.

"We had so many of the same crew people back, and they all felt it," he continues. "We started to wonder, if you did something right to left on the first movie, should we do it in the left to right in this movie? You started to question everything. Our original intention was never to do a sequel. I don't want to say it wasn't fun, because making a movie is always fun, but it became fun plus work. The expectation added the feeling of work. We didn't want to let anyone down, but at the end of the day, you have to assume that we know what's best."

Character actor Wesley Mann remembers feeling a similar degree of pressure while making his *Future* debut in the film. He appeared in a small yet unforgettable role, a character whom the film's end credits refer to as "CPR Kid," the movie's novelization calls "Lester," but most fans of the franchise know best as "Wallet Guy." In the 1955 segment of *Part II*, right before George decks Biff outside the Enchantment Under the Sea dance, Zemeckis was trying to avoid making another compromise with a complicated camera move. "The first shot of that day was a complicated computer-crane shot that starts in the principal's office when he throws the sports almanac in the trash bin," Mann says. "It cranes up to see the car arrive and the altercation with Biff outside the window. That took about three hours to get set up. It was subtle, but there was certainly an air of being watched by the front office. People were wondering if we were going to get this shot. During the shoot, Michael made some allusion to the difference between the two movies. He said, 'We made the first on time. I don't know if we'll make it on the second.'"

Reenacting the Enchantment Under the Sea dance was a unique experience. "When we re-created that scene for *Part II*, I remember it feeling like a sort of time warp," Bob Gale says. "As if I could walk out of our set on Stage 12, which we dressed like the first time we shot it, and find myself in the parking lot of the Hollywood Methodist Church in 1985, where we filmed the dance for *Part I*." The producer's sentiment was felt by a number of those who were present for the filming of the scene for both films. But in addition to feelings of déjà vu, there were also inherent complications that came from trying to re-create the scene in all of its details. The props and costumes from the first film either had to be uncovered from a storage facility or refabricated. Lea Thompson's pink dress had gone missing, but luckily the actress had an extra one she had held on to after filming the first film. While it was easy to resolve the case of the disappearing costume, each small gaffe added to the pressure that everyone was actively trying his or her best to ignore.

As much as "business as usual" was the mandate for the shoot, for Harry Waters, Jr., filming between *Future* and *Part II* couldn't have been more dissimilar. "Bob and the producers were not as accessible during *Part II* because they were having anxiety shooting two movies at the same time," he says. "I remember we were filming the day of the Oscars, and the cinematographer and editor were nominated for *Roger Rabbit*. The entire crew and cast and extras all stopped to watch the awards. When the editor won, there was that moment of, 'Yes, all the people that work on this movie are winners and are going to be an important part of this industry.' Then it was back to work. We felt we couldn't be too crazy while shooting because the powers that be were pretty driven right now. They had a lot on their plate, so it was, 'Show up, do your work, and stop playing around with the extras.'"

Jeffrey Weissman's tenure at the dance was also uncomfortable, but it really was no more so than the rest of his time filming *Part II*. Depending on which side of the argument you choose to listen to, there are a lot of ways to describe Weissman: character actor, imitator, savior, willing conspirator, victim, or scab. He was over the moon about appearing in the sequel, but his enthusiasm subsided when he arrived on set for his first day. "It was odd," he says. "I got really strange reactions from people." Because Weissman had been outfitted in facial appliances made from the molds of Crispin Glover's face and not his own, the result was someone who looked mildly disfigured and certainly unnatural. During a break while filming his screen test weeks earlier, Weissman ran into some actors who were shooting *Dick Tracy* for Disney at Universal. Although several of those actors were in heavy character makeup, Weissman was stared at as if he were the oddity. After he came out of his trailer on the first day the two worked together, Michael J. Fox gave a hard look at Glover's replacement, chuckled to himself, and made a now-prophetic declaration: "Oh, Crispin ain't going to like this."

On some level, Glover's absence may have been welcomed by the Bobs, who didn't have to concern themselves with the actor's curious behavior throughout production on the sequel, but that didn't mean the presence of the original George wasn't felt every day on set. "I think Crispin was weighing on everyone's mind while filming," Weissman says. "While shooting the Enchantment Under the Sea stuff, when Robert Zemeckis would call, 'Action,' he would sometimes shout out, 'Lea!' and sometimes he'd shout out, 'Crispin!' but never 'Jeffrey.' I never felt welcomed. I felt like a scab."

"I was kind of annoyed that Jeffrey Weissman was doing those scenes with me, to be perfectly honest," Thompson says. "That was a little hard for me, just because Crispin was so fantastic. He was a genius in *Back to the Future*, so it was hard that he wasn't there. It gave a real bittersweet feeling to revisiting those scenes. In life, there's always the bad with the good, even with something as great as *Back to the Future*. Crispin didn't do *Part II* and *III* and Eric was fired in the first one, so there's kind of a bad feeling along with all the great feelings of making these great movies. There's always a little thorn in your side. Those two things were it for me."

"I had an inkling that it wasn't comfortable for her," Weissman says. "It couldn't have been good for her, kissing a man in a mask. I was given their screen test to watch, to see Crispin's work and get down young George's mannerisms and everything. In it, you can tell that the two of them had worked hard with each other. They had spent a lot of hours together working on that relationship, and I think she probably was very fond of Crispin. When she found out he wasn't coming back, I am sure it made things uncomfortable."

Weissman's instincts were correct. Throughout production on *Back to the Future*, Lea Thompson and Crispin Glover had grown quite close to each other. Although she acknowledges he was a handful on the set, the two got on famously. They used to have long conversations in their trailers about everything and nothing. He captivated her. At one point, Glover invited the actress over to his apartment to work on their characters for the revised version of 1985 at the end of the movie. When she walked in, she found the walls painted all black, with barely any furniture in the living room. The focal point was a stainless-steel medical examination table. Instead of running lines, he invited her to paint a volcano on canvas with him. Much to his satisfaction, she went with it. For her, it wasn't a big deal; when in Crispin's world, do as Crispin does.

Weissman understood that he wasn't going to replace the actor in her eyes, and he also wasn't making any attempts to. All he hoped for was to be treated as an actor doing a job, a colleague, and not an unwanted consolation prize. "Lea never called me by name," he says. "When we were in the makeup chair in the morning, she rarely addressed me. After the shoot, she brought her mother up to Universal to see the tour. I went to speak to her and she introduced me as 'the actor who played Crispin.' She didn't remember my name."

The rebuke from some on the set might have hurt Weissman's ego, but his greatest pain came from the demands of playing George McFly in the scene in Marty's future home. In the reduced role of the character, Bob Gale constructed a plot device whereby George threw out his back on the golf course, and as a result was suspended upside down in a futuristic back brace. The special effect would hopefully disorient the viewing public and make it harder to realize that it wasn't the original actor on-screen, especially with the old-age makeup required. In order to help with his comfort, a special rig was built so the actor could take breaks between takes, since the crew was unable, or unwilling, to disconnect and reattach Weissman throughout the day. It helped, but the actor, who was not as used to long shooting days as some of the other actors might have been, developed agonizing pain in his back and, consequently, had many sleepless nights. With a 4:00 A.M. makeup call time and shooting days that ended close to midnight, the actor found himself getting even less sleep than Michael J. Fox doing double duty with *Family Ties*, and without any of the pats on the back for his efforts.

Weissman recalls that on one occasion when Spielberg was visiting the set, the executive producer noticed the actor, with his legs up in the air and back resting against a large horizontal surface. "He walked up to me and said, 'So, Crispin, I see you got your million dollars after all,'" Weissman says. "It wasn't until then that I realized I was saving production nine hundred eighty thousand dollars." However, not everyone agrees that this actually happened. "Jeffrey has told the 'Steven Spielberg million dollars' story many times, but I'm not sure it's true," Bob Gale says. "Steven was never part of the negotiations for Crispin, and I'm not sure he was aware of any of the actual numbers discussed. Jeffrey has often exaggerated things, and this may be such a story."

Several months after *Back to the Future Part II* was released in theaters, Weissman received an unsolicited telephone call from Glover. It was a conversation the replacement actor was simultaneously looking forward to, to make sure there were no hard feelings, and dreading, because he feared there might be. Glover never mentioned his replacement's performance. Instead, he went on what Weissman describes as a "whiny diatribe," ranting about his frustration with the way things shook out with the sequel, and his unhappiness with Zemeckis and company, who, in his view, created the problem. "Crispin explained to me how cruel Universal had been to him on the first film," Weissman says. "He said the producers made him cry in front of extras and abused him. Crispin said he was told that he would be paid twice scale, with no negotiation power, to use clips of him from the first movie."

The two spoke at length, with Glover occasionally having hyperemotional moments. Weissman commiserated as best he could, and was asked by Glover if he minded sharing any horror stories he had from the shoot. Dean Cundey's "Crispin without the trouble"? Check. Robert Zemeckis shouting, "Crispin!" while shooting the Enchantment Under the Sea dance? No problem. Steven Spielberg's "million dollars"? Right away. Lea Thompson's cold shoulder? You bet. Without Weissman's knowledge, Glover recounted the telephone conversation to his attorney, who, on October 15, 1990, after *Back to the Future Part III*'s release, filed suit for the misappropriation of Crispin Glover's likeness. The actor maintained that since Weissman was put in prosthetics to look like Glover, and was instructed to mimic his voice and mannerisms, the producers violated his intellectual property and right to publicity. Furthermore, the actor alleged that this was done maliciously because of sour grapes over the failed negotiations. The comments made to Weissman on set were sprinkled throughout the suit as evidence of the *Future* team's ill feelings toward Glover. The actor was targeting Universal Studios, Amblin Entertainment, and U-Drive Productions, a one-off entity created by Amblin for the film in case of situations just like this, to prevent lawsuits going after money or assets for more than one film.

The defendants weren't buying Glover's version of events. They maintained that they had negotiated with the actor in good faith, and besides, George was their character. Unless the actor was making a case that he *was* the character, Zemeckis and company were at no fault for bringing George back for the sequels with a different actor. "He had no grounds, as we had already vetted everything through Universal's lawyers," Gale says. "They confirmed we were entitled to recast the role with another actor and use footage of Crispin from *Part I* in *Part II*." But the case would never be argued in front of a judge. In July 1991, the two parties settled out of court for an undisclosed amount, allegedly in the neighborhood of $500,000. "The insurance company, who would have been responsible for bearing the cost of the lawsuit, decided it was cheaper to pay off Crispin than to pay lawyers and have to go to court, so Crispin took the money and dropped the lawsuit," Gale continues. When adding in the amount he earned from the filmmakers using the footage of him from the first film, Glover likely received the same amount of money he would have made had he participated in the sequels. Perhaps more significantly, Glover has also claimed that as a result of this suit, a rule was instituted within the Screen Actors Guild that movie studios can't re-create an actor's likeness with technical means without that actor's approval. However, some within SAG doubt this rule actually exists, and Glover has never publicly cited the specific rule. Regardless, it all proves that "Crispin without the trouble" can still lead to plenty of trouble.

While the lawsuit was ongoing, and even after its conclusion, Jeffrey Weissman struggled to parlay his major motion picture credit into more high-profile jobs. He was essentially blacklisted after being perceived as a mole and participant in Glover's lawsuit. He managed to get hired on an episode of *Murder, She Wrote*, but was fired and told that he was cast in error. The casting director said she didn't realize that he was "unable" to be hired. Decades later, Weissman, who has continued to work as an actor since the film's release, can see both sides of the situation and has made his peace with his *Back to the Future* experience. "It was disappointing to me that my agents didn't negotiate well," he says. "At the time, Universal and all the studios seemed to be run by attorneys, bean counters, and various other rude people, and I didn't have the great agent I had when I did the Clint Eastwood film *Pale Rider*. I was sad that I was sharing the screen with Lea and Michael, costarring, and I was getting a couple thousand dollars. The studio kept me in the dark until the eleventh hour. I don't know that they would have given me fifty thousand a week if I'd asked for it, but I wish my agent had gone for it. They only settled for a little bit better than what I got on the Eastwood film four years before, which was not all that much.

"I don't think I am bitter that Crispin made more money than I did," he continues. "But I was a little bitter that he didn't at least call me and thank me. I don't want to be full of regrets, but it took a while to get over the shitty thing that Universal did. The studio knew they were doing wrong. Spielberg knew he was doing wrong. The producers knew they were doing wrong. But they were also forced into it by Crispin handcuffing them during negotiations."

From his vantage point, Bob Gale also sees Weissman as a victim, but only as one hoisted by his own petard. "Jeffrey and his agent were given the ground rules from the start," Gale says. "We told him this job was not going to make him a star, he would not be doing any publicity, and he couldn't promote himself because we didn't want to call attention to the fact that Crispin wasn't in the sequels. We also told Jeffrey that under no circumstances should he ever talk with Crispin, so we were all incensed with him when we learned that he did, and even more so when we learned that his statements were cited in the lawsuit. Jeffrey often portrays himself as a victim, but we paid him more money than he'd ever made before—two thousand five hundred dollars a week, which is not a bad salary for an actor in a smaller role, especially in 1989 dollars. Then he knowingly violated our conditions by talking with Crispin, just to satisfy his own ego. Thus, he made himself into a pariah, because no one wants to hire an actor who creates problems. I guess portraying George McFly causes actors to make bad decisions."

The discomfort Weissman felt on set and the subsequent lawsuit stemming from his condemnation of how he was treated during the filming process were not the only hiccups Universal and Amblin had to encounter as a result of *Back to the Future Part II*. As George McFly hung upside down in Marty's future home, shooting was under way on what would be one of the most memorable sequences in the franchise—not only for fans, but also for the team of stunt performers dressed in futuristic costumes who were swinging in the sky from a variety of cables, metal frames, and faux gravity-defying flotation devices.

8. THOSE BOARDS DON'T WORK

Monday, November 20, 1989

*P*art II hadn't even been released yet and already there were phone calls. Scott Ross, the general manager of ILM, had arrived at work with a number of messages waiting for him in his office. He looked through the stack of pink "while you were out" notes that were placed neatly in a pile on his desk. Without exception, each message was about *Back to the Future* and, more specifically, about hoverboards. The curious thing was, as he looked through the names of the people who had tried to reach him, none belonged to people he knew. He was confused, partially because he couldn't understand how these messages had gotten to him, and partly because he couldn't understand why so many people were calling about hoverboards. Before he had a chance to piece together what was going on, his line rang.

"Hello, I wanted to know where I could purchase a hover-board for my son." It was a woman who sounded like she was call-ing from the Southwest. Then it clicked. The preceding Friday night, NBC had aired a three-hour special event starting at

8:00 P.M., *Back to the Future*, followed by a half-hour sneak peek at the making of *Part II*. Leslie Nielsen, from the *Naked Gun* film series, hosted the program. There were sit-downs with cast and crew, along with behind-the-scenes footage of the upcoming film, which was just days away from release. During one interview, after the hoverboards were shown, Robert Zemeckis explained without the slightest hint of humor that the devices were real and had been kept off toy shelves because of concerned parents groups feeling they were too dangerous. The director was kidding, of course, but not everyone watching at home got the joke.

"I don't think you understand. They're visual effects. They don't—"

"Oh, no, we understand that, but my kid wants one. I was wondering if they were dangerous."

"They're not dangerous because they aren't real."

"But I saw them on television and the director said they were." Scott Ross didn't know it at the time, but this was just the beginning of the correspondence he, and several others involved with the film, would field about the movie. The occasional question would be asked about other futuristic devices in the film, but the number one thing that people wanted to know about was the levitating device that Marty used throughout the picture.

The response wasn't so much irritating as it was flattering. Zemeckis and company had felt the omnipotent presence of the audience throughout production. Now, for the first time, the public was weighing in on the filmmakers' follow-up, even before the picture was out. There couldn't have been a better sign that the reception to *Part II* might be just as strong as it was for the first film. "When you set out to make a movie, you're just making the movie," Neil Canton says. "You love it, you give everything you have to it, but it's just a movie. When the movie becomes a phenomenon, it's kind of overwhelming in a way. All of a sudden people are asking questions and want to know things you never really stopped to think about. Of course hoverboards didn't exist, but we made it seem like it was the coolest thing going and people just totally bought into it. Parents would write letters asking where they could get one for their child for Christmas. You go, *Wait a second. I understand that a young child may think that it's a real thing, but how could a parent think that also?* At one point Bob Gale prepared a list of answers to the most-asked questions that we would get, so we could just send that answer. It was very overwhelming for all of us."

Since he was initially approached to design the futuristic elements back in the conceptual stages of the sequel, John Bell continued working on the hoverboards once *Paradox* was officially green-lighted. He took some of his initial sketches to the ILM model shop to turn them into fully realized models. Compared to what materialized on-screen, those early models had a lot more embellishment. They were larger, shaped more like a wakeboard or snowboard, and some even had engines. "From those early stages it just kept getting whittled down, because they knew they were going to have to make a lot of them for the film and they didn't want to blow a lot of money reproducing intricate designs," Bell says. "That's how things got so streamlined. I composed newer drawings for Bob to see, and that's when the hard decisions were made."

As production neared, the designs that would be realized on-screen started to take shape. Griff's "Pit Bull" board was colored an intimidating black and red, adorned with an illustration of a growling dog with a choke collar. The sides were jagged to evoke the look of bite marks, and the front had two large fangs jutting out from it. It was established early on that the main board

Marty uses would be pink, as it was to be originally owned by a young girl and, presumably, toy companies would continue to use gendered hues even well into the future. Initially it was thought that Swatch, the Swiss watch company, would have their name on the boards, but at the last minute it came down from on high that a switch was being made to Mattel, the recognizable company behind Barbie. Nothing fundamentally changed with the design; the company was sent a copy of the sketch with their logo on it and signed off almost instantly.

When it came time to construct the boards, some were built out of wood, while those that would endure less wear and tear were made out of Styrofoam. In order to sell the illusion of their functionality, Zemeckis, along with Ken Ralston and Michael Lantieri, followed a principle that every magician knows: Always keep them guessing. "You had to come up with different methods of cinematic magic to make it look like these boards were hovering," Steve Starkey says. "And so every trick that anybody could come up with was used. It was the most challenging part of the shoot." In watching any of the hoverboard sequences, especially the extended ones like the chase in the Hill Valley square and the tunnel where Biff is trying to reclaim the sports almanac, one can see that a mixture of techniques were used. In some cases, the effects that appear amazing on-screen were really quite low-tech. Thin metal wire legs were placed right in the middle of the underside of some Styrofoam props, so that when Michael J. Fox threw them down, they would wobble as if levitating. In shots where one end of the board was out of frame, the other side was sometimes held by a crew member until Fox grabbed it and tucked it under his arm. When the actors' feet were obscured, they were often shot from the waist up and put on actual skateboards. Sometimes they were pulled on a large dolly. Large sheets of plywood would be added to the ground in order to create additional height in comparison with the rest of what was in the frame.

Of course, there were other, more complicated effects. The actors were also suspended on wires and flown, part of what created the realistic look that deceived so many in the viewing audience. Prior to *Part II*, ILM would have manually rotoscoped the wires out of the scene, a process by which each frame is drawn over by an animator in order to hide the effects mechanisms. For *Part II*, Doug Smythe and Les Dittert at ILM created a way to expedite and improve upon this process digitally. Someone at the effects house would find a wire in a shot and identify it for a computerized system in a few frames, and then the machine would take over and find the wire in each shot. Digitally, the colors in the frame on either side of the wire would be smudged together to effectively paint over each unwanted piece of apparatus. As a finishing touch, the film grain in the treated area would be replicated in order to create consistency across the shot. The process was innovative by 1989 standards, and four years later, Smythe and Dittert were presented with a special Academy Award for Scientific and Technical Achievement for developing the technology, along with their colleagues Mark Leather and George H. Joblove at ILM.

Unlike what would be done today if the film were made, computers helped to remove some of the mechanical elements from shots, but didn't assist in the actual illusion of hovering. The more challenging shots to capture visually were often performed in front of a green screen and then optically created in postproduction. "We were faced with how to make the hoverboards practically," Dean Cundey says. "It was done in a realistic-seeming way. Nowadays, computers allow us to stretch reality past what the audience can understand as being real. It becomes the fantastical. What we were trying to accomplish was something that seemed fantastical, but would be accepted as real. There was something about hoverboards that wasn't so unbelievable. We thought everybody would love to have one, or at least all the skateboarders."

"Now audiences have become so sophisticated because the effects are so unbelievable," Scott Ross, the general manager of ILM, says. "We know Godzilla's not running through the streets and Spider-Man can't jump from building to building. Because of that, the audience has become aware that they were just done on a computer. Back in the eighties, people really didn't get that they were visual effects." Part of the issue, as Ross sees it, is that studios used to go through much greater lengths to conceal the tricks they used in moviemaking. *Michael J. Fox is doing his own singing! Pay no attention to the man behind the curtain.* For those at ILM, there was a constant struggle to be recognized for their work publicly. "The studios wound up owning all of the footage, models, and everything else having to do with the movie because they paid us for our services," he says. "When we did *Who Framed Roger Rabbit,* I desperately wanted the world to know that Industrial Light & Magic really made *Roger Rabbit* happen. There were incredible amounts of work that went into it. Disney was dead-set against it. Particularly back in those days, their public relations department would never allow anybody to do an interview with the visual effects team on any film, because they thought that it would take away from what the film was all about.

"That's obviously changed, because if we look at the top fifty films of all time, all of them are visual effects or animated films," he continues. "Sometime in the late nineties, early 2000s, the studios started to get hip to the fact that Tom Hanks and Sylvester Stallone were not really putting people's butts in the movie theaters; visual effects were. Once they started to realize that, things started to change, at least on the PR side."

For the actors, the experience of being on a hoverboard was unforgettable—but not unanimously for positive reasons. To the untrained eye, the scene where Griff's gang is chasing Marty across the Courthouse Square is perfectly executed; however, to those who were on set the day the crash through the clock tower was filmed, it was a terrifying experience due to a near-fatal injury involving Cheryl Wheeler, one of the stuntwomen hired for the movie. On May 9, 1990, Wheeler and her then-husband, Michael Dixon, filed suit against Universal Pictures, Amblin Entertainment, and more than a dozen others who worked on *Part II*, including Steven Spielberg, Robert Zemeckis, and Michael Lantieri, all stemming from a majorly botched stunt that resulted in a number of expensive surgeries to her arm, face, and jaw. For Wheeler, her time in Hill Valley will always mark a defining moment in her career and life, even though there were many days when she wished she could forget all about *Back to the Future* and the prop that so many people covet.

Several months before the incident, preparation for the hoverboard stunts began at Max Kleven's ranch, a large piece of property that was perfect for a little trial-and-error experimentation. Kleven had worked on stunts on the first *Future* and, afterward, was second-unit director for the scenes shot in the United States for *Roger Rabbit*. Zemeckis was pleased with his direction and invited him to continue serving in that capacity on *Paradox*, freeing up Frank Marshall to devote his attention to *Indiana Jones and the Last Crusade*. Richie Gaona and Gary Morgan, two stuntmen referred to Kleven through mutual friends, assisted in the trial run. "We did about two or three weeks of testing," Gaona says. "They would test for a couple of days, send in the video of what we did to see if the director liked it, then we would come back to make some changes." In the earliest tests, the temporary hoverboard was just a skateboard with the wheels popped off. The base was screwed into the stuntmen's shoes, and the performers were put in harnesses that attached at the hips and were connected to a large crane. But the effect didn't work. It was obvious that the board was attached to their feet and their hover power was coming from a different point in their bodies. The crew tried substituting the skateboard for a long piece of Styrofoam, but the result was the same.

Time for plan B. Wires were attached to the front and back of the immobile skateboard, and a harness was put around the performers' legs, resting at their hips, with two rings on either side that the wires were fed through, giving the performers full mobility to move their legs and bend their knees to help sell the illusion. "It was at a time when wiring was expensive," Morgan says. "So they used really thin wire, but they would snap. We'd be hanging from the other wire, the board would come up, hit our belt where the loop was, and we'd just be dangling." The performers were attached to a large crane, which was moved around in a circle. Although it looked better, there was still something off, and so back to the drawing board they went.

Plan C. No more circular movements. This time, the crane operator pulled back and moved the arm of his machine in a large swinging motion. The move was perfect—the stuntmen looked like they were gliding on air. With the approval of the special effects team and the director's blessing, the tests were wrapped. Along with Gaona and Morgan, David Rowden and Lisa McCullough were hired as doubles for Biff and Spike, the lone female in Griff's gang. McCullough was an accomplished stuntwoman and a dead ringer for Darlene Vogel, the actress hired to play the role, making it obvious why she had gotten the gig.

Once they were on set, they all found the mood to be relatively lighthearted—not casual, but focused and fun. During their first take of the scene in Café 80s, the futuristic answer to Lou's Café in the fifties, where Griff calls Marty a chicken, Michael J. Fox pulled a small prank that cracked up the actors portraying the gang members. It was right after lunch, and Fox had swiped a ketchup bottle from craft services. When Darlene Vogel reached down to grab his crotch—*What's the matter, McFly? You got no scrote?*—she felt the hard glass bottle poking through his blue jeans. Vogel didn't laugh, trying not to break character and ruin the first shot of that scene, but she had to fight to keep her composure.

"Cut!" Laughter erupted out of the actress, and Fox, and then rippled through the rest of the gang. "Yeah, Michael," she said. "You wish."

When it came time to tackle the stunts, the stunt performers watched from their trailer as the effects team tested the big finale of the chase scene: the clock tower crash. The concept was simple. The four members of the stunt team would all be attached to a large crane. It would move to the left, then the right, giving the stunt people enough momentum to swing toward the tower. Once they all made it through the window, a button would be pressed by a member of the effects team, cutting the wires and dropping the performers to the ground, where they would land on large air bags inside, out of the camera's view. During the testing of this process, in lieu of the performers, large sandbags were used to simulate their bodies. There was a move left, right, a swing, push, cut, and drop. One sandbag hit the ground, missing the air bags entirely. "Shit. That one was supposed to be you," one stuntperson said to another. The effects team set up the stunt again: left, right, swing, push, cut, drop. Two sandbags missed the air bags. The other two landed on the right spot, but failed to fall at the same time. When an air bag was hit, it deflated, so if one stunt performer didn't fall on it at the same time as his or her partner, he or she would end up free-falling toward the cement. The tests continued. Sometimes the process worked perfectly, most times it didn't, but what was most alarming to McCullough was that it was never the same. Nevertheless, the performers were willing to give it a shot. The team suited up and gave it a good sporting try.

"It was a wreck," Morgan says. "One time the guy that was on the button cut Lisa and Dave loose. Richie and I swung towards the other air bag. For some reason, he didn't cut the cable right away. He waited until we swung back a little, then cut it, and we went headfirst into an empty air bag. The fact that we didn't break our necks was amazing. I was right over Lisa when he cut me loose and almost landed right on top of her. I was at least twenty-five feet in the air and going headfirst." Part of the problem might have been whose jurisdiction the stunt was left to. If *Back to the Future Part II* were shot today, it is unlikely the special effects team would be responsible for designing the sequence and building the rigging for it to be executed. That would be left to a stunt crew who, first and foremost, would be looking out for the safety of the performers. This isn't to say that Michael Lantieri and his team didn't factor in the well-being of the four performers doing stunts—of course they did—but it's possible the visual impact of the shot might have taken precedent. McCullough voiced her concerns. She said she thought it was unsafe and someone could get seriously injured. Assurances were given that things would be okay, but she wasn't willing to take that chance. That was her last day on set.

Like Gaona and Morgan, Cheryl Wheeler had also previously worked for Walter Scott, the stunt coordinator, and was an acquaintance of Max Kleven's. She was asked to come in and was given a thorough explanation as to why the first stuntwoman had left.

Changes were being made, she was told, in light of McCullough's concerns. If she wanted the job, it was hers, but she should know the situation she was walking into before making a decision.

"Well, I'm not afraid of the stunt," she said. "I just want to make sure it's set up properly."

"We are going to make sure everything is set up properly," Scott said. "You're not going to have anything to worry about."

She stayed silent for a few moments, but there wasn't too much to think about. They were being up front and seemed to have learned from their mistakes. What did she have to lose? "Okay," she said. "I'm on board."

There were more rehearsals in the days before the clock tower stunt. Because tempered glass would have been too heavy, potentially posing a real danger to those underneath when it shattered and rained down from two stories above, sugarcoated candy glass was used. During the practice runs the glass hadn't been installed, but the new method of performing the stunt was being implemented. Each stuntperson was suspended from a rectangular frame, one at each corner. The frame was attached to a large crane through a single wire, which would swing back and forth to cast the four into motion. Each performer held on to a small trapeze that was behind them and that would propel them forward toward the tower when they let go. On "Action," they would let go, fly forward, and make their way through the glass window. A crew member would press a button, the cable would be cut, and they would fall onto the air bags. Unlike the first go-round, this set of tests went off without a hitch. The stunt performers felt good until—

"Wait, you guys have to take all of this down?" Installing the glass would take two full days, and because Zemeckis and his producers were trying to maximize their time, the stunt had to be broken down so shooting of other scenes could continue on the town square. Wheeler was concerned. What was the point of testing it a dozen times if they were going to break everything down and put it back up before doing it for real? "How do you know you took down the marks exactly where they have to be?"

"We did, Cheryl," Michael Lantieri said. "I promise it's marked, and it will be exactly the same when we start it up on shooting day." And that was it. She didn't press any further and he didn't continue the conversation. The two went their separate ways as the effects team continued dismantling. Perhaps foreshadowing the fragility of even the best-laid plans, there was a small earthquake tremor in Los Angeles while the glass was being installed. Everyone on set turned their focus to the clock tower, as the sugared sheets shook in their frame. The crew was panicked, afraid they would vibrate out and shatter on the ground below, but they didn't. Crisis averted. Confidence in the plan was restored, except when shooting day came and there were some deviations from what had been practiced and agreed upon. Right before shooting, Gary Morgan spotted Lantieri making inroads toward Griff's board with props in his hands.

"What's that for?"

"We're going to shoot a rocket as you're going through the window." The idea was that, with the magic of editing, it would look like the sparks were coming from Griff's "Pit Bull" board.

"Really? I didn't know about that."

"Oh, no. We told you about that."

"Hey, Richie, did you know about it?"

"Nope. I didn't know."

"All right. Just don't hit us in the ass with it."

Once again, the matter was settled. Walter Scott, Michael Lantieri, and their crews were doing some last-minute troubleshooting. "Okay, what's the worst thing that could happen?" The performers could hit the back wall when they went through the glass, but the stunt coordinator concluded that was a long shot. For extra precaution, blue pads were added to cover every inch inside of the tower. If someone missed their mark, they would still be covered. Everything was in place. It was time to take to the sky.

Before filming, Wheeler was placed in makeup. She had to wear a wig and a large prosthetic scar on her face, and a red contact lens was put in her right eye, like her counterpart Darlene Vogel. "They actually got the idea because one of my eyes is actually two different colors," Vogel says. "They looked at my eye and they said, 'That's really cool. We're going to do something with that.' They put a full red contact in it, which I had to go get fitted for. It wasn't comfortable to wear that thing. It didn't have a hole in the middle, so you'd see red as you looked out." The process of transforming the stuntwoman into Spike, along with hair and makeup, took over an hour and a half, significantly longer than it took to prepare her male counterparts. When she arrived for the stunt, she was taken aback to see Charlie Croughwell, Michael J. Fox's stunt double, in her harness. He was about the same height, and maybe a little heavier. She could assume what was going on; Croughwell was being tested out in her harness "just in case." Walter Scott approached her quickly, obviously ready to get on with the show.

"Okay, saddle up."

"Are you sure all the marks are right from the other day? How are you sure everything is exactly the same?"

The stunt coordinator looked at her with an odd mixture of compassion and exasperation in his eyes. "Cheryl, you're getting cold feet." She could feel her back stiffening. "I'm going to put Charlie in your clothes and let him do the stunt."

"Walter, I am not getting cold feet at all. I just want to understand. I was in hair and makeup and haven't been out there to see the stunt setup." She wanted to say a lot more. She wanted to put her foot down and insist on seeing the marks. She wanted to say she trusted them, because she really did, but she trusted her eyes and gut more. But she didn't do any of those things. Maybe she bit her tongue because she was relatively new to the business. She had just started doing stunt work in 1985 and didn't want to ruffle any feathers, while Walter Scott had two decades of experience under his belt. Who was she to ask him to prove anything to her? Maybe she was afraid, also, of appearing weak in front of the other stunt performers, or, more accurately, stuntmen. Lisa Mc-Cullough had already left with "cold feet," and now Wheeler was exhibiting similar symptoms. She was as tough as these guys, wasn't she? Why weren't they asking questions? She got in her harness, which Croughwell had already stepped out of.

But her mind still wasn't at ease. She called over Greg Tippie, the special effects team member responsible for pressing the wire-cutting button. She asked him if everything was good to go and exactly the same as last time. "Yeah," he said. "Listen, you do your job and I'll do mine." They were minutes away from starting. She was already dangling.

"Your job and my job are really intertwined here," she said. "I have a right to ask these questions." As it turned out, things weren't exactly the same, not even with how he was planning on doing his job. During the test run, Tippie hid behind one of the pillars of the clock tower and stared up, counting the stunt crew as they made their way through the face of the building—one, two, three, four. Once he could see they were all in, he pressed the button and down they came. But today he decided to move inside the tower. He thought it would be easier to tell if everyone had made it through if he was on the same side. But candy glass isn't transparent. It has a dark tint to it and, because it's made of sugar, actually sparkles in the light. You can see through it, sure, but only shapes and figures. With clear glass, Tippie would be able to see the stunt performers making their way toward the window. But now that would be more difficult, and after the stunt performers made it through the clock tower, the glass would rain down and it would be difficult to tell in a split second if everyone had made it through. He started to walk away, but she called after him.

"What if one of us doesn't make it inside the clock tower?" It was actually the first time the possibility had come to her. It might have been the first time the possibility had come to anyone. "There's going to be all this smoke from that rocket they're using for Griff's hoverboard. How will you know if someone doesn't make it in?"

"Cheryl," he said, "it's the best place for me to be. You have to trust me."

"But that's not how we rehearsed it." She looked at him, he looked back, and their mutual silence and stares terminated the conversation. The debate over the stunt was officially over. It was time to shoot. She was suspended from the far left side of the frame, then Gary Morgan and Richie Gaona. David Rowden was going to land much lower, just above the courthouse steps. The performers were lifted up and clicked in their quick-release hooks. The giant crane started backing up slowly, maybe fifty or sixty feet, while the stunt team was suspended from a long cable. Kleven asked if everybody was ready, and on "Action," the hooks were released. The four started swinging. Wheeler felt the rush of air against her face. They were picking up speed and, to her horror, veering to the left. *I'm going to hit this pillar.* They raced forward. She was headed on a trajectory straight for the set piece. *I'm going to hit this pillar.* Everyone was off course, and she wasn't sure if Gary Morgan was going to make it through the glass either, but she was certain about her fate. *I'm going to hit this—*

She was spinning like a figure skater, parallel to the ground like Superman in midflight. She hit the pillar dead-on, but because she was covered in shin guards, knee guards, elbow pads, and other well-concealed braces hidden within her costume, she felt fine. A little disoriented, perhaps, but fine. As she was rotating, she noticed she was alone. The rest of her colleagues must have made it. This was supposed to be a one-take shot, but whatever went wrong meant they would have to do it again. Maybe they'd be pissed, but she was okay and, most important, Greg Tippie hadn't cut the cable. He must have seen she hadn't made it inside.

Which might have happened if he had stayed outside the pillar. Or if the special effects team hadn't gone with opaque trick glass. Or if there wasn't so much smoke from the rocket. Or if she had gone with her gut and gotten answers to her questions. But that wasn't what happened. He pressed the button and the stunt performers were released. As two other stuntmen headed toward the blue pads, Wheeler fell flat, like she was lying in bed, from thirty feet in the air. She knew she was going to die. She was certain of it, as certain as she had been that she would hit that pillar. She was falling from too high an altitude. She was going to die on the Universal Studios backlot.

Inside, the rest of her team knew something had gone awry. "When we landed, we had to keep our eyes closed, because of the raining breakaway glass," Gary Morgan says. "I was way in the corner, right next to the camera where Cheryl should've been. I opened my eyes and I said, 'Where's Cheryl?' and somebody pointed outside. I got up and Cheryl was laying on the concrete and the pool of blood by her head was getting bigger. I thought she was dead. It was quite a moment, because you prepare for the worst in any stunt, but it just went wrong and nobody expected it to."

When Wheeler woke up, she had three distinct thoughts. She was aware that she was alive, and was thankful for it. She also realized she couldn't move and feared she was paralyzed. Then she wiggled her toes. She wasn't paralyzed. She realized she had been immobilized. When she landed, the stuntwoman's face had slammed against the concrete. She had a concussion, for starters, and everything was crushed on her face between her nose and left ear. "The medics were right there," Morgan says. "They had ambulances, and the minute they rolled her over, she started talking, but she was out cold. She had no idea what she was saying, and sweet Cheryl was just going, 'What did I do wrong? Was that my fault? Did I do something wrong?'"

As the medics on set tended to the stuntwoman, everyone else remained stunned. There was the inherent urge to do something, but there was really nothing anyone on the crew could do. "The rest of the actors and I ended up not even working that day," Darlene Vogel says. "We couldn't believe it. They had to shut down production that day and afterwards."

Wheeler was rushed to the hospital, and the rest of her crew pretended to be her family to get access to see her. "If you had fallen backwards, and the back of your head hit the concrete, you'd be dead," her doctor told her. "Or you'd wish you were dead, because you'd be a vegetable. I've seen people that fall backwards eight feet off a ladder on the back of their head and it crushes like an eggshell." In addition to her body position when she landed, her harness, which had been specially designed for Michael J. Fox, saved her life.

"It was done very old-school, the way the stunt was set up," she says. "It should've been done completely differently, and there should've been pads underneath us outside the clock tower. They had safety people below us, in case something went wrong. An extra took a picture of one of them directly underneath me after I hit the pillar. I still have it to this day. Glass was raining down and she was ducking her head. I was right above her, and she was running and ducking. The glass was two stories high, and so who was going to be able to help me? If I did fall, what was she going to do? I was going to kill her if I landed on her, so she just got out of the way and I hit the concrete.

"It was a big issue in the stunt industry, because Max Kleven and Walter Scott were old-school guys," she continues. "They were real well-known in their early careers. Walter was a cowboy. He was great on a horse, but as far as rigging and a stunt of this magnitude, he was out of his league. He really had to depend on the effects guys. We couldn't figure out why we couldn't put crash pads below, outside the clock tower. Max just said, 'No, we want the lead up. We want the audience to see a big overview master shot, and we can't see crash pads in the shot.' It was one thing after another, and it was just one of those things that went real foul. Everything that could go wrong did go wrong. That was the end of this job for me. I did come back down three or four weeks later. They were still shooting. They had gotten another girl to replace me."

Following the incident, Lisa McCullough came to visit her in the hospital. She reiterated the feelings she'd had about the stunt all along—she may have even used the words "I told them so"—and expressed her condolences for what had happened. Greg Tippie came to visit too. He sat at Wheeler's bedside, saw her badly bruised and broken body, and said, "God, Cheryl, I'm so sorry. I should have listened to you."

"Greg, if you had been behind that pillar, you would have heard me smack it," she said. It was uncomfortable to talk, but she had learned her lesson about staying silent. "You would have *seen* me smack it. You would have seen me dangling there and you wouldn't have pressed that button."

"I know. You're right, but who could have known you were going to hit that pillar?"

Without the presence of social media, and with the diligence of the team at Universal, news of the incident remained sparse. Word spread among those in the stunt industry, but most in the mainstream media and general public were none the wiser. In 1983, Steven Spielberg and director John Landis caught all sorts of hell when a stunt went wrong while filming *The Twilight Zone: The Movie*. Two elementary-school-aged actors, who were hired and paid under the table despite a California law that prohibits child performers from working at night and near explosives, were fatally injured along with actor Vic Morrow. News spread like wildfire and a lengthy trial ensued between 1986 and 1987. Universal did not want Wheeler's incident to receive even a fraction of that attention. They did all they could to suppress a leak of the information, and until her lawsuit was filed, they were successful.

Cheryl Wheeler didn't want to sue Universal, and she too didn't want news of the incident to get out. She was new to the business and wanted to work again, but more important, she had liked working on *Paradox*. She enjoyed the rest of the stunt performers and, save for the day of her drop, had nothing but respect for Max Kleven and Walter Scott. Although she didn't work with Robert Zemeckis directly—most of the hoverboard stunt work that she was involved with was shot second-unit— she thought he was a visionary and full of positive energy. He visited the set from time to time while they were working, and like magic, his presence made everyone work a little bit harder and remember the importance of what they were doing. They weren't curing diseases or sending men to the moon—they knew that—but they were making a sequel to a movie that meant something to many millions of people around the world. Those people were counting on them to give them another experience that they would enjoy and cherish, and that meant something.

But she did sue. She felt she had no choice. Over the course of the next several months, she endured three reconstructive surgeries to repair her arm and face. Her doctor waited a year before the final operation, a particularly arduous one on her jaw, which required that she have three pints of her own blood drawn in advance of her surgery. She filled out a workers' compensation claim and was given $13,000 for her accident, barely enough to make a small dent in the mountain of bills she had acquired while recuperating and unable to take another job. At the time of her incident, the stuntwoman was at the top of her game, earning a quarter of a million dollars annually from the various projects she was able to pick up over the course of the year. Now her career was being sold back to her at a drastically reduced rate. "I was like, 'That's crazy,'" she says. "'You can't just expect me to take workman's comp for something that wasn't my fault. Not only did I not do anything wrong, but I argued about how it was being set up.'" She tried to negotiate, but to no avail. Then she lawyered up. "He just said, 'Ladies and gentlemen, you do not want me to get her on the stand,'" she says. "'Trust me, she is a sympathetic person and you may end up losing a lot of money.' I wasn't asking for a lot. I was asking for what I lost while I was in recovery." The movie studio settled out of court, and within a year the stuntwoman returned to work. Not terribly demanding gigs, but easy ones like riding in the passenger seat of a stunt car. She knew they were "charity jobs" she was being offered by friends and associates who were eager to see her return to normalcy. Instead of feeling sad for what she had lost, she was happy for what she still had. Within a few years, she did return to more rigorous stunts, a career she is happy to still have as a part of her life decades after it was almost ripped away from her. She even worked with Walter Scott again on other projects, but their relationship was forever changed. She asked questions now, not only of him, but also of other stunt coordinators on other projects. "Trust me" were words she no longer accepted.

The hoverboard incident was a horrifying experience, but one the stuntwoman doesn't necessarily regret going through. As a component of her rehabilitation, she worked closely with Lindsey Duncan, a nutritionist whom she married in 1999. She has continued to work and is a motivational speaker who regularly talks about her experiences. "I was at the apex of my career," she says. "When you're in this business, you really do believe that the world revolves around you. A lot of people in Hollywood are like that. It's a funny mentality, but when you're on a big film like that, it just consumes you. It's exciting and there are a lot of big stars. You feel important that you're doubling a lead person.

"Then, all of a sudden, you wake up with your face crushed in and everything that you depend on—your job—is crushed," she continues. "It was a huge wake-up call for me spiritually, or emotionally, or mentally, however you want to look at it. I knew I had to find some meaning for this. Everybody has their type of tragedy, whether it's a car wreck or cancer; we all have been dealt these blows. If we don't get it sooner, we're going to get it later. Life is just that good and that bad."

With Wheeler in recovery, the production continued on. Reshooting that scene was never a serious consideration, and as a result, the stuntwoman's body can clearly be seen descending toward the ground outside of the clock tower in the finished film as the glass is falling. Despite the accident, the production team was proud of the hoverboard sequences in the film, and when filming wrapped on August 1, 1989, they had a strong feeling that they had overcome the pressure they all felt and had made a pretty enjoyable picture. The only unknown was whether or not the audience would agree. There was little doubt that *Part II* would have a strong opening weekend—goodwill from the first film and a strong marketing campaign guaranteed that—but the Bobs didn't just want their movie to turn a profit. For them, it was more important that their fans, the ones who were in the back of their minds every day of writing and shooting the picture, felt good about their return trip to Hill Valley and remained enthusiastic about seeing the conclusion of the story the next summer.

As with the first movie, once the cameras stopped rolling on *Part II*, there was little time to celebrate. There was only a short hiatus before work had to begin on *Three*, the working title for the next chapter in the Marty and Doc story. As *Back to the Future Part II*'s theatrical release neared, Zemeckis and company's excitement was more measured. With filming already significantly under way on the final film in the series, there wasn't the same sense of finality as there was in the summer of 1985.

The test screenings for *Part II* went well, but there wasn't the same overwhelming enthusiasm that had been present in the theater during the first movie's previews. The initial response about the hoverboards on the television special was reassuring, but not as conclusive as screaming test audiences and a rush to release from Sid Sheinberg. Universal spent a lot of money promoting the sequel, including partnering with Pizza Hut for a number of television spots, but their efforts were unnecessary. Rival studios conceded defeat early on, making *Part II* the only major motion picture to debut over the Thanksgiving holiday weekend. In its first two days of release, before the official weekend box office receipts were tallied, the movie made more than $22.3 million. Over the next three, $27.8 million more was accumulated. Even without counting those two early-release days, the sequel's haul was the fourth-best opening weekend of the year, behind *Batman*, *Ghostbusters II*, and *Indiana Jones and the Last Crusade*.

Yet still, money couldn't buy the filmmakers complete satisfaction. For starters, the reviews were generally positive, but not overwhelmingly so. While Roger Ebert kept his thumb pointed to the sky, Gene Siskel turned his upside down. For other critics, as well as several audience members, the film's final scene, which showed Marty returning right after the famous clock tower lightning strike in 1955, was a disappointment. "What I remember most is feeling cheated at the end that we weren't getting a resolution, but a cliff-hanger," Leonard Maltin says. "I had just invested two hours in a story that I didn't enjoy and wasn't even rewarded with a resolution." In recent years, it has become somewhat commonplace for films to spread out their story into two installments. *Harry Potter and the Deathly Hallows*, *The Hunger Games: Mockingjay*, and *The Twilight Saga: Breaking Dawn* were all split in half, with the ending of the first left unresolved. Director Peter Jackson spread out *The Hobbit* over an unprecedented three films. Yet in 1989, audiences were not mentally prepared for a third installment when they walked into cinemas, a decision Universal made that Bob Gale believes cost the filmmakers some of the capital they had earned with their fans, and maybe even some capital at the box office.

"I had a big fight with Tom Pollock, who was the studio chief, about the marketing of *Part II*," Gale says. "I absolutely wanted the audience to know before they bought their ticket that this was part two of three. Pollock wanted the audience to think that *Part II* was complete in itself, even though he knew full well it wasn't, and he couldn't have been more wrong. I remember being disappointed with the ending of *The Empire Strikes Back*—Han Solo in carbon-freeze was a bummer. I had no idea that there was going to be a third one, not beforehand, nor even afterward, much less when it would be released." In order to soften the blow of the second installment's ending, Gale took a page from Alexander and Ilya Salkind's playbook, who had shot 1973's *The Three Musketeers* and its sequel consecutively, and insisted that a trailer for *Back to the Future Part III* appear at the end of the movie. But still, for some, the damage was done. "I lost my fight with Pollock and we lost a lot of goodwill with the audience."

"We knew we were doing a risky ending, but that's what we signed on for," Robert Zemeckis says. For the director, the lackluster critical response was all par for the course. Although he willingly signed on for two *Future* follow-ups, Bob Z had, and has, a generally distasteful opinion of sequels. Of the fifteen movies he's directed as of 2015, with the exception of the sequels in question, *Back to the Future* remains the only one of his films that he has revisited. The less-than-stellar response the picture received in the days following its theatrical release didn't rattle his confidence and, in fact, was probably better than he had expected. "I didn't pay any attention to the reviews. First of all, I was still making *Back to the Future Part III* when it came out, so I didn't have a lot of time to even pay attention. A sequel to a gigantic title like that movie is totally critic-proof, and the critics know it, so you knew they were going to shit all over the movie. They hate sequels, yet we keep making them.

"I hate ninety-nine-point-nine percent of all sequels," he continues. "I just don't like them, so I'm like every other normal critic. I don't want to keep going back and seeing the same thing over and over again. I have no interest in that at all, and I don't really understand the sort of coin of the realm that we have with them in the movie business now. It's like watching somebody else play a video game. There's no emotional investment; you just watch a bunch of shit happening, you know? The two best movie sequels are *The Godfather I* and *II* and the *Back to the Future* trilogy, because they really continued the story rather than just going back and doing the same story and same gags all over. We tried really hard to deliver that premise."

A lot of the criticism of *Part II* stemmed from the Biffhorrific sequences, which many critics found to be too much of a departure from the first film. While Marty and Doc remain central to the story, a lot of the action hinges on the actions of Biff, with the stealing of the sports almanac, the altering of the original timeline, and the final battle for the book in the last act of the movie. Tom Wilson's role in the sequel was dramatically increased, which perhaps set up an inescapably darker tone. "When I look back now, the second parts of a lot of our trilogies have been the dark side," Frank Marshall says, referring not only to the *Back to the Future* films, but also the 1981–1989 *Indiana Jones*, 1993–2001 *Jurassic Park*, and 2002–2012 *Bourne Supremacy* trilogies. "Even George Lucas said that about *The Empire Strikes Back*. The second movie is the hardest because you're setting up the third and it's in the middle. It seems like the critics aren't happy with that."

"Maybe it was dark, but I thought it was great because they were determined by the time," Lea Thompson says. "*Back to the Future* was kind of celebrating the fifties as being an innocent time, but Biffhorrific was not innocent. I love *Back to the Future Part II.*"

"The success of the original put more creative pressure on us, there's no question," Bob Gale says. "*Part I* had been an unknown quantity when it was released. No one had any preconceived notions about it, so it took the audience by surprise. In creating sequels for a movie that was such a huge hit, we had to constantly think about the expectations of the audience. We had set a tremendously high bar for ourselves, and even we knew we could never surpass it."

Despite the mixed reaction, *Back to the Future Part II* was still applauded within the industry both overseas and stateside, although the response was more measured. Ken Ralston, Michael Lantieri, John Bell, and Steve Gawley were nominated for Best Visual Effects at the Academy Awards, and the team won in the same category at the BAFTAs in the United Kingdom. Michael J. Fox and Lea Thompson both took home prizes at Nickelodeon's Kids' Choice Awards for their performances, a testament to the movie's impact with those not old enough to enter Biff Tannen's Pleasure Paradise Casino & Hotel in 1985-A.

As the awards season rolled by, Zemeckis and company readied *Part III* for its theatrical release. The preceding year was a tornado of preproduction and long shooting days, ambitious camerawork, and the occasional misstep. Filming the two sequels back-to-back was a smart decision fiscally and creatively, and although *Part II* was not as well received as its predecessor, its strong box office performance further vindicated the idea to split the original long script into two. With the final installment just months away from hitting theaters, Zemeckis and company hoped that the public would show up to see them strive to reach the bar they had set for themselves for the conclusion of the *Back to the Future* trilogy.

9. IT'S A SCIENCE EXPERIMENT

Thursday, May 24, 1990

The crowd outside the Cinerama Dome Theatre on Sunset Boulevard had grown considerably since 2:00 A.M. Several dozen people had skipped work, or cut classes, and forgone sleep during the twilight hours to be among the first in the world to see Robert Zemeckis's last installment in the *Back to the Future* saga. Some were dressed as Marty McFly and Doc Brown, long before cosplay became en vogue. An hour or so before the morning rush, Bob Gale arrived at the movie house, surprised to see people already lined up. He turned back around, and returned a few minutes later with coffee and donuts—enough for all who had been waiting. The fans appreciated the gesture, but it was clear that the producer appreciated them more.

The group that had assembled marked a nice beginning to the end of a long week, and an even longer five-year odyssey. That Monday, the cast and crew had assembled for the world premiere of *Part III*, which was held at the Cineplex Odeon in Los Angeles. It was a star-studded event, with celebrities like

Kurt Russell, Goldie Hawn, Matthew Perry, and Sally Field in attendance. Several women wore brown suede or leather boots, and the men skipped their silk neckties. Not to be outdone in terms of fashion or statement-making, Steven Spielberg wore a light blue button-down shirt with a maroon Aztec sweater with an array of colors woven into the design. He wore a silver necklace with a large piece of turquoise and, topping off his getup, a yellow wide-brimmed hat and black reflective sunglasses. This was not your typical red carpet event, and all in attendance seemed grateful for a little change of pace.

To generate an added bit of publicity, Universal organized "Back-to-Back-to-Back" marathons in nineteen cities across the United States and Canada on the eve of *Back to the Future Part III*'s official theatrical release date. The results were just what the studio had hoped for and, perhaps, even better than the Bobs had expected. In New York City, outside the Cineplex Odeon National, the line stretched over a block from Broadway to Forty-Third Street. In Los Angeles, more than a hundred more patrons had joined the group that Gale had brought refreshments to, waiting six hours before the screenings were to begin. A DeLorean was parked outside, and musicians who looked like ZZ Top, the band that provided music for this installment of the series, were playing "Doubleback," *Part III*'s answer to "The Power of Love." A woman on horseback was doing rope tricks near a juggler passing pie tins from hand to hand. As the start time neared, the rodeo circus reached a fever pitch when Robert Zemeckis, Bob Gale, and Neil Canton arrived. Their congregation greeted them with rapturous cheers, not knowing that the three unexpected guests had one more surprise in store. They pulled out white T-shirts with the *Back to the Future* logo outlined in red. Underneath, the Roman numeral IV was printed within a large circle with a downward diagonal line splitting its diameter. If a silkscreen top can say a thousand words, three of them must have spoken volumes. *It has been fun, but just in case you crazy kids are wondering, the ride is over.*

The director and his producers were hoping for the best, and the attendance at the trilogy screenings firmed their backbones a bit, but they always knew *Back to the Future Part III* was going to be the hardest sell of the three. The second film in the trilogy was released just six months earlier, and while many fans of the franchise loved it, the picture failed to garner the sort of widespread support and success of the first. The box office receipts for the sequel were strong—$118 million domestically, nearly $332 million worldwide—but significantly lower than the original's mammoth success. Internally, there was some concern that some audience members might not show up for round three. Putting a teaser at the end of the second movie was a smart idea, and piqued the interest of die-hard fans, but it also revealed an inescapable problem in terms of marketability to the masses. The final film was a western, and by and large, moviegoing audiences in 1990 did not kick off their summer by watching cowboys and Indians on the big screen. The Bobs had faith in their story and Bob Gale's screenplay, but as they were reminded by the tepid critical response to *Part II*, there are no guarantees in Hollywood.

The process of bringing the last chapter to the screen was a marked difference from the preceding adventures. Unlike *Part II*, where a significant number of the shots were technically demanding and the high potential for continuity errors kept Arthur Schmidt and Harry Keramidas on their toes, the last film was simpler. There were no flying cars and far fewer hoverboard sequences, and no scenes from the previous films to re-create.

There were still technical challenges, complicated camera shots, and long nights, but compared to the precedent set on the first two films, making this *Back to the Future* was a vacation.

While some of the third picture was shot at Universal, *Three* was mostly a location shoot. The exterior of Doc's 1955 mansion was filmed at the Gamble House in Pasadena, while the sequence with Marty and Doc at the drive-in movie theater was shot in Monument Valley, home base for many John Ford/ John Wayne films. However, most of the picture saw Zemeckis and company taking their show on the road to Sonora, more than three hundred miles northwest of the comfortable confines of the Universal backlot. The town is not only a beautifully versatile blank canvas for filmmakers to use, but it is also a well-tested piece of real estate. By the time the DeLorean rolled its wheels across the terrain, hundreds of movies and television series had been shot in the town, including *Bonanza* and *The Lone Ranger.*

The beginning of making the film provided the most stress for the filmmakers. When production on *Three* started, Arthur Schmidt and Harry Keramidas split up so they could divide and conquer, as both sequels were being cut simultaneously. Initially they both went to Sonora, where Zemeckis was working with them on the final edit of what was now being referred to as *Back to the Future Part II*, but the director's focus was sporadic. He was shooting during the day and during nights and weekends was sitting in with his two editors. It was great to have his collaborators on site with him, but Zemeckis's head wasn't completely in the game, and he knew it. The editors did too, but there was nothing that could be done. Once again, they were racing against the clock toward not only one release date, but now two.

After a while, Artie left for Los Angeles, to assist with the sound dub recording of *Part II*, while Harry stayed behind in

Northern California to continue piecing together *Part III*'s climax, an elaborate and lengthy sequence that took place on an antique steam locomotive and was shot over the course of several weeks. Things might have been rough on the director beforehand, but they were about to get significantly more challenging. With *Family Ties*' run concluded, Michael J. Fox reveled in his ability to play an eighties kid-turned-cowpoke without having to spend his days as Alex P. Keaton. Now it was Zemeckis's turn to make the long commute, and this time the transportation was even more intricate than being chauffeured around in a station wagon. For a three-week period, as Bob Z was shooting the climactic train sequence by day, Bob G stayed in Los Angeles to supervise the dub of *Part II*. After the business on the rail line wrapped for the day, the director would take a private plane south, where a driver would meet him at the airport in Burbank and take him to the dubbing stage at the Hitchcock Theatre at Universal. Zemeckis would eat dinner there, review the footage that had been worked on that day, and make notes. He'd turn in at the Sheraton Universal Hotel, get dropped off at the Burbank airport in the morning, return to the Old West, lather, rinse, and repeat. Several weeks later, back in San Jose, the test screenings for *Part II* started. More edits were required before the film was locked, and all the while, work on *Three* continued.

When *Part II* failed to connect with some viewers, Zemeckis wasn't completely surprised. It was a different film—a darker film—but, also, a less refined one. "When I say it suffers from editing, I don't mean that it should have been shorter or should have been longer," Zemeckis says. "I just didn't have enough time to sit with my film. The editing process is really delicate, and it's different for every film. If you have too much time to edit, you can start to be self-destructive, but if you don't have enough time, you maybe don't get the rhythms just right. You don't have enough time to let it gestate, which is what it needs, but if you've got too much time on your hands, you can start to think about things you shouldn't worry about. I just felt I didn't have enough time, which doesn't mean that I should have cut more stuff out. It might have been that I should have let more things breathe. I just didn't have that time to do that final little polish because we were too busy in the middle of making this other gigantic movie."

"It was an extremely difficult time, and it was very difficult for Bob creatively," Arthur Schmidt says. "It was extremely demanding on him. Maybe that's one of the reasons why *Back to the Future Part II* suffered a bit. He just didn't have the time that he usually has, and likes to have, to devote to the postproduction and editing of his film. I've had a chance to sit back and look at it more objectively and say, 'Oh, I wish I had more time because I would have done this. I would have changed that. I would have brightened it up here.'"

While hindsight has since kicked in, there was little time for reflection on the second film while the third was in motion. For several of the actors, the experience of making *Part III* was one of the highlights of making the trilogy. Many welcomed the change of scenery, and being among the dirt and the mountains. Sure, the Sonora shoot had the occasional discomforts—the morning call time was 6:00 A.M., when the temperature was often hovering around twelve degrees—but the cast and crew did manage to have a lot of fun. "Over a period of time, we really developed the town into almost a resort for the crew," Dean Cundey says. "We began to develop little areas behind the set for different kinds of interests and activities. Some of the drivers built a little pitch-and-putt driving range for golf. There were three or four of us who were interested in old firearms, myself being one of them, and we built a nice little shooting range off to one side. There was a horseshoe pit. Hidden behind this set that appeared to be out in the middle of nowhere was what we called 'Cup BTTF,' our playground where everybody would relax. We had a great caterer, but everybody would rush through their meal so that they could get off to spend the rest of their lunch hour in their favorite activity. And at the end of it, we were all delighted to go back to work. We all came back revived. Everybody remembers that production on location fondly as being a great experience. It was not only the fun of making a film, but just the fun of being there, the camaraderie, and the fact that you spend your entire time having a really rewarding experience."

Without the rigors of having to race to and from the *Family Ties* set, Michael J. Fox was able to kick back and enjoy being a movie star. He joked that Zemeckis enjoyed coming up with new ways to abuse him during the making of the *Back to the Future* films—skateboard stunts on the first film, hanging from a harness while filming the hoverboard sequences on the second, walking atop a moving train on the third—but the actor enjoyed the challenge. He couldn't help but feel impressed with himself when he found out that at one point he traveled at thirty-five miles per hour while on horseback, something he never expected to do when he was a young kid growing up in Canada.

Meanwhile, Christopher Lloyd was able to bask in the spotlight as one half of the romantic focal point in the film, the other half being Mary Steenburgen, who was cast as Clara Clayton, Doc's love interest. Playing Doc had become almost second nature to the actor by this point, but he relished the opportunity to explore a new side of the wide-eyed scientist. "I could relate to the desire to have a romantic experience, but Doc had never even thought about it," he says. "He was so involved and obsessed with his various projects—time travel and all the rest of his little things that he was constantly involved in. I don't think it was on his agenda. It wasn't until he rescues Clara and their eyes meet, then suddenly the whole world changes. I just thought, what a wonderful situation for the guy to be in. He is totally smitten. He does not know how to handle it, but it has taken control and he has discovered himself, in a sense."

Working with Mary Steenburgen was an added benefit for the actor. The two had worked together before in her screen debut, the 1978 film *Goin' South*, which was written and directed by Jack Nicholson. Lloyd couldn't have been happier to have another opportunity to spend time with the actress both on- and off-screen. "I confess to having been infatuated with her, and I think it was mutual," he says. "We never got involved at all in any kind of relationship, other than being on the set and enjoying each other's company. We had fun, and that chemistry was already there. I was delighted to hear she was going to play in the film, she was delighted to be there, and we continued to have this wonderful experience for the sake of Clara and Doc." Working with Steenburgen on *III* also marked a milestone in Lloyd's career: The actor had been in nearly three dozen films and close to a hundred episodes of television series, including the memorable role of Reverend Jim Ignatowski on *Taxi*, yet the actor had never kissed on-screen. Christopher Lloyd and Mary Steenburgen may have kept their real-life relationship strictly platonic, but Doc and Clara were able to share one sweet moment of family-friendly physical romance under the stars.

The *Three* shoot also brought about a first for artist Drew Struzan, the creator of the franchise's iconic promotional art: He was able to have actors pose for him for a movie poster. Since the original film, Struzan had been an integral addition to the franchise's branding and marketability. His one-sheet poster for the film, with Marty staring at his watch, standing with one foot in the DeLorean, the other on the ground, while trails of fire run underneath his legs and a smoky blue and orange sky fills the frame, had become an emblematic representation of the series. While the image became iconic almost instantaneously, arriving at the winning concept required a lot of time and effort.

Prior to designing the art for the *Back to the Future* poster, Struzan hadn't read the script or seen any of the shot footage. Instead, the Bobs, along with Spielberg, talked him through the major beats—there was a teenage kid played by Michael J. Fox, a mad scientist played by Christopher Lloyd, Crispin Glover and Lea Thompson play his parents, a portion of the film takes place in the 1950s, there's a time-traveling DeLorean, and lots of clock imagery. He was provided with three-ring binders stocked with hundreds of Ralph Nelson's photographs from the set. Struzan came up with six or seven ideas and presented them to the production team, who, fortunately, saw potential in everything the artist had created.

"They were very respectful and open-ended," Struzan says. "It's why they were great to work for, because they respect other people's creativity. That's why they came to me. They'd seen other things I'd done and liked what they saw. It wasn't one of those jobs where it was hell and I couldn't figure out what they wanted. I had a whole lot of freedom. I think that's why I remember it fondly, because it was so respectful and so easy to do."

The Bobs and Spielberg liked all the artwork and couldn't decide which concept they wanted to proceed with. They asked for Struzan to work on full-color paintings for each concept, or comps, as they're called in the business, short for *comprehensives*. Then there were notes. One painting had Marty sitting on an oversize watch, but they suggested the artist change it to an older watch. Wait, how about a futuristic watch? What if his parents were reflected on the outside face of an antique pocket watch? In the end, there was quite a bit of trial and error, and none of those paintings were commissioned.

It would be easy for him to take credit for coming up with the winning idea, but even decades later, Drew Struzan still concedes that he doesn't know where the concept came from. As *Back to the Future*'s release date was nearing, Spielberg had another thought in mind that he wanted the illustrator to test out. He liked the artist's style and work on *Future* to date, but wanted him to try his hand at an idea that had been pitched by someone in-house at Universal—Marty looking at his watch in disbelief. The executive producer presented Struzan with a photograph of Marty standing in his now-familiar pose. This was the image the production team wanted to represent their film. The artist completed a comp, which the Bobs and producers loved, and a finished one-sheet soon followed.

Part II's poster includes Marty in a similar pose alongside the now-flying DeLorean with Doc joining him, and it took longer to arrive at that design than one might expect. "Everybody seems to have his own recollection and his own memory of the circumstances," Struzan says. "Usually they will say, 'We wanted to keep the concept to have a nice consistency through the three of these pictures.' The fact is, I did about thirty-five drawings, pursuing every concept for the second one that I could think of. I did tons of these drawings. It wasn't until the very last among those drawings that there was one with both of the guys standing there. At the very end they decided, 'That's what we should do. Everybody loved the first one—why not just repeat it?'"

With the design concept in tow, Struzan got to work on *Back to the Future Part II*'s final one-sheet. Production on *Three* was already under way, and with Michael J. Fox significantly more accessible than he was during the first two films, the producers hired the illustrator to not only work on the promotional art, but also pose the actors the way he wanted them so he could take reference photographs that he would use while working on the painting at his studio. For Struzan, this was an attractive offer. Over the course of his long career, he had never had the opportunity to have an actor pose for him before. For the first film, someone had posed Fox in order to take the photograph that Spielberg had presented him with, but it was virtually unusable as a working guide for his painting. The artist found the pose unnatural and unsuitable to help sell Michael J. Fox as an emerging movie star. "He did such a rotten job on the photo session that—and this is something I've never told anybody—I reposed for that picture," he says. "The body is my body with Michael's head. The picture the other guy took was poorly lit—it just didn't have any soul. So I redid it to my pleasure, to my taste, to my feelings. Apparently it was the right decision, because they've used that pose ever since."

But this time, things would be done his way from the start. The artist made the four-hour drive to Sonora, with a photographer alongside him, and spent the day on set. Michael J. Fox and Christopher Lloyd changed out of their western costumes, back into their outfits from *Part II*. The photographer set up the lighting, and all moved into their respective roles. Struzan played art director, instructing his subjects to adjust their stances as he exuded the enthusiasm of a fashion photographer. "Okay, stand over here. That's right, right here. Do the watch pose. Okay, now both of you do it. Move to the left. A little more. No, Chris, stay there. Michael, a little more to your left. Michael, can you—"

"Wait a minute—" Fox threw his hands in the air. Everyone froze. The actor took center stage as Struzan's heart dropped. He had offended the star of the movie. He would be packing up and heading home within minutes. The actor looked him straight in the eye and walked toward him.

"Are you *the* Drew?"

"I'm Drew, yeah."

"I'm your greatest fan." Fox knew Struzan had provided the artwork for the first film, but he had no idea the man who had shown up with a photographer here in the middle of the desert was the same person whose work he so admired. The artist appreciated the compliment. It was a fantastic first impression of what it was like to be in the presence of Michael J. Fox.

When it came time to work on the one-sheet for *Part III*, Struzan was once again invited to pose and photograph the actors. Like most aspects of the trilogy, it was easier the third time around. This time there was a concept—Marty and Doc would be painted next to the DeLorean while the car was on train tracks. The actors remembered him and greeted him warmly, with Fox even taking a few moments to chat Struzan up about some poster art for other films.

The shoot for the *Part III* one-sheet was done at Stage 12 at Universal, where several pickup shots were being done. Before Struzan arrived on set, the scene was lighthearted, as Zemeckis was preparing to shoot the sequence with the DeLorean in the cave on the soundstage. "Wait, now. Wait a minute. Wait, wait, wait." The director was watching as the crew was setting up the lights. It was supposed to be dark in the closed-off cavern, and Bob Z thought the aesthetic was wrong for what he was trying to accomplish. "Where's the light coming from inside of this cave?"

"From the same place the music is coming from." Dean

Cundey didn't skip a beat. Just as the audience would accept Alan Silvestri's score coming from some unseen place, the cinematographer knew questions about the source of the light he needed to properly cover the scene were equally irrelevant. Moviemaking is about selling an illusion, and as long as you operate within the realm of reality, the audience will go along for the ride. Zemeckis accepted the gentle ribbing from his friend, acknowledged that Cundey was right, and the crew continued about their work. In the meantime, Struzan was free to borrow the two lead actors. Fox and Lloyd got into costume, photos were taken, and the artist returned to his studio. The basic visual motif from the first two films would be repeated for the third installment, but there was an element of the concept that spurred uncertainty and debate. "We went through, like, sixty comps before they could come up with it," Struzan says. "Their idea was to have three 'somethings,' but they didn't know what. How about Marty, Doc, and horse? Marty, Doc, and train? How about Marty, Doc, and— it was just all these crazy ideas. In the end, they were printing the poster of just Marty and Doc and the westernized car. While it was on the printing press, they finally made up their minds and said, 'Wait a minute, I think we really should add Mary Steenburgen in it.' Once again, when they're up against the clock, they made a good decision. Obviously, it was the right one to make, but it took many, many incarnations to get to that point."

By the time the decision was made, Struzan was unable to photograph the actress. Instead, the illustrator described what he needed to the producers, and they arranged for Steenburgen to be photographed by a third party, using the pictures that were previously taken of her costars as a guide. When the stills were sent to Struzan, it was too late for him to redo the entire onesheet. Instead, he took out a separate piece of illustration board, painted Steenburgen's image on it, cut his work very carefully out of its canvas, and pasted it into the main artwork. Thankfully, the final product was seamless and audiences who saw the posters displayed in their local multiplexes were none the wiser.

In addition to Alan Silvestri's score, which put western variations on some of the familiar *Back to the Future* musical themes, the producers wanted to find a way to integrate a recording artist of the day into the film. Chosen in large part because of their easily recognizable extra-long beards, which looked right at home in the Old West, ZZ Top was asked to make an appearance and provide a song for the soundtrack. "My favorite sequence in terms of the filming was the festival in *Part III*," Bob Gale says. "We had live music on the set, the weather was decent, and the entire atmosphere of the scene was very upbeat and positive. Because it was night, it really felt like we were back in time. Everyone enjoyed seeing the ZZ Top guys jam with the local musicians."

"ZZ Top was very different from Huey Lewis, just in terms of the sound of their music," Neil Canton says. "I'm a big fan of ZZ Top. I'm also a big fan of Huey's, but we needed to get someone to be in the movie and write a song that was appropriate for the plot. ZZ Top look like they belong in the West, and so that was that. In theory, you would think that would have been a hard group to get, but because of the success of the first movie, they were very receptive to it."

"Me and the band—you know, the five black guys—we knew that we wouldn't be in the third one because there was no way they could write us into the Old West," Harry Waters, Jr., says. "We did have a conversation with Bob Gale, who said that they were trying all sorts of ways to figure out how we could be there, but it just couldn't happen, so that was a bit of a disappointment. I was pleased that it took ZZ Top to replace us."

Jeffrey Weissman also found himself disappointed to not have a greater role in *Part III*. Michael J. Fox played the part of Seamus McFly, Marty's distant relative, in a part that was originally offered to Crispin Glover as a negotiation tool back when there was a chance he might have been involved with the sequels. But the gag wouldn't work as well with Weissman in the role. While Weissman maintains that he was initially told he would be playing that role back when he was hired for *Paradox*, Bob Gale disagrees, claiming the actor was never considered for the role of Seamus. Either way, the end result was the same—Zemeckis and company harkened back to a memorable effect from *Part II* to realize Seamus on-screen. In the second film, there was a sequence where Fox played his son, daughter, and an older version of Marty in the same scene. The shot was achieved with a VistaGlide camera, which was revolutionary technology at the time of production. Greg Beaumont of ILM built the camera specifically for the needs of Zemeckis and the film crew. The camera, which was about the size of a small refrigerator and noisy as all hell, would enable an operator to take multiple exposures on a single frame of film. The negative for the VistaGlide was four times the size of a standard thirty-five-millimeter frame, so that it could be photographed on that many times. Each time the film was developed in the lab it was reduced in size until it was the same size as all the other footage. "If you look at a lot of *Back to the Future Part II*, it's a lot of big, sweeping, high-concept camera stuff," Robert Zemeckis says. "The actors have to do that dance with the camera. I've been very fortunate to work with actors who don't chafe under that." Since the effect was successful and seamlessly executed in the second film, the idea was just to reproduce it for the third.

"I'm especially proud of how we pulled off some of the motion control work with multiple Michael J. Foxes," Bob Gale says. "I love the tracking shot of Marty and Seamus at the festival, and the shot in *Part II* in the Café 80s in which Marty takes the hat of Marty, Jr., and puts it on his own head. It's brilliant and goes by so quickly that the audience doesn't even stop to wonder how we did it."

One of the elements of the picture that received the most attention was the lengthy sequence near the end where Marty and Doc try and power a steam engine up to eighty-eight miles per hour. Like the hoverboard stunts from the second film, the spectacle was achieved with a mixture of both special and visual effects, practical and optical. The actual locomotive used during filming is Sierra Railway No. 3, which made it easy for the prop department to convert it into No. 131 for the shoot. It had been built in 1891 and had appeared in over a hundred films and television shows. Shooting the train sequence took seven weeks, nearly as long as the hoverboard work on *Part II*, and provided another opportunity for the lead actors to do some minor stunt work of their own. Christopher Lloyd may have had trepidation about standing on the ledge of the clock tower for *Part I*, but he was more eager to attempt the riskier shots for *Part III*.

"There was a sequence where I was chasing the train on horseback, galloping along the tracks," Lloyd says. "I had to hang on to the train, and pull myself off of the horse onto the locomotive. They would not let me do that because there was a risk involved. You can see me in one of the takes galloping along, and it was a lot of fun. I have ridden a lot, so I felt comfortable. I could easily have gripped the handle on the train and pulled myself up. I almost did it, but I thought, *What if it doesn't go right?*" Although he has a general fear of heights, Lloyd is not altogether risk-averse. He and Michael J. Fox had the opportunity to run on top of the train, although they did not actually jump from car to car. Lloyd actually prefers to do his own stunts whenever possible, as it gives the director more options when filming and the editors more material to cut together. His thrill-seeking had been relatively limited in the trilogy until that point, but on *Part III*, even the Doc got to ride one of the sought-after hoverboards, as he and Clara glided away from the locomotive, moments before it crashed into Clayton (or Eastwood) Ravine. "Those steam engines are such amazing creatures, these huge iron gadgets with all these moving parts," he says. "It was pretty heavy. I forgot how they rigged the hoverboards to the train, but I loved it, I absolutely loved it. I felt comfortable. I felt safe. You had to pay attention working on those parts, but I really liked doing those sequences."

For their third go-round making a *Back to the Future* film, *Part III*'s unique take on what had, by 1990, already become a very familiar story kept the experience fresh. "I'd like to make it sound like it was an awful, arduous experience and that we were fighting heat and sleep deprivation at all times," Dean Cundey says. "But I have to say, we turned it into really sort of a great, fun adventure for all of us. We were lucky to have that location up in Central California. It's the famous gold country, where gold was discovered and most of the gold rush took place. It was chosen because there is the old train museum up there and they still keep alive the steam trains on a section of track and let them run through a visually perfect little valley. We took over the town on the edge of the train line. We were staying in small, rustic little hotels and stuff. They were very comfortable, very scenic and interesting."

In a lot of ways, *Three* was almost a victory lap. Even the DeLorean time machine, for all of the headaches it caused during work on the first film, was relatively easy to work with, thanks to some much-needed enhancements from Tim Flattery. In total, seven DMC-12s were used during production on the trilogy—three for the first film, one additional for the second, along with the fiber-glass car, and two more with extra oomph for the last installment. "The DeLorean was definitely not a performance vehicle," Bob Gale says. "Having learned this during *Part I*, we had our people do some work on some of the cars to make them more powerful, more stable, and tougher."

"We built an off-road chassis from the ground up with a Volkswagen engine in it, and put the DeLorean body over the top of that," Flattery says. "If you look at that vehicle in the film, you'll see that it sits higher than a normal DeLorean would, just because of the suspension system on it. We had to make it taller so it could drive through that desert with all that rough terrain. It got the car to the point where it was ready to go and just needed the exterior dressed to match the other DeLoreans. I drove it up to Sonora with transportation, stayed up there for two days to make sure everything went smoothly, and then left after that."

That conclusion of the trilogy reached its fitting end when the DeLorean B car was smashed by a train at the end of the film, once Marty returns back to the present time. For those on set, the experience was somewhat emotional, but also pretty exciting. "It was mostly a sweet moment, because we didn't have to worry about it anymore," Neil Canton says. "It was like a character in the movie, but movies are like that. As you get towards the end of principal photography, there's someone who you've been with every day for months, and then it's their last shot in the movie and then they're done. It affects you. You know that you may never work with them again. It was kind of like that. The DeLorean was captured in the movie, so you felt sad that it was done, but at the same time you were happy because it got to the finish line. I think some people grabbed pieces of it. I just know we were going to make darn sure that no one else could work with it, so we were going to destroy it."

"It wasn't bittersweet at all," Bob Gale says. "It was a perfectly executed wreck. After all, it wasn't the A car. But it's a testament to the power of these movies that the audience reacts so strongly to its destruction, as if it was a character. That day is vividly etched in my memory. I mean, come on, how many people ever get the chance to see a car get hit by a train—and for a good reason?"

With the DeLorean in shambles, our hero returned to 1985, and with the two-hour mark nearing in the movie theater, there was only one more thing to do—send Doc Brown and his new family back to the future in a custom time-traveling steam train that also didn't need roads. Marty Kline, an animator at ILM, designed the train, following the directive from Robert Zemeckis that the locomotive be evocative of the *Nautilus* from Disney's 1954 film *20,000 Leagues Under the Sea*. To create the various moving parts and time slice animations, John Bell and Wes Takahashi worked together to decipher how the train was going to move and react on-screen. "The train was modeled," Takahashi says. "To do the time slice, I would just get a background plate, then look at it forwards and backwards, frame by frame, trying to figure out what I could do to it. The train had many more moving parts, so we had to figure out what all these parts would do once we added the ILM magic to it. I worked very closely with John Bell on that. He gave me a photograph of what he thought all the bells and whistles on the train were doing. On certain parts, they'd be emitting sparks; on other parts, they would be emitting glows. There would be smoke coming off of it. I was following John's lead. By *Back to the Future Part III*, I could do the time slice in my sleep. It wasn't that different from doing it on the DeLorean."

Principal photography wrapped in early 1990, giving the postproduction team a little bit longer to work on the finishing touches. For the first time, Arthur Schmidt, Harry Keramidas, and the effects wizards at ILM didn't have to move heaven and earth to make their theatrical release date. Zemeckis polished the film, gave some promotional interviews—as did several of the lead actors—and awaited the response. On May 27, 1990, just days after the Bobs and Neil Canton publicly declared that there would be no fourth installment with their custom-printed white T-shirts, it seemed like audiences had yet to have enough of *Back to the Future*. Universal and Amblin had pulled off a hat trick: For the third consecutive time, their time-travel film debuted in the top spot at the box office in the United States. When the dust cleared, the overall haul for its inaugural weekend was less than that of its predecessors, $19.1 million, but they had still struck gold. Perhaps even better than their commercial success was the acclaim the film received from both fans and reviewers alike. Siskel and Ebert both pointed their thumbs toward the heavens, and unlike with the second film in the series, *Entertainment Tonight*'s resident movie appraiser was back in support of the Bobs' story. "I just thought it was great fun," Leonard Maltin says. "I happen to love westerns, and I was happy to see a big, splashy shot in Monument Valley with a great railroad train. I thought it was great fun from start to finish. It captured the spirit of the first film while going in a totally different direction, and it had so many funny ideas. One of my chief disappointments with *Part II* was that it got serious. *Part III* lightened the tone again, and even though it was markedly different from the first film, it had the same panache and ingenuity."

The initial reaction may have been better than *Part II*'s reception, but the third volume did fall a bit short of expectations.

Although it was predicted by some in the industry to surpass *Part II*'s domestic gross due to better word of mouth, there continued to be diminishing returns at the box office. *Back to the Future Part III* grossed $87.7 million in the United States, making it the only film in the franchise to not reach the coveted $100 million mark. Overseas, the picture made $156.8 million, an impressive number, but significantly less than *Part II*'s $213.5 million. Perhaps adding slight disappointment, the filmmakers' dance cards were mostly left blank come awards season.

To the unsuspecting eye, it may have seemed that *Back to the Future* was going to go away not with a bang, but a whimper; however, that couldn't have been further from the truth. With three films in the can, Marty and Doc were charging full speed ahead toward more adventures—this time at Universal Studios theme parks and on Saturday morning television.

10. YOUR KIDS ARE GONNA LOVE IT

Thursday, January 23, 2014

Robert Zemeckis sat at his computer before starting the day's work. There was nothing too pressing on the agenda, which, for all the hustle and bustle of his schedule of late, was just the way he liked it. He opened his email and saw a message from Bob Gale. He read the short note, clicked a link, and was transferred to FunnyorDie.com. Just days earlier, Warren Buffett, the fourth-richest man on the planet, offered $1 billion to anyone who had predicted a perfect NCAA basketball bracket. The headline on the site announced that a winner had been crowned, and when the director scrolled further down, he saw a photograph of Buffet and Tom Wilson—dressed as the Biffhorrific version of his character—holding up *Grays Sports Almanac*. The director couldn't help but laugh, taking his glasses off to wipe away a tear. "Of course it's gotta be Biff," Zemeckis says. "I love that people are still thinking about *Back to the Future*."

Time has been very kind to the Bobs following the stagger-ing success of their three time-travel movies. Following *Part III's* release, Bob Z continued his long-standing working relationship with Steve Starkey. Together, the two brought films that pushed technological limits, like *Death Becomes Her*, *Cast Away*, and *The Polar Express*, to the big screen. A number of other *Future* crew members, including Rick Carter, Joanna Johnston, Ken Ralston, Arthur Schmidt, and Alan Silvestri, have also continued to work with the director on a number of projects—and some have even won Academy Awards during the process. His parents may have initially been skeptical of his decision to be a film director, but it's safe to assume they had since changed their minds by the time he won an Oscar for *Forrest Gump* in 1995, almost a full decade after he first made box office history with *Back to the Future*. He was right about films all along—they do have the power to captivate, bring people together, and change the world.

Working on *Back to the Future* has also been life-changing for Bob Gale. Not only did he also gain his parents' support—"My father has taken to introducing himself not as Mark Gale, but as the father of the writer of *Back to the Future!*"—but he has also been instrumental in preserving the integrity of the trilogy and stoking the fandom flames throughout the years. Over the past three decades, Universal has continued to consult with Gale on all matters involving the trilogy, a responsibility the cocreator has happily accepted. For the film's fans, Bob G is "Mr. Back to the Future," the go-to expert and authoritative keeper of the franchise's history. He isn't just a multi-hyphenate behind-the-scenes creative, but the movies' number one fan. The credits may state that the movies are all Robert Zemeckis's films, but as anyone who has chronicled the trilogy's ascent in our popular culture—and Gale's role in it—can attest to, they are equally Bob Gale's babies.

By the time the Bobs exchanged Internet memes via email,

the last film in the *Back to the Future* trilogy had been released twenty-five years prior. Unlike on a television show, where the same cast and crew can work together day in and day out for years, moviemaking is much more ephemeral. Yes, a director or producer may invite some of his team on Project A to work with him or her on Project B, which was what happened with some of the various members of the *Back to the Future* team who had crossed each others' paths before and after filming the trilogy, but that is by no means expected. Hollywood is a fleeting place, often built on fragile relationships.

Which makes it all the more phenomenal that so many members of the *Back to the Future* family have remained in touch and loyal to the film series throughout the years. As conventions have become more mainstream, many of the cast and crew have met with fans, posed for pictures, and signed glossy eight-by-tens in major markets and small towns around the United States. While some have done the rounds more than others, virtually all of the key cast members have sat behind a table at one point or another since the early 2000s. At the 2006 Hollywood Bowl, an annual convention celebrating popular culture, an unprecedented *Back to the Future* reunion was staged. Two dozen *Future* alums, including Michael J. Fox, Christopher Lloyd, and Lea Thompson, spent hours hearing stories from fans about how these three films impacted their lives.

"I've been hanging out with Chris Lloyd at conventions for a few years, and I think he's surprised that he's so beloved," Thompson says. "I mean, he is massively loved. Thousands of people hang on his every word, and he's hilarious. It's interesting to look out at two thousand people, and a good half of them weren't even born when the movie was made. It's such an amazing feeling."

"When I am sitting at the table signing, the parents that come up who have kids, they were kids when the first movie came out," Lloyd says. "They are just so affected by the film and the story, and entertained by it. It is amazing for them to actually meet Doc, and they all go on repeatedly about how it was part of their growing up. It was their world."

While he has frequently traveled the convention circuit as a lone wolf, Crispin Glover has chosen to abstain from any events commemorating the film since its release. From as far back as the late 1980s, the actor has been critical of the first film and, especially, its subsequent sequels. *Back to the Future* was a boon to his career, he'll be the first to acknowledge, but he doesn't consider the movie to be among the work he is most proud of. In recent years, Glover has taken to touring the country promoting *What Is It?* and *It Is Fine! EVERYTHING IS FINE*, two independent films he's written and directed. The actor's official website currently has a somewhat lengthy explanation of why the actor didn't appear in *Part II* and *Part III* of the trilogy, but besides that, little mention is made of the film that helped make him a star.

Coincidentally, Tom Wilson used to be one of the most readily available actors to make public appearances in conjunction with *Future*-related events, but he has also chosen to abstain from making the reunion rounds in recent years. The actor, who was a staple of the late-night talk show circuit around the time of each film's theatrical release, appeared at a number of conventions between 2001 and 2003; however, since then he has significantly distanced himself from his affiliation with the films. For Wilson, it has been a delicate dance that has inspired debate and some frustration among fans of the franchise. During his stand-up act—Wilson started his career as a comedian and continues performing comedy gigs to this day—he has taken to performing

"The Question Song." The number, an infectiously jaunty tune that Wilson sings while strumming an acoustic guitar, is designed to answer all of the questions about *Back to the Future* that audience members may have. *Yes, Michael J. Fox is a nice guy. No, the hoverboards don't really work. Yes, Crispin Glover was unusual. No, the manure wasn't real.* Some have seen the song as a sign that the actor is unappreciative of the fans who have given him the biggest hit of his career, while others can empathize with the actor's frustration with receiving the same queries on a daily basis about three films he acted in decades ago. It seems unlikely that Wilson isn't proud of his work on the *Future* trilogy—his official website still sings the film's praises—but he probably would prefer if he wasn't requested to call someone a "butthead" on every day that ends in a *y*.

However, despite the few notable exceptions, most of the cast and crew of *Back to the Future* remain happy to speak about the film whenever asked. Claudia Wells, who owns a discount high-end men's fashion store, Armani Wells, in Studio City, is often visited by tourists from around the world who stop in to speak with her about her role in the first film. Although far fewer people realize his connection to the film, fans also chat up Bob Schmelzer, who doubled Eric Stoltz in the early days of the first movie's production, at Circle-A, the skateboard shop he owns in San Jose.

"By and large, almost everyone who worked on our films had a good experience and has great memories," Bob Gale says. "I hear it from our veterans all the time—that the *Back to the Future* experience was one of the best, if not *the* best, time they had on any show. Certainly, part of that is because the movies are so good. When you tell someone you were part of *Back to the Future*, they usually want to hear more about it. I certainly love the fact that this happens to me, and I don't get tired of talking about it. There aren't many films that attain 'classic' status, so it's very rewarding to be associated with one."

All of these recent displays of *Future* fandom might seem like a recent phenomenon, but their roots can be traced back at least to the late 1980s and a superfan named Dan Madsen, a man who was no stranger to gathering the troops. He was the president of both the *Star Trek* and *Star Wars* officially licensed fan clubs, two franchises that also have endured well past their debut. When he heard that there would be sequels to *Future*, he and his partners approached Universal to see if the studio could use his assistance in putting together an official fan club. It was the ultimate win-win situation: Madsen would have the opportunity to visit the set and interview some of the actors, while the movie studio would have a de facto publicity campaign for its upcoming films run not only for free, but also by a fan who knew how to attract other like-minded folks to join his flock. Madsen and his team flew out to Los Angeles to meet with someone at the movie studio, who told them, pending the Bobs' blessing, Universal would be happy to have their involvement.

"Once they saw what we were doing with *Star Wars* and *Star Trek*, and realized that we could do something fun like that for *Back to the Future*, they agreed to get on board and support it as well," he says. "It really just kind of evolved from there. It was a traditional licensing deal. We got the license to do it, and then we kicked it off and started marketing it around. When *Back to the Future Part II* went into production, that's when we got on the phone and started talking to everybody."

Madsen knew speaking with some of the actors and key crew members would be a perk of the project, but he was struck by just how informative, and how much fun, his interviewees were. Even after several decades, he has never forgotten the warm treatment he received from even the biggest and brightest stars on the project. "We had a whole list of everybody that we wanted to talk to, and they were good about getting us everybody that we wanted," he says. "At the time, Christopher Lloyd was not an easy person to get an interview with. He was kind of a quiet guy. We were told he didn't do that many interviews, but since this was the official publication for the fan club, they thought he would do it. It took a little while, but we got him, so I'm most proud of that interview, there's no question about it. Mary Steenburgen was also one of my favorites. She's such a sweetheart. I was really impressed with her and loved being able to interview her. And of course, Michael J. Fox is a class act all the way."

Unlike with Madsen's two previous fan club ventures, the *Back to the Future* official fan club folded by 1990, after having four magazines, one released each quarter, featuring dozens of articles and previously unseen photographs, becoming the first outlet of any kind to take an in-depth look behind some of the more technical aspects of the trilogy. There were two more surprises that Madsen left as parting gifts before he went back to dedicating himself fully to *Star Wars* and *Star Trek*. Universal had quietly been developing a theme park ride for its Florida location, as well as an animated series inspired by the trilogy. A sneak preview of the ride appeared in the final issue of the fan club magazine, before it was officially announced in *The Secrets of the* Back to the Future *Trilogy*, a half-hour special hosted by Kirk Cameron that was included in the first VHS box set of the three films. The ride opened May 2 of the following year in Orlando, with thousands of excited fans flocking to the park to be among the first to ride in one of the eight-seater DeLorean time machines.

The ride was created with a relatively simplistic functioning concept. The patrons would line up and watch a preshow video featuring Christopher Lloyd, Tom Wilson, and Darlene Vogel, who traded in her Spike costume from *Part II* and now was playing the role of the ride's "spokesperson." The basic premise was that Biff Tannen had stolen the time machine, after breaking into Doc's Institute of Future Technology, and was now traveling throughout history, potentially disrupting the very fabric of the space-time continuum. The "volunteers" at the institute, the riders, would then make their way into an auditorium and sit in one of twelve DeLoreans, which were on pistons that allowed them to bend, tilt, rise, and fall. A large-format film was projected on an IMAX screen, placing the volunteers right in the middle of the action. At the beginning, flight was simulated as the front section of the car rose eight feet in the air. The attraction was an unmitigated success, which led to identical versions opening at Universal Studios in Hollywood on June 12, 1993, and at the company's theme park in Japan on March 31, 2001.

One of those patrons who visited Back to the Future: The Ride in its early days was Stephen Clark, a self-described "country bumpkin from Alabama." His first venture was eight months after it opened, in January 1992, and from that moment he was hooked. He had seen the films in theaters several times and fancied himself a real enthusiast of the trilogy, but there was something about sitting in a DeLorean time machine, placed in front of the action, that sparked something in him. "I just really threw it into high gear as a geek fan," Clark says. "I could not get enough information about *Back to the Future*. This was before the Internet, before any of that stuff. When I came back from the ride, I just thought, *I have got to find me a copy of that footage*." His quest for his holy grail led him to Universal. He called the studio and was directed through the bureaucratic channels to Bob Gale, who still had an office in the backlot while *Back to the Future: The Animated Series*, which debuted in September 1991 and ran for two seasons on CBS, was in production. The two got to talking. Clark had a background in computer programming and thought he could be helpful in revitalizing the fan club, but in a different form for fans who remained just as interested as him in the trilogy. With the assistance of technology, perhaps Stephen Clark could not only help keep interest in the franchise high, but also provide a forum for fans to connect with others from around the world. Gale agreed that it was worth a shot and assisted Clark in getting hold of some of the cast and crew.

As the Internet took off, Clark was among the first to have a fan site for the trilogy, and he undoubtedly had the one filled with the most content. On January 22, 1997, BTTF.com was born. It's doubtful that anyone could have predicted it that day, but the website—which is now more appropriately at home at BacktotheFuture.com—became the go-to online resource for all things about the trilogy. Stephen Clark remains surprised to this day at how influential his website has been, acting as an informative resource about the films and significantly helping to impact *Future*'s standing in our popular culture.

"Three distinct moments really stick out in my mind when it comes to the website's impact," he says. "The first was in August 2000, when Universal invited me to write the pop-up trivia featurette for all three films' 2002 debuts on DVD. The second time was at the twentieth-anniversary screening at the ArcLight Cinemas–Hollywood in February 2005. I was a sponsor and did some heavy advertising for it online. We sold out two showings, with each followed by a Q&A with the cast. During both, the host asked the audience of over three hundred fifty people how many heard about the event through BTTF.com. Both times, about seventy-five percent raised their hands. That blew me away—that an Alabama-based site could have such an influence on audiences in California.

"The third one—and the one I'm most proud of—was in December 2007," he continues, "when the Library of Congress selected *Back to the Future* for the National Film Archive. The yearlong write-in campaign was my brainchild, and we succeeded on the first attempt. The Library of Congress said that they had never had such a large number of votes come from the public. I was interviewed by the *Hollywood Reporter* about it soon after, and the journalist who interviewed me said he had been trying to get *Caddyshack* nominated for a decade. He was jealous that we succeeded in just one year!"

In addition to exclusive interviews and photographs, fans also flock to his site to access the two things they covet most: a sense of community with others who love the movies, and tons of collectibles. *Back to the Future* was not designed to be a heavily merchandised film. Unlike with Joel Schumacher's 1997 disaster *Batman & Robin*, there was never a suggestion that toys would play a part in the marketing of the films, even with all of the gadgetry in *Part II*. If the films were made today, Mattel hoverboards would have been on sale in toy stores around the nation in advance of the film's theatrical release, but that was not standard at the time. But demand drives supply, and over the decades since the first film's release, more products have come out for the *Back to the Future* franchise. Since the early 1990s, Universal has struck licensing deals with McDonald's, Lego, and Hallmark, to name just a few. The merch caters to fans of all ages who enjoy die-cast DeLorean scale models, flux capacitors, Christmas ornaments, T-shirts, and a seemingly unending litany of other collectibles. Some of the most coveted items are those that were inspired by props for *Part II*. As "the future" of 2015 neared, the fan community worked hard to make some of the more fantastic technological inventions in those sequences a reality. There have been several attempts to create functioning hoverboards, some of which have been reported about in internationally renowned news outlets like the *New York Times*, but it seems that true hoverboarding like Marty does on film is not going to become a reality anytime soon.

Like others before it, Mattel, the toy-manufacturing giant, responded to the fans' call for a hoverboard. In 2012, the company's MattyCollector division, which caters specifically to collectors in the twenty-five- to forty-five-year-old demographic, thought it was time to bring everyone's most desired handheld prop from the movie into fans' homes. "The hoverboard, being an item that was made by Mattel in the film, seemed like a very natural item to do," Scott Neitlich of Mattel says. "We approached Universal about doing a line of *Back to the Future* items, and the first one we wanted to do was, of course, the hoverboard. It really just came out of passionate folks at both Universal and Mattel who felt this was the right time and the right way to do this item. It made it easier to sell internally, being able to show images of it from the film and reminding everyone it was made by Mattel. That was sort of the straw that kicked it over. We needed to do this. It was too cool not to."

Throughout March 2012, hoverboards were put up for presale at a price of $120 on the MattyCollector website. For legal reasons, the company does not release actual sales numbers, but it's safe to assume the hoverboards sold extremely well. To date, the collectible remains one of the top three items MattyCollector has ever sold. Bob Gale gave an early endorsement, which no doubt helped persuade some fans who might have been riding the fence, and Stephen Clark heavily promoted the toy via his website.

It seemed to be a match made in heaven, that is, until the hover-board was released and the product disappointed more than a few people. "This is one of the areas where there was a lot of contro-versy," Neitlich says. "There were over thirty different boards used in the film, depending on the shot. There were boards that were screwed to Michael J. Fox's foot. There were boards for close-ups. There were boards for far away, and no two boards looked the same. The colors, the stripes, the lenticular surface, the font—completely different from board to board. We started off by look-ing at images online and freeze-framing the film, but we were fortunate enough to have Michael Lantieri and Bob Gale visit Mattel. They brought several of the screen-used boards for us to look at. We actually filmed a segment, and it was online, of us meeting with Mr. Gale and Mr. Lantieri, and it was great because we were able to take measurements, but I think that led to a lot of expectations for the fans. Which of the thirty boards was it going to look like? We really tried to go for a composite of all thirty, sort of what the board looked like in your head versus exactly what it looked like shot to shot, since it changed so much.

"The two biggest challenges we had was, one, a lot of fans expected the board to actually float," he continues. "Of the nega-tive feedback we received, the number one complaint was, 'Why doesn't the hoverboard fly?' Floating technology doesn't physi-cally exist. It was meant to be a fun thing for your wall or to hold in your hand or throw across the floor. We did promote that it would glide across carpet, which it does do, but I think a lot of fans wanted it to do something that's just physically not possible, especially for a hundred-and-twenty-dollar item. I got emails from people sending me things from Harvard and Caltech and these think tanks in Germany and the United Kingdom that were developing hover technology, saying, 'Why don't you add this technology in?' Well, A, that's extremely experimental, and B, we're trying to mass-produce something for a hundred and twenty dollars. You're talking about experimental technology that costs tens of thousands of dollars per square inch to make something hover. I always told fans that DeLoreans also don't time-travel. You have to kind of let go of fantasy expectations."

While a lot of criticism was directed at the device's inability to function as it appears on-screen, the second-biggest complaint Mattel received was that it failed to affix a lenticular coating that, in the movie, gives the hoverboard its shine. For many fans, this exclusion was particularly baffling. How difficult could it be to put coating on a piece of plastic? Apparently, Neitlich says, pretty difficult. "Lenticular is incredibly expensive," he says. "If we had a full lenticular sticker across the entire surface, it would have more than quadrupled the cost of the toy. We really wanted the board to be under a hundred and fifty dollars. We did not want to produce a five-hundred-dollar board, because that really limits the customer base. We had to go with a less lenticular sticker that sort of replicated the shine, but not exactly in the way it looked in the film. People questioned, 'Well, how could they make it lenticular and shiny in 1989 when they were filming the movie, but you guys couldn't reproduce that?' The very easy answer is that the boards for the movie are movie props, and while there were about thirty of them made, I could probably guarantee they weren't made for a hundred and twenty apiece. All of these handmade movie props cost hundreds, if not thousands, of dollars to produce. When you're mass-producing an object for consumers, there have got to be some concessions, and one of those was how shiny the lenticular could be."

Among those who worked on the film, the hoverboard received mixed reviews. Bob Gale publicly withdrew his support via Stephen Clark's website, citing many of the same criticisms that fans had voiced to the company directly and in online forums. Among others responsible for bringing hoverboards to the big screen in the *Future* sequels, the reaction was more mixed. John Bell received a board as a gift. He thought they were re-created well, but he also cited disappointment with the lack of lenticular decal. Robert Zemeckis was generally pleased with the look and functionality of the Mattel hoverboard, although he has been on record as stating, perhaps jokingly, that he might have the only one that works.

The criticism over Mattel's prop replica is likely due to the increased fascination with hoverboarding as the "future" of 2015 neared. While many fans may be disappointed that hoverboards don't exist, at least not like they appear in the *Future* sequels, Bob Schmelzer, who worked on the skateboarding stunts on the first film, is happy life hasn't imitated art. *Back to the Future* did wonders for skateboarding in America and throughout the world, raising the visibility of the sport and mainstreaming it from an activity for rebellious teenagers in the suburbs to something even the good kids wanted to try their hands at. But with the advent of hoverboards, the franchise drifted away from what initially made the movie so cool to begin with, at least to many in the skateboarding world. "When people talk to me about *Back to the Future*, the first thing they almost always ask me about is 'hoverboard this' or 'hoverboard that,'" Schmelzer says. "I had nothing to do with that. There's no skateboarding there, but people just remember that. When I think about *Back to the Future*, I remember the first movie's actual skateboarding scenes more. People always ask me, 'Well, aren't you getting excited for when hoverboards actually exist?' Well, no, because, one, it's never going to happen. Two, it would never be close to the level of what skateboarding is. I'm no physics major, but I understand how skateboarding works in a pool and in the streets. I also understand how a hovercraft works, and it's never going to happen. Give it up."

As popular as the films were three decades ago, it seems as if each year the cult of devotees grows a little wider and the cultural impact becomes a bit more apparent. In addition to conventions celebrating the film, there are also DeLorean car shows. There is no question that the film resuscitated air into the lungs of the DMC-12, which had been left for dead following the company's bankruptcy and John DeLorean's trial. However, *Back to the Future* made the vehicle en vogue again, a fact that DeLorean himself acknowledged in a letter he sent to Zemeckis and his production team shortly after the first film's release. Since fewer than ten thousand DeLoreans were made in the early portion of the 1980s, they have become even more coveted in recent years—especially ones in good running condition. Currently, a company based out of Humble, Texas—also named DeLorean Motor Company, although it has no direct ties to the car's creator or original company— has continued making the vehicle and celebrating the uniquely designed car in shows across the nation.

At such shows, it is often not hard to find someone who has tricked out their own stainless-steel vehicle in an attempt to match the A car from the film. The luckiest of fans have had an opportunity to have their vehicle appraised by Bob Gale or Kevin Pike at one of these events. "You have to understand that when we built the cars, twenty-some-odd years ago, we weren't thinking about having them replicated into the future," Pike says. "I guess we should have got in one of the cars and gone forward. I have people ask me, 'Where'd you get this part? Where'd you get that part?' and I tell them, 'Listen, if I knew you were going to ask all these questions about how to build the DeLorean time machine, I would have written a book on it.'"

Ken Kapalowski and Joe Walser are two fans who know firsthand what it's like to meticulously reproduce the DeLorean time machine's many exterior elements. The two met online in a forum for DeLorean enthusiasts. Both had DMC-12s they wanted to convert into a replica of the A car from the film, and a friendship was quickly formed. Ken made frequent trips from the East Coast to go visit Joe, look for parts, and work on their respective vehicles. When their DeLorean time machines were finished—and yes, they earned the endorsement of Bob Gale—it was somewhat bittersweet. Kapalowski's trips to California often doubled as sightseeing missions. *Back to the Future* filming locations were hunted down, and he fell in love with retracing as many of Marty McFly's steps as possible while on the West Coast.

"I call Joe a 'jaded Hollywood guy,' because he sees movie stars in line at coffee shops in the morning and he's just like, 'Yeah, whatever,' but for me, seeing the tunnel where McFly rode on a hoverboard was just like, holy shit, it was awesome," Kapalowski says. "I thought it would be a cool experience to share that with everybody, and that's what Joe and I talked about doing. Universal wasn't really planning anything big for the fans for the twenty-fifth anniversary, so we said, 'Let's do it.'"

Proving the maxim that necessity is the mother of invention, from November 5 through November 12, 2010, the two friends held "We're Going Back," a weeklong *Back to the Future* convention. Over two dozen of the trilogy's cast and crew members were guests of honor. There were sightseeing tours, panel discussions, and even an opportunity for fans to strap into a harness and ride a hoverboard, which was rigged in the way the stunt was done in *Part II*, but this time on a much smaller, and safer, scale. The experience was enjoyable for both fans and honored attendees alike. The convention's culminating event, a re-creation of the Enchantment Under the Sea dance, was unforgettable for A. J. LoCascio, a *Back to the Future* fan who managed to become a part of the franchise in his own right.

A year or so earlier, the New Jersey native was working in Manhattan at a dead-end office job he hated when he saw a posting online by Telltale Games. The company was looking for someone to do voice-over work for a *Back to the Future* computer and video game it had in development. LoCascio couldn't wait to play it once it came out. There had been other game adaptations of *Back to the Future* made for Nintendo in 1989 and 1990, but both fans and the filmmakers considered them to be embarrassing blemishes on the franchise's legacy. "We had no input whatsoever into the Nintendo games," Bob Gale says. "The game people were dismissive of us and said we didn't know anything about games, even though Bob and I had been playing video games since *Space Invaders*. For the second one, my recollection is that the company simply repurposed an existing game by putting some *Back to the Future* iconography in it." But the Telltale game seemed different altogether. LoCascio was familiar with the company and its quality of work. He made a mental note to keep close tabs on the game's progress.

Two days later, his cousin called. "Did you hear there's a *Back to the Future* game coming out? You should do the voice of Marty. You do a fantastic impression." LoCascio hadn't even considered that, as it seemed so out of his realm, but his cousin's comment stuck with him. He visited Telltale's website, and called the first telephone number he found. "I left a message and didn't hear anything. Then I called up Rhoda Gravador, who is their financial person. I left her a message: 'I have to be in this game.

It's my density.' It was some crazy fan message that I was certain would never get a response. I got an email back a week or so later: 'Hey, send us an MP3 of you doing some Marty McFly stuff?'"

LoCascio got the job. Providing the voice for one of his favorite movie characters was a surreal experience, especially since it meant costarring, at least vocally, with Christopher Lloyd, whom Telltale hired to reprise his role as Doc Brown. To LoCascio's pleasure, his instincts were right. Telltale's game is incomparable to the Nintendo ones, at least partially because the company went out of its way to ensure that it would be. "I was involved from the very beginning with Telltale," Bob Gale says. "The team were not only big fans of the trilogy, but actively sought my input. I worked with them to develop the story line in all five parts of their game." As a testament to its quality and the strength of the fan response to the game, Michael J. Fox agreed to voice Marty's great-grandfather William in Telltale's fifth installment.

While *Back to the Future*'s presence has only continued to grow in the United States, its popularity has similarly exploded overseas. In the United Kingdom, Secret Cinema staged a full-scale re-creation of Hill Valley and screened the film in a sold-out run of twenty-one dates in 2014, complete with actors in costume and facades erected in the image of several key locations from the first movie. BacktotheFuture.com has sold more of Marty McFly, Jr.'s rainbow hats from *Part II* to France than to any other country. Michiel Sablerolle, a Dutch collector, owns the taxicab made from a 1972 Citroën DS that John Bell and Michael Scheffe designed for the second film. The car has even been the subject of two short documentaries filmed in France, Holland, and San Francisco. In 2011, Garbarino, a large Argentinian electronics store chain, hired Christopher Lloyd to appear as Doc Brown in a series of television commercials. The response was so strong that the company paid for a replica DeLorean time machine to travel to each of their stores—a two-month adventure—where thousands of fans greeted it at each stop.

For all of the support worldwide, Japanese interest in the trilogy has always been strongest by a long shot. To date, both sequels are on Japan's list of top-grossing films, with *Part II* at number thirty-three and *Part III* at number fifty. "I think *Back to the Future Part II* is the most successful of the three in Japan because of the intricacies and complications of the story," Harry Keramidas says. "Who knows why, exactly? Maybe they just pay more attention; maybe they like details; or maybe they're more educated about time travel. Maybe they just didn't have such high expectations." In between the release of the first and second sequels, a collection of props, costumes, and production art was shipped to the country and put on display in the Hollywood SFX Museum's *Back to the Future* exhibition, which traveled to four different cities. Every visitor received a 121-page full-color program with information about each item, which has since become highly sought-after by collectors. It is not uncommon to find one going for north of $400 on eBay. As a testament to the enduring impact of the film in Japan, Back to the Future: The Ride is still open in the country, while both American theme park attractions closed in 2007.

The international presence of the film hasn't been lost on the filmmakers, who remain appreciative of and humbled by the support that still cascades at conventions, via email, and on social media from people all over the world. "So many times over the years that I have been doing these conventions, someone will come up and say, 'I was watching that film in Kenya being projected on a wall,' or some other country, and it gave them the idea to be a scientist," Christopher Lloyd says. "It is amazing that people who are in the very remote areas of the planet see this film and are touched by it. That is extraordinary."

"What's so interesting about this movie is that it truly is a crossover," Lea Thompson says. "It means something completely different to a seven-year-old and a fourteen-year-old and a twenty-seven-year-old and a forty-year-old. A young person would be like, 'Oh, my god, I love the car and the hoverboards.' That's what they think they love, but there are so many deep themes in it. It's so poignant, the whole idea of going back and seeing your parents before you were born and what happened to them and how having courage in a single moment can change your life.

"That's really powerful," she continues. "And it's something you need to remember to be a good person every day. That's why people watch that movie over and over again. You need to remember every day that your actions count. It's one of those amazing pieces of art where it all kind of came together and worked. We all know most movies aren't like that. It's like lightning in a bottle. If it was just hoverboards and a time machine, it wouldn't have endured, but the ideas of friendship, and how you'd better live your life great or you're going to be miserable when you're forty-seven years old, these are universal themes that are interesting and inspiring to people."

As a testament to the widespread familiarity of the film and the franchise, several advertisers have used *Back to the Future* as a means to sell products, sometimes only tangentially related to the film. In the fall of 2012, General Electric hired Michael J. Fox to provide a voice-over for a television spot called "The Future Is Now," which included a flying DeLorean time machine. The commercial received a significant amount of attention, airing during highly rated broadcasts of NFL games, *The Daily Show with Jon Stewart*, *Saturday Night Live*, and NBC News. However popular the General Electric ad was, the commercial was only the latest in a number of television advertisements inspired by the film. In 2007, Christopher Lloyd starred in a DirecTV ad for satellite television that used some material from the first film—that clock tower sequence, once again—alongside new footage of the actor, in costume as Doc Brown, seamlessly mixed in.

Four years later, the scientist turned up in another spot that quickly went viral on the Internet, for Nike Mag shoes, inspired by *Back to the Future Part II*. The sneaker company made fifteen hundred limited-edition kicks and sold them at auction to benefit the Michael J. Fox Foundation for Parkinson's Research. In addition to celebrating the films, one of the most significant and poignant ways *Future* fans have banded together has been by supporting Michael J. Fox, who, since very shortly after he last appeared on-screen as Marty McFly, was diagnosed with Parkinson's disease. "He is such a beloved actor, and when he made his illness public in '98, it devastated fans across the world—myself included," Stephen Clark says. "But it was brilliant on his part to set up a foundation in his name where fans could get involved and fund-raise on his behalf to help Parkinson's research."

To help attract attention to their auction to support Fox's foundation, Nike shot an elaborate spot designed to make *Future* fans go wild. The commercial shoot was a small reunion for some alumni who worked on the trilogy on both sides of the camera. The clip starred *Saturday Night Live*'s Bill Hader and professional basketball player Kevin Durant, but the uniqueness of the ad came from seeing Christopher Lloyd and Don Fullilove, who played Mayor Goldie Wilson in the first two films, alongside each other again. Frank Marshall directed, in a throwback to his days on the first film's second unit, and Dean Cundey returned in his old capacity of cinematographer. The promo spot recycled some of Alan Silvestri's instantly recognizable score, and yes, there was a time-traveling DeLorean. With the Bobs executive-producing and Huey Lewis and the News' "Back in Time" over the end credits, the commercial helped the campaign raise more than $5.6 million for the actor's foundation, and thanks to a matching grant from Google cofounder Sergey Brin, the total amount exceeded $11 million. Not surprisingly, the Nike Mags that were released for the charity auction didn't actually have power-lacing capabilities, but shock waves were sent throughout the fan community when, in August 2010, the company registered a patent for the technology to make sneakers tighten on their own around one's foot. Perhaps the future is only just around the corner, after all.

Among those assisting in the effort to find a cure to end Parkinson's disease are Terry and Oliver Holler, a couple who have traveled to different conventions, benefits, and *Back to the Future* screenings around the world in a DMC-12 outfitted to match the time machine from the film, raising funds for Fox's foundation. Following a diagnosis of terminal cancer in 2001, Oliver made a bucket list of how to spend his last six months on earth. Topping the list was something he had wanted to do for decades—buy a DeLorean. He had been a big fan of the film since he had seen it in theaters as a kid, and like so many whose curiosity was piqued when they first saw the vehicle disappear into the space-time continuum, he dreamed of owning one. With his wife's blessing, he purchased a used vehicle and started modifying the car to match the one in the film. To everyone's relief, the doctor's diagnosis proved incorrect, and Terry and Oliver still drive the DeLorean around to this day. Their fund-raising method is simple—they attend events and take pictures of interested parties posing with the car. Fans are encouraged, but not required, to make a small donation in exchange for the photo opportunity.

Some dress up as Marty McFly and Doc Brown, re-creating the famous pose of the two looking at their wrists from Drew Struzan's *Part II* one-sheet. To date, the couple have visited more than four countries and every one of the United States with their vehicle, raising a total of more than $250,000 for Team Fox, a branch of the actor's foundation.

The Hollers aren't the only ones who have used *Back to the Future* as a means to bring awareness and funds to Parkinson's disease. In 2011, Joe Maddalena, president and CEO of Profiles in History, a memorabilia auction company based in Calabasas, had an idea. His company had become the basis of a reality television show on the Syfy cable network, *Hollywood Treasures*, and Maddalena and his producers thought it would be interesting to do an episode where they tracked down *Back to the Future* props and sold them at auction. As an added bonus, it was decided that the funds raised should be given to Team Fox. There were lots of benefits. The episode would attract more attention to the foundation, which might cause a spike in donations. More important, the association with Fox's organization might make those who had been holding on to props for the past several decades more willing to part with them, and probably also incentivize those interested in bidding to spend more cash on those items, knowing that the money was going to a good cause.

The company contacted Bob Gale, who was ready to part with some of the items he had taken home after production wrapped on each film. There were *USA Today* newspapers telegraphing that Griff's gang had been jailed, a "Pit Bull," and lots of Mattel hoverboards. Maddalena asked Gale if he would be willing to donate some of his items to an auction to benefit Team Fox. Bob G couldn't have said yes any faster if he tried to. With the promise of some props, Profiles in History reached out to

Fox's nonprofit. They explained the idea, and without hesitation, Team Fox was happy to participate with whatever the company and show needed. At auction, the props did gangbusters. A screen-used *Grays Sports Almanac*, which had been Gale's, was appraised at $3,000 to $5,000 and ended up fetching $15,000. The two copies of *USA Today*? Two thousand dollars and $3,000. A copy of the *Hill Valley Telegraph* with "Doc Brown Committed" as the headline? Four thousand. In total, Bob Gale's lot raised $49,500 in total, an impressive number that exceeded the items' appraised value. But Gale's items weren't the only things that were sold at Profiles' Team Fox auction. The screen-used resizing jacket Marty wore in *Part II* was appraised at $25,000, but sold for three times as much. The crown jewel of the auction, Joe Walser's DeLorean time machine replica, sold for $95,000.

Given the uniquely mammoth success of the *Back to the Future* trilogy, it is no surprise that Profiles' Team Fox auction exceeded its projected net gross. Regularly, replica props—not only of DeLorean time machines, but also of the Café 80s Pepsi bottles, blue clock tower flyers, and, yes, hoverboards, along with every other artifact from the films one can think of—pop up on eBay. There are debates among the fan community as to how screen-accurate a particular repro is, and then the inevitable bidding war as the auction's expiration time nears. There are individuals around the world who have spent many thousands of dollars to collect, and preserve, cardboard standees from the first film's original VHS release and photocopied production notes sold on websites like ScreenUsed.com, a must-visit page for authentic movie props. Children at heart never grow too old to play with toys, especially conversation pieces evocative of one of the most globally successful film trilogies of all time.

But what is it exactly about *Back to the Future*? Revisionist historians will claim that the film's success was guaranteed, but that's not true. The movie's screenplay was truly exceptional—the perfect cocktail of an original idea, memorable and distinct characters, and sharp dialogue. There are colleges and universities throughout America that use the Bobs' final draft of the first film as an instructional tool for budding screenwriters. For all of the technical achievements of the films, the cast and crew still point to Zemeckis and Gale's ability to craft a wonderfully realized story, especially in the first film, but not exclusively so, as the franchise's most significant achievement. Similarly to other high-grossing summer films that have come afterward, like 1993's *Jurassic Park* and 2008's *The Dark Knight*, *Back to the Future* explored themes universal to a wide swath of the moviegoing public. However, while many of the top-grossing films of all time have been sequels or adaptations of books or films, the Bobs deserve credit for not only crafting a good film, but also one that had no inherent built-in audience on opening day.

Back to the Future's success could be due to any number of other factors. Perhaps Robert Zemeckis earned his sea legs at the right time, and happened to have the right opportunity to flex them. Maybe it was the cast—the confluence of Michael J. Fox's youthful energy, Christopher Lloyd's precisely calculated manic facial expressions, Tom Wilson's brute idiocy, Lea Thompson's naughtiness encased behind a disarming facade of sweetness, and Crispin Glover's often-misunderstood brilliance. Perhaps older people just enjoyed seeing their childhoods relived on-screen during the 1955 portion, while young people could see themselves faced with Marty's dilemma and imagine what steps they would take to get back to the present. Maybe it was the film's subtle commentary on our culture—did we *really* just elect an actor president of the United States? Or perhaps it's the sum of all these parts synthesized together, along with a million other factors.

"It is such a family picture," Lea Thompson says. "It doesn't seem to matter how old you are. Young people in their twenties, who saw it when they were adolescents, get married, have kids, their kids see it, and then they see it over again. There are so many fans I have run into saying they have seen *Back to the Future* a hundred times, or they just watched the whole trilogy last night. It is amazing. I feel very fortunate to be a part of something that has had that impact."

Of all the factors that led to the film's critical, commercial, and cultural successes, the most significant may just be that the right team was assembled to do the right job and made the right calls while doing so. After *Romancing the Stone*, Zemeckis could have chosen to direct any number of screenplays that arrived at his desk, yet because of his convictions and confidence in his project, he went back to *Future*, even though it had been rejected dozens of times over. Before shooting, the Bobs kept revising their work—with Gale often doing minor rewrites and delivering fresh pages even during the shooting process on all three films—and didn't rest on their laurels. They took a chance on Eric Stoltz, had the strength of character to admit the error of their ways, and made the exponentially riskier decision to cast Michael J. Fox, a sitcom actor with no record at the box office worth writing home about—a choice that cost the studio millions and, if unsuccessful, would have gone down in Hollywood history as one of the poorest decisions ever made. The commitment and devotion to the project, from all parties involved, resonates in every frame of the movie. *Back to the Future* was not only the defining movie of that time, but of all time—a unique case study in how to defy the odds and prove, as Doc Brown says in the last film, that no one's history is written.

"We had a blast making the film," Frank Marshall says, "and I think a lot of times that translates up to the story. Certainly Bob is a great storyteller. We had just a lot of great elements, and of course, Michael J. Fox was fantastic."

"If you look at the tone of that first movie, just as a comedy, it's heightened, but it's also grounded," Peyton Reed, who worked on *The Secret of the* Back to the Future *Trilogy* promotional documentary and wrote the script for Back to the Future: The Ride, says. "And it's also science fiction. It's really hard to mix those two genres. It's really only been done successfully a handful of times, and *Back to the Future* is the poster child for how to do that. It has just got such energy and this incredible heart."

The filmmakers who worked on the trilogy, by and large, have continued to cross paths, collaborating on other projects and significantly shaping the film industry. When Steve Starkey accepted his Oscar for Best Picture at the Academy Awards for *Forrest Gump*, he thanked his friend and colleague, whom he cordially referred to as "Bob Z" during his speech, for being a visionary. Earlier in the ceremony, when Zemeckis was honored with the Best Direction award, he used that opportunity to thank not only Steven Spielberg, but also Bob Gale. That moment was a victory for both of them, as they entered the movie business together as partners and, in many ways, have remained that way.

Despite their hectic schedules, the Bobs still speak regularly— sometimes to work on *Back to the Future: The Musical*, the big-budget stage production that is forthcoming, and other times just to reminisce and bask in the glow of their accomplishments. When an interesting video pops up on YouTube that references the trilogy, another company claims that it has almost perfected the technology to make functional hoverboards, or a new crop of rumors about the trilogy come out that need debunking, the two still can't believe it. "That's like mission accomplished," Zemeckis says. "To have made a film that two guys thought up in some shabby little one-room apartment in Burbank and it becomes this thing, this cultural touchstone—I'm very proud of that. That means it was all worthwhile. It's great. I'm very proud of that. Very, very proud of that."

Acknowledgments

I have to give the greatest thanks to Peter Steinberg of Foundry
Literary + Media, the best literary agent I ever could have had
on board for this project, for his support of this idea at a time
when I needed it most, and Kate Napolitano, my fantastic editor,
for all of her wisdom and guidance in maximizing my potential
and making this the best book possible not only for me, but also
for all of the *Back to the Future* fans out there like Peter, myself,
and you, our readers. I have learned so much from both of you
and hope we all have an opportunity to do this again sometime,
after a well-deserved respite. Also, to Rachel Bressler and the
entire team at Plume and Penguin Random House, I can't thank
you enough for all that you have done to make this book what it
has become, especially considering our condensed schedule. I
couldn't have asked for a better home for this project.

There are two people who significantly went above and
beyond to help me in my journey to tell the most accurate and
comprehensive story I could. Bob Gale, coproducer and cowriter
of the trilogy, was an early supporter of this book and was always
available for my litany of questions and requests for assistance in
getting a hold of some hard-to-reach cast and crew. His memory

is impeccable, and if over the course of this book you've wondered how I could have possibly known some tiny detail, it's likely thanks to Bob. Additionally, Stephen Clark, executive director of BacktotheFuture.com, has similarly been helpful in corroborating my information, assisting in my hunting down of people, and generally being a soundboard for my ideas and frustrations. I can't imagine what this book would have been without you both, but it certainly would not have been written as quickly as it had to be.

Between April 2013 and January 2015, I interviewed more than fifty people whose reflections largely informed the narrative I've constructed. Though all may not have been quoted substantially throughout this book, every conversation I had and email I exchanged with those who contributed to the *Back to the Future* phenomenon added something to the way I thought about this trilogy and bettered my grasp of what transpired on the set and beyond. With all of my heart, I would like to thank the following people for their time and access: Isa Alsup, John Bell, Clyde E. Bryan, Mark Campbell, Neil Canton, Tamara Carrera, Rick Carter, Stephen Clark, Ron Cobb, Darold "Doc" Crotzer, Dean Cundey, David de Vos, Mike Fenton, Tim Flattery, Charles Fleischer, Don Fullilove, Courtney Gains, Bob Gale, Richie Gaona, Paul Hanson, Melora Hardin, Oliver Holler, Terry Holler, Bones Howe, Joanna Johnston, Kenneth Kapalowski, Harry Keramidas, Huey Lewis, Christopher Lloyd, A. J. LoCascio, Ricky Dean Logan, Joe Maddalena, Dan Madsen, Leonard Maltin, Wesley Mann, Frank Marshall, Frances Lee McCain, Marc McClure, Gary Morgan, Scott Neitlich, Larry Paull, Kevin Pike, Elsa Raven, Peyton Reed, Scott Ross, Michael Scheffe, Bob Schmelzer, Arthur Schmidt, Sid Sheinberg, Tom Silknitter, Steve Starkey, Drew Struzan, Wes Takahashi, Lea Thompson, James Tolkan, Darlene Vogel, Joe Walser, Harry Waters, Jr., Jeffrey

Weissman, Claudia Wells, Cheryl Wheeler, Bob Yerkes, and Robert Zemeckis.

Several of the people listed above have fantastic agents, assistants, managers, and publicists who helped connect me with them. The greatest challenge in writing a book like this is clearing the gatekeepers, believe me, and I am thankful that the following people passed my request and proposal along to their clients and helped me reach them: Sarah Bauer, Michelle Bega, Nina Bombadier, Beth Comstock, Pearl Evidente Feldman, Andrew Freedman, Lily Gibbs, Julie Groll, Samantha Hill, Derek Hogue, Mary Hulett, Hannah Jacobson, Karin Martin, Evan Miller, Paul Miller, Judith Moss, Monique Perez, Maxine Pezim, Sabrina Propper, and Ivan Savic. Additionally, thanks are owed to Roni Lubliner and Jessica Taylor for their assistance on this project.

When I read a book, I often find myself turning to the acknowledgments first, especially if the author is someone I know. From personal experience, I know many of my friends do the same. I can practically see some of my favorite people quickly scanning these paragraphs, seeing if I've shouted them out, so, friends, you can stop skimming—this is your section!

I have to give extra-special thanks to Johanna Calle, who is frequently on the receiving end of my random bursts of creativity, frustration, excitement, and disappointment—whether she wants to be or not. Her patience and love is something I never take for granted. I also have to thank Christopher Ryan, Toney Jackson, Mathew Klickstein, and Dina Nasr-Heerema, fantastic friends and even better writers, who serve as a constant source of inspiration for me, often just through seemingly normal conversation. Also, my unending appreciations go out to Reeshelle Sookram, for running that top-secret errand for me in Los Angeles while I was trapped on the East Coast.

Terecille Basa-Ong has the best eyes when it comes to spotting typographical and grammatical errors, which she has been generous enough to share with me in order to make my books the best they can be. Fiona Sarne remains a fantastic source of help and guidance for me throughout the writing and publishing process. Jen Hale, and the whole crew over at ECW Press, I am still so amazingly grateful for the opportunity you afforded me with my first two books. Thank you all for your continued support of my endeavors.

Several of my friends have borne the brunt of my talking about the interviewing and writing process more than others, and for that, I want to say thank you for understanding when my thoughts could no longer be contained within my head and by my mouth. I can't really repay you for the time you spent listening to me go on, but I hope seeing your name in print serves as a small bit of compensation: Josh Bellocchio, Phil Brophy, Daniel Carola, Angela De Gregorio, John and Rose Frontignano, Rasha Jay, Gregory Liosi, Vanessa "Curly Fries" Matthews, Steven Pfeiffer, Melissa Rotolo, Wendy Salkin, Stephanie Shaw, Michele Stein, Jared Wexler, and Anthony Zisa.

Last but certainly not least, I have to thank my family—especially my parents, Bernadette and Curtis, and my brother, Curtis Gaines III—for their unending support, love, and encouragement. I am so blessed to have you in my life presently and in the future.

To be continued . . .

Caseen Gaines
caseen@caseengaines.com
www.caseengaines.com
www.facebook.com/caseengaines
Twitter: @caseengaines

Sources

The overwhelming majority of the information in this book is from a series of original interviews conducted by the author. In order to best corroborate the information provided by the interviewees, as well as to fill in some necessary gaps, some additional sources were consulted. What follows is a list of resources that were helpful, either in small or large part, to the overall accuracy and scope of this project.

Books

Baxter, Meredith. *Untied: A Memoir of Family, Fame, and Floundering*. Waterville, ME: Thorndike, 2011.

Fox, Michael J. *Lucky Man: A Memoir*. New York: Hyperion, 2002.

Goldberg, Gary David. *Sit, Ubu, Sit: How I Went from Brooklyn to Hollywood with the Same Woman, the Same Dog, and a Lot Less Hair*. New York: Harmony, 2008.

Klastorin, Michael, and Sally Hibbin. *"Back to the Future": The Official Book of the Complete Movie Trilogy*. London: Hamlyn, 1990.

McBride, Joseph. *Steven Spielberg: A Biography*. 2nd ed. Jackson, MS: University Press of Mississippi, 2011.

Struzan, Drew, David J. Schow, and Frank Darabont. *The Art of Drew Struzan*. London: Titan, 2010.

Films (this includes all applicable audio commentaries and special features)

Back to the Future. Dir. Robert Zemeckis. 1985. Universal, 2011. Blu-ray.

Back to the Future Part II. Dir. Robert Zemeckis. 1989. Universal, 2011. Blu-ray.

Back to the Future Part III. Dir. Robert Zemeckis. 1990. Universal, 2011. Blu-ray.

I Wanna Hold Your Hand. Dir. Robert Zemeckis. 1978. Universal, 2004. DVD.

Looking Back at the Future. Dir. Darold "Doc" Crotzer. Agenda Films, 2006. DVD.

Used Cars. Dir. Robert Zemeckis. 1980. Sony, 2002.

Online Articles and Interviews

An interview with J. J. Cohen. Audio of the interview is available at http://moviehole.net/img/jjcoheninterview.mp3.

An interview with Tom Wilson. Audio of the interview is available at http://www.nerdist.com/pepisode/nerdist-podcast-125-tom-wilson.

Brad Jeffries's response to "What was it like to work on the *Back to the Future* movies?" on Quora, which can be found at http://quora.com/What-was-it-like-to-work-on-the-Back-to-the-Future-movies.

Empire Online's *"Back to the Future*: The Oral History," which can be found at http://www.empireonline.com/interviews/interview .asp?IID=1084.

HollywoodChicago.com's "Interview: Lovely Lorraine Lea Thompson Is 'Back to the Future,'" which can be found at http://hollywoodchicago.com/news/10067/interview-lovely -lorraine-lea-thompson-is-back-to-the-future.

Movieline's "Meet the 'Real' Crispin Glover," originally published on December 1, 1989. It can be found online at http://www .movieline.com/1989/12/01/meet-the-real-crispin-glover.

Tom Wilson's 1989 article for *Us Weekly*, "Back to *Back*." The original publication date is unknown, but full text of the article can be found at http://www.bigpopfun.com/Biff_to_the_Future.shtml.

Uncut's article "'I Met Andy Warhol at Madonna and Sean Penn's Wedding': An Interview with Crispin Glover," which can be found online at http://goo.gl/70WkXc.

Periodicals

Associated Press. "Movie Sequel Arives [*sic*] This Weekend." *The Nevada Daily Mail*, May 25, 1990.

Benson, Shiela. "Movie Review: An Underpowered Trip 'Back to the Future.'" *Los Angeles Times*, July 3, 1985.

Dogherty, Conor. "Hoverboards: A Story 25 Years in the Making." *New York Times*, October 24, 2014.

Lyman, Rick. "*Back to the Future* Director Found Path to Success a Rocky Road." *Orlando Sentinel*, July 12, 1985.

"Stoltz Out-Foxed on Film Role." *Wilmington Morning Star*, April 23, 1985.

Strauss, Bob, *Los Angeles Times*. "Fox Seeks Challenge in Dramatic Roles." *Pittsburgh Post-Gazette*, August 25, 1989.

Thomas, Bob, Associated Press. "Eric Stoltz Hits 'Up,' Again." *The Gainesville Sun*, March 12, 1987.

Thomas, Bob, Associated Press. "Zemeckis Film Took Long Road to Screen." *Park City Daily News*, July 2, 1985.

Websites

Back to the Future—http://www.backtothefuture.com.

Back to the Future Filming Locations—http://www.seeing-stars .com/Locations/BTTF.shtml.

Billboard Music Charts—http://www.billboard.com.

Box Office Mojo—http://www.boxofficemojo.com.

Crispin Glover's Official Website—http://www.crispinglover.com.

Futurepedia: The Back to the Future Wiki—http:// backtothefuture.wikia.com.

The Internet Movie Database—http://www.imdb.com.

ScreenUsed—http://www.screenused.com.

Tom Wilson's Official Website—http://www.tomwilsonusa.com.

YouTube

Bob Gale (*Back to the Future*), Page One Writer's Conference, 2013, Part 1—http://youtu.be/t_Kqe49o9y4.

"Car Crash: The DeLorean Story"—http://youtu.be/uMUXZaROJKM.

Crispin Glover, "*Back to the Future* Controversy"—http:// youtu.be/gmuGyHb4iHE.

Crispin Glover, "Zemeckis Got Really Mad at Me," SiriusXM, *Opie & Anthony*—http://youtu.be/lcG61w474zY.

BTM UNCUT, "Director Robert Zemeckis on the Mattel Hoverboard Prop Replicas"—http://youtu.be/oa0GkcPDdOc.

Hollywood Treasures, "DeLorean Time Machine"—http://youtu.be /QUVO5qsyBYI.

The South Bank Show, "Robert Zemekis [*sic*]"—http://youtu.be
    /o6UMUYv1AJM.

Additionally, a number of the production reports, call sheets, concept art, and costume designs from the three *Back to the Future*
films—most of which were shared by Bob Gale, John Bell, and
Joanna Johnston—were also useful.

INDEX